PLAYLAND

Greetings From Ocean City, Maryland

A Summer Story

EARL SHORES

onewayroadpress.com

Earl Shores/One Way Road Press
P.O. Box 371
Media, PA/19063
www.onewayroadpress.com

Cover Design by Earl Shores

Playland: Greetings From Ocean City, Maryland/ Earl Shores – 1st ed.

ISBN 978-0-9892363-6-2

LCCN: 2019902501

To Robin and Andy, Mom and Dad, and to my Grandmother, Aunt, and Uncle. To Mrs. and Mr. Bunting, and the Bunting family. To Greg and Rick, and everyone I worked with at Playland. To anyone and everyone who worked at Playland during the park's existence. And finally, to the wonderful people in Ocean City who treated my family like family, and made the memories that inspired this book.

Phil,
Hope this bring back
some cherished "Beach"
memories!
Best,
Earl Shore
7/30/19

CONTENTS

Introduction

OUTSIDE
Free Parking — 1000 cars | **FREE ADMISSION**

OCEAN PLAYLAND
65th St. & Philadelphia Ave   Ocean City

Playland was a real place. Located on a strip of land out in the bay at 65th Street, Playland first opened for business in 1965. I was lucky enough to work there in 1980, which, sadly, turned out to be the park's final summer. It was by far the best job I've ever had, with nightly sunset views that people pay a lot of money for these days. We were getting paid to be there. How crazy was that?

So this is my story of that summer and my love letter to an Ocean City that no longer exists. Much of what I've written is exactly what happened during the summer of 1980. My descriptions of the rides, how they ran, and the events that took place on them, all of that information is factual. A forgotten part of Ocean City history I wanted to preserve.

Some names have been changed, and some haven't. Some names I simply couldn't remember anymore. While for others, it was important to me that their identities were known. These people are not only part of my story, but they're also part of Ocean City's story. Hiding them behind made-up names just didn't seem right, even though it might open me up for trouble because I'm not declaring that my book is a "complete work of fiction" and that "any resemblance to actual people, living or dead, is completely coincidental."

That said, not everything in the book actually happened. But it could have. And I guarantee that the next time you get on a ride, you will consider the ride operator in a much different light.

Just be sure to smile and say "hi."

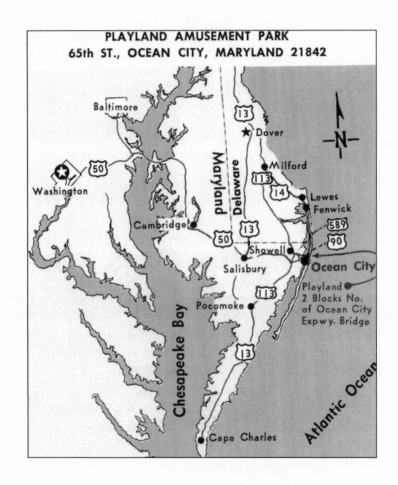

PLAYLAND AMUSEMENT PARK
65th ST., OCEAN CITY, MARYLAND 21842

Baltimore

13

Dover

Milford

113

14

Lewes
Fenwick

50

Washington

Maryland

Delaware

Cambridge

50

13

589

90

Showell

Ocean City

Salisbury

Playland
2 Blocks No.
of Ocean City
Expwy. Bridge

Pocomoke

113

Chesapeake Bay

13

Atlantic Ocean

Cape Charles

CHAPTER ONE

Chosen

"Green is the gas, red is the brake!"

My opening line, which I'd shout numerous times throughout the night. Shouting was necessary to be heard over a sextet of sputtering go-kart engines whose dissonant carburetor-cantata filled the night air with irregular rhythms that defied notation. I took my usual "dramatic" pause in case somebody decided to try out the green pedal sitting under their right foot – no takers this time. Thank God. My shouted spiel continued.

"Keep your feet inside the car and your hands on the steering wheel at ALL times. There's no zigzagging, no cutting people off and absolutely NO bumping! Not following the rules will end your ride early."

By this point in the summer, I wanted to add that the bumper cars were down by the roller coaster and that anybody who couldn't or didn't want to rein in their bumping impulses was welcome to exit their kart – immediately. Full ticket refund included. I'd even point the way down to the ride. Hell, tell Dodgem Denise that I sent you. But neither the paying guests nor the park management would appreciate my late-July cynicism. And unlike my previous jobs, I liked management. Mark was a good guy.

So I stepped aside and waved this puttering group off onto the flood-lit confines of our "L"-shaped go-kart track. The largest one in Ocean City, Maryland, or so our radio ads claimed, even though the layout would have fit easily onto the dirt infield of any high school baseball field. As the six riders passed to my left and accelerated down to the first turn – a 90° left-hander – I didn't *see* any obvious trouble. The first four riders were males in their early 20s. Regular looking guys in cutoff jeans and t-shirts, they weren't drunk, weren't obliviously loud, and had actually paid attention to my instructions without revving the gas pedal. All good signs. The final two riders were tanned and halter-topped mid-teen females. That category barely registered on my go-kart trouble continuum, other than making sure their long hair wasn't hanging over the back of the seat into the engine area. For some reason, our track's perpetual pungent haze of single-cylinder Briggs & Stratton exhaust fumes only seemed to impair the judgment of riders with a Y chromosome. And I'd even witnessed this impairment in riders whose Y-chromosomes were old enough to know better.

Making my way through the pit area to a vantage point where I could see the entire track, I felt confident this would be a "clean" group. Already following the progress of the first lap was my ride running partner Pat Hodges, who was positioned about twenty yards to my right at the end of our back straightaway. We had been working the go-karts together for over six weeks now and had developed an easy going and trusting relationship despite our age differences. Actually, our ages weren't all that different, we were just a couple years apart. But we occupied different stages of life that made those years significant.

Pat was a local who grew up not far from the park, and still had a year of high school to finish. I was a seasonal transplant heading into my junior year of college, having not lived at home since packing up my car two summers earlier. Not that I was all that more worldly than Pat, but my name was on the phone bill, the electric bill, and the apartment lease. So through moves, roommates, and monthly check writing, I'd spent significantly more time in the adult world than Pat had – not that spending time there meant you were actually being an adult.

To Pat's credit, he was mature beyond his years. This was his third summer working in the park, and his nightly presence on the go-karts was a testament to his maturity. Despite the grime, noise, and smell, they were one of the park's featured attractions. And they were considered a serious ride to run.

This was something I discovered after my initial unbroken three-week streak of working the karts. In general, the park schedule had most of the staff rotating across different rides through the course of a workweek. A handful of park veterans had dibs on their favorite rides, where they would be fixtures all summer long. But the rest of us, at least what I was told initially, would move around and work all over the park. After a brief early June debut in Kiddie Land running the Antique Cars, I was assigned to the go-karts. Permanently it seemed.

When I finally asked for the chance to run a different ride, even just for a night, I was informed in thoroughly complimentary language that I had been "chosen" to run the go-karts.

Chosen?

It was all news to me. Why didn't Mark – the assistant manager – tell me? Because it turned out it wasn't Mark who did the choosing. The chooser was Dave the mechanic. Dave was a towering man who had an amazing knack for appearing out of thin air at your ride. Word was that he'd been quite the sports star at the local high school, which you could sort of see in his still slim build and the long graceful strides that propelled him stealthily through the park. In his mid-thirties now, always dressed in navy colored mechanic's clothes (complete with an oval "DAVE" patch over his left breast pocket), his main job was keeping our fleet of go-karts healthy and running. During my early days of working the go-karts, Dave and I barely exchanged a full sentence, but he apparently was impressed with the way I collaborated with Pat to limit the abuse our paying guests inflicted on the karts. So Dave informed Mark that he wanted me on the go-karts. Given the special status of the karts, and the weight that Dave's skill and opinion carried behind the scenes, I'd spent the entire month of July stuck on the go-karts.

I was past ready for a break, unlike Pat who seemed to have some part of himself tied to running the karts. This was just a summer job for me, one that conveniently kept me on the beach or on my surfboard when I wasn't working. Pat went home over the bridge at night and really didn't have a lot of interest in the beach or the ocean. He could have been living in Pennsylvania or Missouri and still been happy. As long as he was working the go-karts.

The first three laps went by without an incident or even a hint of a problem. With everything seemingly under control, I walked back through the pit area and stepped over the dilapidated picnic bench the park had given us to sit on, taking the opportunity to size up our growing line. Maybe it was time to add a seventh kart to our lineup. Then I heard it – the squealing skid of locked-up tires and the almost simultaneous metallic thump-thump-thump of bumpers making contact. Only four karts came out of the far corner of the track, which was currently out of my sight. Pat went sprinting through the infield of the track, while I had to wait until the quartet of still running karts passed me by before running down to where Pat had originally been standing. It was a minor tangle on the sharpest turn of the track, a place where it was easy to get spun if the front driver slowed down unexpectedly. From what I had observed, it was just one of those things. The main give away came from the faces of the guys in the karts. They looked embarrassed about being embedded in the loose tires lining the track. Problem People, the ones who mess around and cause accidents, would be sitting there snickering like Muttley from the Wacky Races.

So I was surprised to hear this...

"You're both off! Done! Take it into the pits!" yelled Pat, as he pushed a sideways kart back out onto the track.

"My foot slipped off the gas," pleaded the stunned looking front driver. "That's the only reason we got tangled up. He didn't have a chance to avoid me."

The other driver's face changed from stunned to angry as his eyes narrowed. "He stopped right in front of me – I couldn't miss him. It was an accident."

Pat didn't back off. "You're both off for the night. Take it in." A profanity might have been uttered as they pulled away, but it was lost in the accelerating growl of the engines. I hustled back to the pit area to make sure they pulled in, and they did, one behind the other, in the pit lane nearest the picnic bench. As they began to get up out of their karts, the other two friends pulled into the adjacent pit lane.

"What's up?" asked the recently arrived driver in the front kart, using a voice loud enough to be heard over the idling engines.

"They're kicking us off," came the reply from the rider who caused the accident.

I got a sideways dirty look from the sitting driver as the conversation continued.

"He's kicking you off?"

"No, not him, the douchebag out on the track. My foot slipped off the gas – that guy thinks we were screwing around."

"What do you think?" asked the still sitting driver, aiming at me a question, and also an incriminating index finger.

"Sorry, I didn't see it. I have to go by what he says," I said, pointing my own index finger at Pat, who was still out on the track fixing the tires that had been displaced by the accident. Like I really wanted to be in the middle of this. I was so desperate to be running a ride where I had full control of the riders.

"Yeah, figures," he said, rising up out of his kart. The driver in the kart behind him got up too. He'd been silent until now, but pithily finished off this moment of escalating tension with a "Fuck this."

"You know, we paid a lot of money to come in here and ride the go-karts. You tell your friend we're going to get it back from him at the end the night," said the driver whose foot slipped off the gas.

I wasn't exactly sure what he meant, but the most unsettling part was that he didn't sound angry at all. He was very matter of fact in making it clear there was a score to settle.

"We'll be waiting for you guys later. Don't worry, you won't miss us," he finished with a chuckle. The three other friends had a chuckle too and began walking toward the chain link exit gate.

"See you later," he said with a smirk and a malice that put a lump in my stomach.

I hadn't noticed Pat guiding the two girls into the pit area. They seemed to think the ride was simply finished, not even aware that there had been any commotion. It was part of the seamless way Pat and I could handle things. Neither of us took a moment off during a shift. Things could go wrong very quickly on the go-karts – like what just happened. We were alike in that we prided ourselves on being ready for anything. But while I appreciated Pat having my back, I thought he got this one wrong. From all that I had seen, they hadn't been messing around. Maybe in the far corner one of them did something stupid, but overall, they hadn't done a single thing up to that point to even earn a hard "I'm watching you" stare from Pat or myself. Since I was already standing near the entrance gate, I should have opened it and let the next group of riders in. Instead, I circled back to Pat who was standing in front of our six idling and empty go-karts.

"Pat, what the hell happened out there?" I asked.

"Those college assholes didn't respect the karts. They needed to go," said Pat, looking back at me through his lightly tinted aviator-style pre-scription glasses. As usual, he was wearing jeans despite the oppressive humidity of the night, and no hat. This was his standard work outfit, even when our shifts started in the skin frying rays of the midday summer sun.

"Well, they didn't take it very well. They said they're going to wait for us and get their money back at the end of the night," I replied.

"I'm not giving them anything."

"I think they plan on being, shall we say, 'persuasive.' You know, there's four of them – only two of us."

"They're going to wait for us in the parking lot?"

"Yeah, I'm pretty sure that's their plan. Although, being just a college asshole, I could be wrong."

Pat's face dropped a bit under his bushy red-brown pageboy haircut. Then he regrouped with a weak smile. "No, no, not you. I didn't mean..."

"I know Pat, I know, but man, those guys were pissed off. Scary pissed. They weren't even yelling."

"Well, they can wait around if they want. Dave's got a revolver."

My head twitched an involuntary double take at Pat, and the world seemed to stand still as my brain caught and reassembled each individual letter of R-E-V-O-L-V-E-R somewhere in the depths of my cerebral cortex.

"What...wait...revolver?"

I needed to find a different ride to run. And fast.

CHAPTER TWO

A Job at Playland

The already intensifying June sun hung just over my left shoulder in the mid-morning sky, sitting at an angle that nearly matched the time of the day. It served as backlighting to the sand trail kicked up by my tires, and as I watched the expanding shape drift away and dissipate on the warm westerly breeze, I wondered whether flip-flops were appropriate attire for a job interview. They were, after all, top-of-the-line Rainbow flip-flops, the ones with the leather footbed and straps. And their tan color matched with my brown Ocean Pacific shorts and my yellow short-sleeve Ocean Pacific shirt – complete with two button collar and cool orange going to red accent band around the chest – in a very Garanimals kind of way. This was my best "out for the evening" surf wear, a thoroughly sophisticated beach look that showed I was taking the occasion seriously. Which was a major accomplishment considering how last minute the arrangements all were. A quick glance at my watch showed that only 25 minutes had passed since I gathered my nerve and made a cold call to a phone number in the Yellow Pages. That meant I had five minutes to spare before my appointment with the assistant manager.

As the sand settled down into the mix of asphalt and gravel covering the ground, I could finally see all the way back to Coastal Highway. It took some serious squinting plus an assist from my right hand to shield the sun, but once everything came into focus...man, this parking lot was *enormous*. Probably bigger than the lot down at the inlet. It was easily two football fields, side by side before you reached the spaces in the farthest eastward stretch of the gray expanse. Then it was another football field in length before you made it out to the traffic light for the highway. In addition to its size, the lot had another unusual feature. Or to be more accurate, it was missing a very usual Ocean City feature. Parking meters – there wasn't a meter in sight. It had to be the largest free lot in the whole damn town.

Yet parking wasn't the only oversized thing in the immediate vicinity. As I began walking the perimeter of a head-high chain link fence, it was impossible to ignore what soared skyward on my right like some kind of eccentric seaside cathedral spire. Standing at least 20 feet tall was a colossal fiberglass man, a man whose already impressive visual impact was amplified by the fact that, in addition to being 20 feet tall, he was also mounted 20 feet off the ground. From this very lofty perch, he was clearly "Lord of The Lot," a Lord with a single and specific purpose – to attract attention from far off Coastal Highway.

He'd started his Ocean City landmark life in the mid-1960s as a pirate. A smiling, welcoming, bearded pirate, complete with black boots and a black buccaneer style hat. (Yet oddly missing the sword that his arms and hands seemed specifically designed to hold.) Then somewhere along the way, he'd received a makeover. He was now clad in a white long sleeve puffy polka dot shirt, red and white striped balloon-at-the-bottom pants, and a retrofitted jester hat. And his once empty hands now had something to do, as they were busy juggling four large, brightly colored balls – the silver and orange ones seemingly suspended in mid-air. It wasn't necessarily a bad makeover, maybe a bit forced. Where he once was 100% pirate, he now seemed to be equal parts clown and genie. These dueling attributes, however well-intentioned, left him with a whiff of creepiness that was absent from his previous pirate persona.

But this nearby giant-in-the-sky wasn't just hovering starkly in mid-air. His feet were planted at the midpoint of a narrow black billboard-shaped sign that was at least three times as long as he was tall. Stretching across the length of the sign were eight large yellow letters, done in an all-capitals format that could easily be read by passing cars on Coastal Highway.

Those letters composed a single word.

"PLAYLAND"

My first sighting of the Playland amusement park came from a backseat car window in 1965. It was summer, and my parents had taken the "scenic" route to Ocean City instead of making the usual inland drive from suburban Philadelphia. The scenic route was Delaware Highway 1 through the beach towns of Dewey, Bethany, and Fenwick Island. This was my favorite way to get to Ocean City – it felt like your visit started early thanks to the 40 minutes of sand dune scenery you took in before hitting the Maryland state line.

This scenery included a series of abandoned concrete lookout towers, tall turret-like structures that kept the coastline safe during WWII, and then there was the dream-inducing view of the Atlantic Ocean from the Indian River Bridge. Plus, you could often smell the ocean on this route. I always wondered why my family bothered with the dreary farm field and sometimes manure-smelling monotony of two-lane travel in southern Delaware. I guess it was easier to reach my aunt's West Ocean City trailer, which sat just off Route 50 in a makeshift mobile park that some enterprising individual had stuffed into a sandy backyard between Villani's Furniture and the Sea Isle Motel.

Playland was hard to miss back then, especially when driving south from Delaware. This was a time when "up the beach" ended at about 30th Street, so other than Bobby Baker's Carousel Motel, there really wasn't much of anything in northern Ocean City, especially on the bayside. So from a long way off it was easy to see a "speck" sitting out in the bay. As you drove closer and reached the streets numbered in the 90s, a silhouette became visible. There was something obviously round toward the highway – a Ferris wheel? – and what was that large structure that seemed to be sitting out in the water?

Moving down into the streets numbered in the 80s, this form became easier to make out. A roller coaster, a wooden roller coaster – the first in Ocean City. And as you closed in on 65th Street, where the park stuck directly westward out into the bay on a man-made strip of sand, it was easy to see the smiling Playland pirate and the sign he was standing on.

And also the elevated monorail track that emerged from each side of the sign.

You had to give the park creators credit. The monorail, which ran around the rectangular perimeter of the park, was always one of Playland's most distinguishing features. Monorails were definitely "in" when the park first opened in 1965, considered part of the future of transportation. Disneyland had a monorail, and one of the top attractions at the 1964 World's Fair had been the AMF monorail, which even had on-board stewardesses (or so my cousin had told me). It seemed like only a matter of time before one was coming to a city near you. So Playland was certainly forward thinking in putting a monorail in the park. Just like the wooden coaster, it was an Ocean City first. Yet the U.S. monorail revolution never took place. And here in 1980 this once futuristic mode of travel seemed dated and faded – much like the sun-bleached and salt-eaten maroon paint now clinging to its track. But taking a ride around the park – and from what I remembered, it was a slow ride – still offered one of the coolest views in all of Ocean City.

I turned the corner of the fence and, as instructed during my phone call, began walking up the gravel-covered access road toward the open service gate in the front of the park. On the other side of the fence was a sizeable go-kart track, which sat just outside the park's original boundaries in what used to be a prime corner of the parking lot. The last time I was in Playland, the go-karts were still on the inside. But that was three or four years ago. Now there was an ongoing go-kart arms race with the Jolly Roger Park on 30th Street. That's why in the first week of June I'd already heard multiple Playland radio ads for "OC's largest go-kart track!" Whether the claim was true or not, it was a smart decision to move the incessant lawn mower growl and noxious exhaust of the kart engines to the parking lot. It would make the interior of the park a quieter and more inviting place.

Also removed from the park was the smell of rubber, as lining the bottom of the other side of the fence were dozens and dozens of old tires. They served as borders and bumpers for the track, giving wayward drivers a cushion from any direct encounters with the fencing – or each other.

I continued walking toward the service gate, trying not to break too much of a sweat while keeping my flopping at a minimum to prevent loose gravel from lodging under my feet. Off to my right the main entrance was shuttered and locked, with the park beyond being eerily silent and still. The Ferris wheel was the most prominent ride in my vision, sitting directly behind the Playland mascot. My view of the Ferris wheel disappeared as I closed in on the gate, replaced by the side of a building with a bright yellow wall. Painted on this wall, now staring directly at me was a smiling life-size version of the Playland mascot's face. Life-size being 20-foot tall life size.

At the threshold of the service gate I felt my heart speed up, not that I was nervous about the interview, but with one more step, I'd be backstage at an amusement park. It was a fantasy that had rattled around inside me since those summer nights when I'd fall asleep in the back cottage of the Ocracoke Apartments on Dorchester Street while listening to the whooshing metallic serenade of the Wild Mouse coaster just blocks away at Trimper's Rides. I tried to be as casual as possible, with no reveal at all of the eight-year-old inside me, and then...I was inside the park. Behind the scenes at Playland. A full-on rush even if the single-story buildings lining both sides of the service road now blocked my view of the park. I continued walking, passing between two tall blue stanchions that held up a curved section of the monorail track before heading toward the building on the left side of the road. A white door took up the near corner of a rose-colored wall, and over the top of the doorframe was a white sign with black letters: "Office." Yep, I was in the right place.

I reached to grab the door handle, then pulled my right hand back. I should probably knock first. But as I raised my arm and readied my knuckles for contact, I was frozen by the oversized yellow serpent filling the horizon at the end of the service road. It was the Hurricane, Playland's wooden coaster. As coasters go, it wasn't very big. Maybe a 60-foot drop that wasn't all that steep and a tight Figure 8 circuit that wasn't all that long. But it was still the only wooden roller coaster in Ocean City. Which was a little surprising, considering the go-kart competition now underway with Jolly Roger. In the 15 years since the Hurricane debuted neither Trimper's nor Jolly Roger had tried to one-up Playland, at least in terms of a wooden coaster. And the coaster's landmark status had only been enhanced since the Route 90 Bridge opened in 1972. On any drive into Ocean City across Route 90 – which intersected Coastal Highway just three blocks to the south at 62nd Street – the coaster was *the* main point of reference. Especially when lit up on summer nights.

With my focus back on the door, I gave it three solid knocks.

"Come in," said a slightly muffled voice. I pushed the door inward and stepped inside. A pleasant glow of natural light streamed through the partially drawn metal blinds on the east-facing window, and there was a refreshing coolness thanks to an air conditioner mounted on the back wall. Quickly standing up from a desk in front of the window was a tanned and trim man with a coffee colored mustache and thick curly hair of the same color. He was dressed casually in a white golf shirt with a small Playland logo, and dark blue shorts. Almost exactly my height, we were pretty much eye-to-eye as he extended his hand. He was definitely older than me – maybe almost thirty.

"Earl, right? I'm Mark Davis," he said with a smile that put me instantly at ease.

"Earl Shores – thank you for asking me to come in," I answered while reaching to grab his hand firmly.

"So...you're a friend of Jack Wainwright?" asked Mark.

"Yes, he had nothing but great things to say about you and Playland all last summer. I think he was sorry he didn't come back to work here."

"Have a seat. How is Jack these days?" Mark inquired.

I wasn't sure if this was a test or not, but fortunately, Jack and I had surfed together just a couple of days earlier. And even if it was a test, I liked Mark immediately. Jack said he was a good boss, not to mention a pretty cool guy.

"He's doing well," I said while lowering myself into the gray folding chair in front of Mark's desk. "We surfed together on Monday. He can't come back to OC this summer because of his military obligations." It was certainly nice to start things off with an authoritative and honest answer.

"Oh, that's right, he was at...ah, I can't think of it. A military college, right?" said Mark.

Again, I wasn't sure if this was more testing on Mark's part, but there was no hesitation in my answer.

"Yes, he's at VMI," I replied.

"Right, right..." said Mark, letting his words drift away into dusty rays of sunlight filling the office. "So, you guys worked together last summer at...I'm sorry, where did you say?"

I had been proud of myself for cold calling Mark and pitching him for employment. It had been a quick conversation. Jack guided me on what to say, so I must have said enough "right" things, or perhaps Mark was just desperate enough to invite me in for an interview. On the phone, I had mentioned where Jack and I had worked together, but now I was hesitant to repeat it. Of course, I had no choice.

"Phillips – at the Crab House on 21st Street," I said.

"And you didn't go back?" said Mark, inflecting his voice up a bit to show his surprise. The reality was, I couldn't go back. Jack and I, along with two other guys, had walked out of the Crab House on a busy Saturday night in late August and gone on an impromptu surf trip to Cape Hatteras, North Carolina. It was something I had absolutely no regrets about doing – until this moment.

"It was a real hectic place, especially at the end of the summer. Jack made it sound like Playland was a much more fun place to work," I said, feeling good about an answer that didn't fib the events of the previous summer. But God, if he asked for references...my underarms began dripping like a leaky faucet.

"Yeah, we like to think that working at Playland involves a good bit of fun. We're definitely different from Phillips. How many kitchens do they have there?" said Mark.

"Last year, at least, there were seven."

"Yeah, that's hectic alright. So this year you didn't try to line up a job before the summer started?" Mark certainly had a knack for asking good questions, and he held my eye as he asked this one. Again, I was unsure if he was just curious or probing harder. It was a fair question because it was already June, with Memorial Day having fallen on the previous Monday. Most seasonal transplants – like my roommate, who had rushed right out and gotten a job the day after we moved in – were already working. My approach had been more leisurely, based on what I experienced the previous year when I donated every weekend from Easter onward to Phillips. Donate was the operative word because I barely made back my weekend expenses despite working three full shifts. This was on top of the hassle of rushing to Ocean City immediately after my final Friday afternoon class, then hurrying back to school late Sunday night to catch up on lessons that didn't get taken care of in my hotel room. Essentially, I ended up paying for the privilege of a guaranteed summer position. And I wasn't going to do it again this year.

Since it had worked so far, I gave Mark another completely honest answer.

"Umm...I discovered last summer that there were still plenty of jobs available after Memorial Day."

Mark opened his desk and was looking down when he said, "Smart. You could focus on school throughout the spring." He then pulled out several long pieces of paper out of his top drawer, as well as a square bright yellow booklet.

"Jack's a good guy. I enjoyed having him at the park. If he's recommending you, that's good enough for me. Here's an application and an employee handbook," Mark said, offering up a smile that felt even more welcoming than the one he'd greeted me with. My smile was involuntary and embarrassingly wide, but I didn't care. I'd always wanted to work at an amusement park. And what a relief that Mark didn't ask for a Phillips reference.

"Thanks, Mark, thanks a lot!" I said, reaching across the desk and shaking his hand. He handed me the paperwork, along with a pen.

"You can just lean on the front of my desk and fill things out. Do you have a phone?"

"Yes, yes we do."

"Good, not everybody does. Kind of hard to believe in 1980, isn't it? Oh, and one more thing – you're going to have to lose the beard. Page two of the employee manual."

Mark was being kind about the beard, or at least calling it a beard. Being just a few weeks shy of birthday number twenty, my shadowy scruff looked like the dirt a kid would pick up while playing in the backyard.

I smiled, "Yeah, I'll be sure to get a washcloth on it when I go home."

"Can you start tonight?"

"Absolutely."

"Ok, be back here at 5:30 pm. Do you have navy colored shorts?"

What luck, I had two pairs. A pair of OP's and a new brand called Sea Breeze.

"Sure do."

"Good, good. I'll give you your shirt tonight. Be sure to bring a sweatshirt too. These early summer nights can be chilly, especially with the park sitting out in the bay like it does."

Mark turned around to look out the window, as the sound of tires on gravel grew louder. A dark blue panel van pulled through the service gate, and stopped just outside the office door, idling in place. Mark got up from his chair and headed for the door.

"You'll excuse me, I have to deal with this delivery. You can just leave the application on my desk when you finish," Mark said, twisting the doorknob to step outside. "See you tonight!"

CHAPTER THREE

Mouse Ride

My family really wasn't much for storytelling or passing down family yarns. But one story they did tell was about the first time my stroller was rolled in to see the carousel at Trimper's Rides, and how on the way out, I sat in front of the curved carnival mirrors giggling uncontrollably at my shrinking and enlarging image. This recounting always finished with great laughter (and my embarrassment) as my family described in detail the tantrum I threw as my stroller was wheeled back out onto the boardwalk. "You could hear him screaming all the way down to Thrasher's" was the side-splitting punchline. Being just over a year old, I had no actual memory of the event. What I did carry, thanks to the repeated retelling of this tale, was a reconstructed and faux stroller recollection of thrashing my arms and my legs as I was helplessly pushed away from the mirrors. Clearly, I had a "thing" for Trimper's from a very young age.

Once I could walk on my own through the garage door-like openings of Trimper's carousel building, this "thing" turned into a fascination with all of the amusement rides inside. From my earliest days, I had an inborn inclination to absorb and categorize every ride that I saw.

Just a few steps inside was the whip, a vintage 1920s kiddie whip, complete with red velvet seats. Now that was a ride worth riding. Always full of laughs, I hated when the cars slowed down and I had to get off. The kid-size boats that floated leisurely in an oval of water around a tall lighthouse structure – they were pretty neat, but the murky water they floated on was creepy. Was it safe to get wet? How deep was the water if I fell in while trying to get in or out of the boat? I was always relieved when the ride was over, and my feet were back on concrete. The old canopy-covered miniature Navy boats that moved quickly over a circular "wavy" track? Mostly fun. I always wondered how the tiny wheels under the boats stayed on the narrow wooden track. When sitting in the front seat I kept my eyes focused on the well-worn path the wheels followed. The fighter airplane ride was fun, you did get pretty high in the air. And they were really noisy, thanks to the buzzer that went off when you fired your battle gun. (These buzzers could be heard throughout the entire interior of Trimper's!) As for the fire engine ride...that was my least favorite. The circle you went around in was too small, and the bell clanging was annoying. It got old quickly

The main attractions for me on the inside part of Trimper's were the Dodgem Cars (which I was still years away from being big enough to ride), the noisily rumbling and spinning Tea Cups (which I would hopefully soon be able to ride), the kiddie Ferris wheel, and of course the classic merry-go-round. The best part of the Ferris wheel was that near the top you entered a little addition to the roof that had been built to accommodate the height of the ride. You couldn't really see down anymore, only out, thanks to windows on all four sides of the addition. And your view was of the big rides outside. Looking straight ahead as the wheel turned in its counter-clockwise direction gave you a view of Trimper's real Ferris wheel; looking out to your right gave you a view of the Wild Mouse, one of the earliest coaster rides in Ocean City. Like the Dodgem Cars, these were all rides I aspired to. They would all be part of my natural progression through the amusement ride world.

This ride fascination was nurtured by how our visits to Ocean City were set up. Home base in the 1960s was my aunt's trailer in West Ocean City, so we had to drive over the Route 50 bridge to get to the beach or the boardwalk. Driving meant that most visits usually began and ended in the inlet parking lot in downtown Ocean City. This unique three-block stretch, besides having a beach and public parking area, was bordered by the inlet jetty to the south, the Ocean City boardwalk to the west, and the Ocean City Pier to the north. There was also the Pavilion (which offered shade and public restrooms), and multiple mouth-watering options for lunch (Dayton's, Dumser's, the Alaska Stand, and Thrasher's). So this was the beach we always used.

But in addition to spending a day in the ocean, it was also spent in the shadow of the rides on the pier, which had been rebuilt after the 1962 Ash Wednesday storm with an area specifically for amusement rides. The most prominent rides at the time were the Paratrooper and the always-intriguing Loop-O-Plane. The Loop-O-Plane was the first upside down ride I ever saw. (Trimper's had one too.) On some hot sunny days these rides didn't run a whole lot, but every so often you'd hear the diesel engine of the Loop-O-Plane fire up. Even if I were in the water, I'd turn my attention to the pier and watch, first as the cars built up the momentum to move upward, then complete that first upside down loop. How did the people stay in their seats? And then either mid-ride or end-ride, the operator would catch both cars in the upside-down position. Skilled Loop-O-Plane operators could really stall the cars in that full vertical position for a while. Other times, with what were obviously less experienced operators, the cars moved upwards a little too quickly. You knew they weren't staying at the top. They'd get there, seem to almost stop, and then the excess momentum would carry them over. And it seemed like there was one shot at doing this trick. If it didn't work on the first try, it was time to finish the ride.

Pulling into the inlet parking lot in the evening...it was full-on ride city. Besides the rides on the pier, Trimper's complex of indoor and outdoor rides anchored the south end of the boardwalk. So Trimper's Ferris wheel would be turning, as would the Paratrooper and the Octopus on the pier. The pier also had a Satellite ride, which was something to see when lit up and elevated in its unique full spin pattern. I watched them all carefully as I knew these were rides that I would take on in the, hopefully, not too distant future.

There didn't seem to be a lot of ride height limits during this time. So the "when" of me challenging some of these serious adult rides came down to when an adult – either my father or, surprisingly, my grandmother – judged that I could hold on, or that they could hold on to me, during the duration of whatever spinning and gyrating the ride dished out. The first big ride I got on was the Tilt-A-Whirl at Trimper's. I remember sitting in the seat, leaning against the padded back of the clamshell-shaped car, and pulling the curved restraint bar over my lap. The bar was heavy but seemed so thin, and not really substantial enough to hold you in your seat. But once the ride started up, slowly at first, and gravity began making the cars sway and spin, it became obvious that you weren't coming out of the seat. With that worry gone I was on to my next worry, and that was, would I survive the ride without getting sick. I closed my eyes at first, but as it became more apparent that I was surviving just fine, I opened them and watched the world spin by. There was Trimper's Ferris wheel, then the Loop-O-Plane, then the Octopus (yes, Trimper's had one of those too). When the ride slowed down, and our car gently spun to a stop in one of the small valleys of the circular track...I had survived. My first "real" amusement ride had been a success. Fun even. I was hooked and ready to move on.

It wasn't long before I hit the Ferris wheel – which I found scarier than the Tilt-A-Whirl thanks to my newly discovered fear of heights. So the Ferris wheel was okay, but maybe I should stay closer to the ground. On one sunny afternoon my dad and I hit the Tilt-A-Whirl, then decided to expand my ride experience by going on the Octopus. I thought the ride was fantastic. From having the ride operator open the car – where the front half dropped down and formed your own personal little step up into the seat – to the small rubber-ended handles that slid out for you to hold onto, to all the tight turning and spinning...the ride was a completely new experience. At the end, however, my dad barely made it out to the perimeter fence before leaving part of his lunch in the gutter. The Tilt-A-Whirl-plus-Octopus sequence was just a bit too much for him. Once he recovered and regained his equilibrium I overheard him telling my mom that it had been a pretty scary experience, as he was doing all he could do to keep me in the seat. Of course, I never noticed. It was no surprise that Octopus rides were put on hold for a couple of years. That was okay, as Trimper's red-and-white Merry Mixer became my favorite ride.

The most monumental ride of my life happened in this early period. One of the unquestioned heavy-duty adult rides in all of Ocean City was the Wild Mouse behind Trimper's. The Mouse had a massive block-long skeletal support structure featuring a forest of strikingly thin white wooden posts that rose starkly up into the air. Running between and connecting these posts were narrow wooden crossbeams and long silver metal rods that crisscrossed the entire ride in a thicket of oversized "X" patterns. Yet despite having this very dense wooden frame, the Wild Mouse wasn't your typical wooden roller coaster. The track was made of metal, and very, very narrow. It also, in places, ran out and away from the ride, so there were no walkways or handrails along the side of the track to create any illusions of safety. The track just ran "naked" in what seemed like 10 different directions, weaving in and out of support posts that looked much too spindly to hold up the ride.

Another difference between the Wild Mouse and a traditional coaster is that it didn't have a train of multiple cars. Instead, it had individual cars that seated only two people. That made a ride on the Wild Mouse an individual rather than a community experience. You couldn't borrow any composure from a more relaxed rider seated nearby. The fear and bravado quotient of a trip around the Wild Mouse was all up to you.

The ride fronted South Division Street in downtown Ocean City, just a block from the boardwalk, and on any approach to the ride – from the boardwalk or the street – the most prominent features were the two tall fiberglass archways. Easily 15 feet tall, both were painted bright red with "Wild Mouse" spelled out in black letters on white tiled blocks. (Each letter had a block that was tilted slightly to the right or the left.) Topping off each archway was a nearly human-sized 3-D mouse figure (or at least the upper torso of a mouse), with large gray ears, a far-off zombie stare, and a strange blue uniform that looked very much like a space suit. Each mouse pointed a glove-covered right hand down to the blocks spelling out Wild Mouse, while their glove-covered left hand pointed upwards – as if they were inviting you onto the ride. The left archway was marked "Exit." The right archway, the one just steps away from busy Baltimore Avenue, was marked "Entrance."

Walking through the Entrance archway for the first time – the "mouse hole" into the den of these bizarrely clad fiberglass figures (a mouse with gloves?) – and up the ramp to where the individual Wild Mouse cars awaited, was a scary experience. My legs felt weak and my heart was beating so hard, like I was sitting in a doctor's office waiting for a booster shot. I wasn't sure I wanted to do it, but at the same time, I really wanted to do it. Actually, I wasn't even sure if I could do it because my dad had a discussion with the ride operator double-checking that it was okay for me to ride. As long as I rode with my dad – that had been the plan all along – it was okay. So we handed him our tickets and got ready to climb into our own personal mouse.

It really did look like a mouse, with a rounded back end, a narrow oblong "body," and a cone-shaped front end that finished off in a circular silver "nose." A single horizontal bumper on the front of the car looked like a mouth, while a trio of vertical bumpers on the back end gave the appearance of a tail. All it needed was a set of eyes (I guess that was us). Although the colors weren't very mouse-like – the car was mostly dark blue with a splash of yellow on the rounded backside – they were comforting, as blue was my favorite color.

The ride operator held the mouse steady as my dad got in first and leaned against the padding in the back of the car. I then stepped over the side and sat down, sliding my legs forward as I leaned back against my dad and shifted to get my body into the compact space. There were no actual seats – we were both sitting directly on the padded floor of the car, which left me craning my neck upward to see over the front of the mouse. Most of what I could see was the gauzy fiberglass pattern of the car's interior, and my dad's legs stretching down into the shadowy darkness of the bowels of the mouse. With my smaller legs wedged between his, the fit was pretty snug, but there were no bars or straps to hold us down, so I quickly scanned around for somewhere to put my hands. There were long metal handles protruding up from the sides of the car, and what looked like a circular handle around the front of the car – but I was never going to be able to reach that one. I was still scanning when my dad reached his much longer arms onto the side handles and braced himself for the ride. At that point, there really wasn't much left for me to grab onto. All I could do was lean back into my dad's chest, brace my arms down against the floor...and hope for the best.

I had been watching the Wild Mouse intently since my earliest days of riding Trimper's kiddie rides. I knew that it was my amusement ride destiny, so I had already memorized its entire path, its turns, its hills, even its sounds. Especially the chattering metallic sound it made as it swooped over the loading area in a long extended left turn as the track headed back into the lower level of the wooden post forest to finish the ride. But it was a much more intense experience to hear that sound while seated directly under the car making it. And not only to hear it but to watch the speeding car pass by just above you...I just swallowed hard and looked straight.

Then the ride operator barked "Ready?" to which I shook my head while my dad answered "Yep" and our car coasted slowly forward for a second or two before making an easy left turn to drift down a gentle grade to catch the pull chain, which ran along the right side of the track. As the car started pointing upward the chain hesitated, jerked slightly, and then we were on the chain moving effortlessly up the lift hill.

We kept going up, up, and up, higher than I'd ever been in my life, with the orange glow of a sunset illuminating the sky to our right. At the top of the chain we had time to glance down at a three-story house below us, then take a quick look out at Trimper's turning Ferris wheel – which had already turned on its distinctive blue-and-white "star" lighting pattern – before the first 90° turn of the ride wrenched us to the left. This put us on a straightaway that had our mouse picking up speed as we headed for a tight 180° turn that sat just inside the wooden framework at the far end of the ride. Approaching fast was the roof of Trimper's carousel building, and my stomach involuntarily dropped as the front of the mouse dangled out over the edge of the track before throwing us hard against the insides of the car as it turned onto the next straightaway, pointing us back in the direction we had just come from. The force of the next 180° turn at the other end was even stronger, but less scary because the lift hill was just below and beyond us.

Heading into the next turn it felt like we were on the verge of control. The sharply bent track disappeared beneath us, and for a moment it seemed like we were suspended in the air, surely heading off the end of the ride and onto the ground four stories below. Then the car whipped around – we were still on the track! – with sideways momentum that conjured the possibility of tipping off the side. Yet in an instant we were heading straight again, and into the next gut-wrenching 180°. I'd had enough, but of course, there was no way at this point to get off. I was sorry I got on. Again, it felt like we were going to run right off the end or tip over sideways, but we survived and were now headed for the final turn on the top layer of the ride, a long looping slightly-inclined left-hander that would deliver us to the first hill of the ride.

It would also drop us into the second layer and more serious part of the Mouse, where things really got "wild." We were going so fast now that all I could focus on was the track stretching out in front me – all of the side scenery had become a blur. I saw the first hill coming, and we were going up the other side before my body knew what happened, as it was just a quick dip. Then we hit a 90° left-hander that threw both my dad and me hard against the right side of the car. Now on the back straightaway of the ride, the next 90° left-hander would put us onto the biggest hills of the Mouse, two of them in succession, in fact. This turn was just as jarring, except we were now looking down, straight down it seemed, into the pit of hell, and I felt my body come off the floor and away from dad as the car went vertical on the hill.

Oh, no, I was going to fly out of the car!

But I reconnected with the floor and my dad when we got the bottom, the force pinning me to my dad's chest as the car made it up to the top of the second hill. And then a funny thing happened at the top – I felt like I was floating. Not that I was going to come out of the car, but just for a second, it felt like gravity didn't exist. It was such a cool feeling that I...quickly felt again like I was coming out of the car as we started down the second hill, then was again pinned back into dad as we went up the other side. The feeling of floating wasn't as dramatic at the top of this hill, which connected to the long sweeping left turn that rocketed us over the Wild Mouse loading area and into the third and final layer of the ride.

A quick right turn set things up for a quick dip of a hill that – whoa, there's that weightless feeling again! Then a sharp 90° left put us into the short lower level back straight away, which was followed quickly by another sharp left and smaller dip, then a fast right, a lightning left, and...SCREEEEETCH! The car came to a stop in the Wild Mouse unloading area. It was time to get off.

I had survived. Not only had I survived, I felt kind of good. Pushing myself up and out of the car, and taking my first step on the wooden exit ramp out of the ride, I was a little light headed. My heart was certainly beating hard, too. But I felt good. Excited and exhilarated. Taking stock of all that happened over the last two minutes...life had changed. I'd taken a step into the grown-up world, and I liked it. The Wild Mouse, heck, it was fun. Thrilling, too. The closest to "cheating death" that I'd ever come in my young life. Walking out of the bright red fiberglass Wild Mouse exit portal there was only one thing on my mind.

"Dad, can we go on it again?

Chapter Four

First Shift

I eased my left foot off the clutch, allowing the nose of my Pontiac Sunbird to poke out onto the shoulder of northbound Coastal Highway. Getting out from 122nd Street usually wasn't much of a problem. There was just empty marshland directly across from us, and the block to our south was sand and beach grass except for three scattered houses. The only things remotely near us on the other side of the highway were The Sauté Café, and the looming fiberglass shapes of the Rolling Thunder Skate Park up at 125th Street, although so far this summer, the park appeared curiously deserted. Not that it was ever a major contributor to traffic, unlike the Montego Bay Shopping Center and the Gold Coast Mall, Ocean City landmarks that our first-floor condo was conveniently equidistant between. Our location's "convenience" wasn't all that apparent at 5:15 pm on a Friday in early June. But then a window opened in the southbound traffic, and I hit my Michigan-built V-6 for all it was worth. Finally, I was on my way to my first shift at Playland.

Despite the traffic, I was walking up the access road to Mark's office by 5:25 pm. A number of cars were already grouped along the eastern edge of the go-kart track fence – where I had parked this morning – in what was obviously the employee parking area. And walking just a few yards ahead of me was a pair of yellow-shirted Playland workers. I moved at their pace to keep a comfortable distance as we entered the park, then watched as they continued walking along the backside of a long building on the right side of the access road. I veered left heading for Mark's office door.

I reached for the doorknob, then had déjà vu, and put three more knocks on the door in just about the same location I had this morning.

"Yes, come in," answered Mark. I pushed the door forward and stepped inside.

"Ah, early, I like that," he said, getting up from his desk and heading toward a tall file cabinet in the back corner of the office. Mark opened the second drawer and began rustling around inside it with his right hand. "You look like a medium – here ya' go!"

Mark frisbee-ed me a plastic-wrapped package that was flat and bright yellow. It was my Playland shirt. "You can just change it here, then I'll walk you up to the employee lounge. You did bring something warm for later?"

"Yes, in my backpack," I said. "What do I owe you for the shirt?"

"It comes out of your first paycheck. So don't be alarmed."

"That's fine," I said, admiring the cool looking navy Playland logo on the right breast of the shirt. "Is my hat ok?"

Mark looked at my hat, a brimmed baseball model that was the same navy color as my shorts, but featured a white patch with black letters saying "Montego Bay Hardware." I was also a little worried that I hadn't done enough with my razor, leaving my mustache (allowed by the employee manual), and a small patch of blonde whiskers growing under my lower lip. The manual didn't offer specific instructions about this area, so I figured Mark could just tell me to shave it off. Which he now had the opportunity to do.

"Yeah, it's fine. Local. And you look good. Good job with the razor."

"Thanks," I said while tearing the cellophane wrapper from my shirt. Mark went over to his desk and picked up several pieces of paper.

"I'll be outside. You want to undo those buttons at the collar. Otherwise, you'll never get the shirt over your head," he said while opening the office door. I quickly undid the top buttons, stuffed my T-shirt into my backpack, then pulled on my Playland shirt while holding my hat in my left hand. It was a perfect fit. The yellow color and polo shirt style was much more inviting than the almost black Phillips T-shirt I had to wear the previous summer. The restaurant put us in a dark color because we were supposed to be invisible. Only the bus boys in their bright red shirts, or the waitresses in their white uniforms, were supposed to be "seen" by the customers.

I put my hat back on and opened the door.

"Looking good! Follow me," said Mark.

We made a sharp left from Mark's office and started walking up the access road toward the back of the park. Stretching out on our left was a continuation of the building that held Mark's office. It appeared to have several more offices before ending in a small shop area where the go-karts were being worked on. Next came a knot of well-worn picnic tables, beyond which there were only monorail stanchions and water – lots, and lots of water. This was the demarcation point of where Playland became a peninsula in Assawoman Bay. The only thing farther out in the water was the millipede-like structure of the Route 90 Bridge just to our south at 62nd Street.

On our right, a long cinder block wall was about to end, leaving a narrow corridor before the next building started. Through this opening came my first glimpse into the park – a quick snapshot setting the imposing erector-set inspired Spider ride against the colorful red and yellow umbrella canopies of Playland's kiddie rides. We kept moving forward as the surface transitioned from gravel to hard sand, the wood framework of the Hurricane now blotting out a significant chunk of the horizon. I was struggling, happily, I might add, to take it all in when Mark grabbed a door handle on the back of the building.

"Here we are, the employee lounge."

It was a square fluorescent-lit room with benches along the walls, and eye-level mounted pegs where hats, jackets, or sweatshirts could be hung. On the wall straight ahead was a punch clock surrounded by time card racks both on the left and the right. Just inside the door, three yellow-shirted young men were discussing the prospects of the Orioles, who had fallen to 6th place after Wednesday night's 3-2 home loss to Milwaukee. While the Orioles were my favorite American League team – I became a fan watching their games on television during the previous summer in Ocean City – I was a Philadelphia Phillies fan, born and bred, however painful that allegiance proved to be.

"Ah, the O's will be fine," said Mark. "You'll see."

"I don't know," said the tallest of three, who looked like he spent a couple of hours too long working on his summer tan.

"I say they sweep the Angels over the weekend," said Mark.

"You're crazy," said a guy who missed the memo on the navy shorts. His shorts were brown. At least his socks were navy.

"What's it worth to you?" propositioned Mark.

"We're not working enough hours yet to have any money," said the tall, sunburned guy. This got a laugh from everyone, including Mark.

"How about, if they don't sweep, you get the weekend off?" said Mark addressing the tall guy directly.

"Man, I need the hours..."

"And if they do sweep, I get you for a week on the monorail."

"Hell no!" came the immediate retort, which triggered a cascade of loud laughter. It nearly drowned out the "I'm not spending any shift in that suffocating fishbowl" concluding clause of the sentence.

"Okay, okay," said Mark with a big smile. While it was clear he had a good relationship with his employees, I made a mental note to beware of the monorail.

As the trio of still chuckling Orioles fans went out the door, Mark called out to a young woman sitting on the bench near the time clock.

"Lindsay...Lindsay," said Mark.

Lindsay got up and walked over to us. She stood half a foot shorter than Mark and I, with shoulder-length brown hair, a nicely tanned, round face, and wide set yellow-brown eyes that captured your attention. She was older than me, though certainly not as old as Mark, carrying a not quite bikini-ready roundish build under her official navy Playland windbreaker (the logo blazing out in bright yellow). Her orthodontic-aligned smile was bright and warm.

"Lindsay, this is Earl Shores, our newest hire. He's actually a friend of Jack Wainwright's. He's going to work the Antique Cars tonight."

"Nice to meet you," said Lindsay, holding out her right hand. I shook her surprisingly firm grip. "Yes, I remember Jack – glasses, crew cut, kind of built like a weight lifter."

"Yep, that's Jack," I answered.

"Hard worker, too."

"For sure. A good guy."

"You're all set, Lindsay? I need to get going," Mark interjected.

"Yes, I'll get him all set up," answered Lindsay.

"Great. Earl, I'll check on your later. Trust me, you're in good hands," said Mark as he moved toward the door.

Lindsay and I both blurted an almost simultaneous "Thanks!"

She quickly moved over to the punch clock and began scanning the time cards on the left side of the clock, which stuck up vertically out of the gray metal racks like a paper version of Ocean City's Condo Row.

"Let's find your time card," said Lindsay, as she continued examining the cards. About a third of the way down the rack she pointed to a card with my name on it.

"Here it is. Now punch it in the time clock and move it to the rack on the right."

I pulled out my card, which was about as long as a dollar bill, slid it into the slot in the time clock, and heard and felt the "ka-thunk" of the time stamp.

"Just anywhere?" I asked, trying to make a conscientious impression on Lindsay.

"There's a slot for each ride, but we've got kinda' lax with that over the last couple of years." Lindsay went quiet for a moment like she didn't want to tell me the wrong thing or start exposing the park's warts just 30 seconds into my first shift. I quickly scanned the slots and found the one near the top that said "Antique Cars."

"Got it."

"Great. We're supposed to punch in 15 minutes before the park opens. That's 5:45, at least tonight, but it's okay to be a little early on your first day. When you punch out at the end of the shift, move your card back to the left side. That way we know everyone's out when it's time to close."

Lindsay then reached up and removed a clipboard from a hook on the wall. I could see it was a chart with ride names in a left-hand column, days of the week across the top, and last names written in the boxes underneath to designate who was running a ride on a given day. The schedule sheet started on Sunday and ran to the following Saturday. My last name was penciled in for the Antique Cars tonight, but that was it. I didn't ask why.

"The new schedule gets posted every Saturday – it's always fun to see what you're going to be running each week. We open at 6:00 on weeknights right now, and 1:00 on Saturday and Sundays. Closing time is 11:00, or whenever someone official like me comes over and tells you to close your ride. We're rarely open until 11:00 in the early part of the summer."

I was still engrossed in the clipboard, looking at the endless possibilities for the summer. The "coaster" and the "mouse" caught my eye, the mouse being Playland's Monster Mouse, which was a more intense version of Trimper's Wild Mouse. It actually had a bigger first drop than the Hurricane, and probably the biggest and steepest drop in all of Ocean City. How cool would it be to run that?

"Are you ready?" asked Lindsay.

"Think so," I answered, trying to hide my actual excitement. "Should I leave my backpack here?"

"What's in it?"

"Just a sweatshirt for later and my sunglasses."

"You can bring it and put inside the fence of the ride. If you need the sweatshirt it has to go under your Playland shirt. The guests have to be able to see that you're a park employee."

"Oh, right, that makes sense. Thanks."

"Ready then? Let's go!"

We made a left out of the lounge, then another left into the corridor, and in an instant were in the park, the Spider ride dead ahead. It was still oddly quiet as we entered into the park proper, our footsteps the most prominent sounds as we moved across the southern "midway," one of the two main thoroughfares that ran the entire length of the park. Nearby on our right was the front entrance (overseen by the giant Playland genie), while off in the distance to our left was the bay, a tall chain link fence and the elevated monorail track serving as the boundary marker between land and sea. Peeking out from this westernmost corner of the park was the lift hill of the Hurricane, as well as the tall, squashed rocket shape of the Rotor, better known throughout the amusement world as the "Hell Hole."

I followed Lindsay around the waist-high boundary fence encircling the Spider. Jack told me the ride was brand new when he worked here in 1978, and it still looked shiny and almost new two years later, its hefty black metal support framework contrasting attractively with the fluorescent green ladybug-shaped cars sitting on the end of each arm. Helping this contrast were the white interiors of the cars, which seemed to glow against the green and black color scheme of the rest of the ride.

Besides the Spider's visual appeal, I also knew there were some distinctive marks on the control panel, left there by Jack and his Spider running partner on a blistering Bermuda High afternoon when Playland hosted a private corporate picnic. Maybe one evening this summer I'd get a chance to confirm Jack's version of the day.

As we rounded the Spider into the northern park-length midway, a life-sized brown bear stood in our path, being part of the "herd" of fiberglass animals posed throughout the park. To our right now were the distinctive giant red and yellow umbrellas of Kiddie Land. Playland owned a pair of these popular kid's rides, one with spinning silver tubs under the canvas canopy and another with beeping and flashing fiberglass space vehicles. Right behind them under a blue and white circus tent-like covering sat the kiddie boat ride, complete with a shallow circle of water. But Lindsay and I were going to stop just a few yards beyond the bear, in front of a long arched wooden sign that sat well above human height level. Topped on each end by miniature turn-of-the-century street lamps, its two support posts connected together with the ends of a thigh-high brown picket fence. And framed between the uppermost portions of the posts, on a background of all white, were large black letters saying "Antique Cars."

The large opening under the sign was divided in half, with the chained off right side being the entrance, and an inward-swinging thigh-high wooden gate on the left being the exit. A short wooden ramp led up to the chain, which Lindsay unclipped, letting me go in first. She put the chain back across the opening, and there we were, standing beside three shiny scaled down antique cars, all parked end-to-end on a long straight section of track that served as the ride's loading area. Considering this was just a kid's ride, the details of the cars were stunning, complete with thin tires on oversized wood spoke wheels, striped canvas "convertible" tops, and narrow squared off front ends with large headlights and old-fashioned external radiators. The radiator grills even said "Opel." I had a faint recollection of riding them during my earliest Playland visits in the 1960s, but I was too young to appreciate how realistic the cars actually were. As an almost grown up 19-year-old, I thought they were pretty cool.

While I stood there gawking at the cars, Lindsay walked around the back of the last one and began crunching over the loose gravel that filled in the interior of the ride. When she reached a pole mounted gray electrical box near the back of the ride, she pulled on a handle on the side, then walked back over to me.

"That's your power. The cars are sitting in a dead zone here in the loading area, that's why they're not moving yet," Lindsay said, nonchalantly adding, "Just put your backpack down on the other side of the ticket box. Uh...you're not a smoker, are you?"

"No, I was too busy with sports to ever get interested. Plus, I'm too cheap."

"Good. Then you won't go into withdrawal before your evening break comes. There's absolutely *no* smoking while we're working the rides."

Lindsay then walked toward the front car – a bright blue one with a blue and white striped top – and motioned me over to look inside. The car was surprisingly large, an adult could sit inside comfortably. A steering wheel and metal gearshift were in the front seat, and there was a steering wheel in the back seat, too. Both steering wheels were positioned on the right side of the car.

"There's no gas or brake," said Lindsay, who leaned over inside of the car and began pulling the front steering wheel back and forth. "These don't do anything but spin inside the car. The kids are just along for the ride turning the wheel and pulling the gear shift."

Lindsay then pulled her head out of the car and began gently pushing it forward out of the loading area.

"Now for the magic..."

As the car neared a sharp right-hand turn the engine came on, the headlights lit up, and it began moving on its own, driverless at a fast walking pace, guided by the electrified rail in the center of the track. After a few seconds on a gentle "S" section the car ran under the white wooden Exit ramp of Playland's monorail station and made a sharp 180° turn back toward the loading area.

"Now would be when you start the next car," instructed Lindsay, looking directly at me. I nodded to acknowledge that I got the directive, and we watched as the car made a teardrop-shaped loop back out toward the monorail track, then a final 180° for an inward run to where we stood.

"Come on," said Lindsay, and I followed her past the rear bumper of the last parked car (a bright red one with a red and white striped top). Lindsay stood waiting on the outside of the track just where the final turn sent our driverless car into the loading area. When the car got even with the nearby spinning tub ride, it slowed down like someone applied a brake. Lindsay grabbed its front roof support post to slow it further, then pushed it to gently bump the red car, moving the two parked cars slightly forward.

"You don't have to catch it each time, but you should try," she said with emphasis. "It's going to be a quiet night. You can see we only have three cars on the track," she said, pointing to two other dormant cars sitting off on the gravel interior.

"Okay, now it's your turn. And I want you to get all three running at once."

This was *so* different than the previous summer, which I spent in a claustrophobic kitchen standing over a sweltering steam table or in front of a hissing six-foot-tall Vulcan industrial steamer, an instantaneous flesh-melting monster that never ceased to unnerve me. Now I was standing out in the fresh air and golden glow sunshine of an early June evening, a gentle ocean breeze making the temperature about perfect. My view through the monorail stanchions on the far side of the ride consisted of acres of undeveloped marshland, and the North Ocean City skyline against a background of cloudless blue. And all I had to do was get these three cars out onto the track? Not sort through a clothesline full of barely legible seafood orders?

Was this job for real?

Following Lindsay's explicit instructions, it was easy to get all the cars out and back again. Compared to digging my way out of the "weeds" at Phillips on a summer Saturday night it was a piece of cake. ("The weeds" being a term for having so many order forms hanging in front of you that you couldn't see the waitress when she returned to pick up her food.)

"Seems like you're all set. I'll check back a little later. And I'll be walking around the park throughout the night. If you have a problem, let me know."

"There's no height limit or tickets to collect?" I asked, again trying to be the conscientious newbie.

"Oh – right. Good questions. No, there's no height limit. Just remember to hook the strap in front of them. If they can sit still, they can ride, and the smaller ones can ride with their parents. We have a set admission fee. Guests can ride all the rides as many times as they want."

"OK, thanks," I said, hoping I'd be able to discern the kids who were "sit-stillers."

"Just be sure to look for the stamp on their right hand."

Watching Lindsay walk away past the bear, it was still hard to believe I was here, standing outside on this beautiful evening, in my official Playland shirt, at a ride that I was going to run. This was something I had long dreamed of doing...and it was actually going to happen!

In trying to take in everything from my new post, the nearest ride to me was the Spider, about 30 feet away just on the other side of the midway. I watched as the two dark haired guys manning the ride methodically rotated each of the six curved arms down into the loading area and carefully checked the locking mechanism on every pair of cars. A black-handled lever stuck out from the front of each car, and when it was pulled on, the entire green front half dropped down, exposing a white bench seat while at the same time creating a step for riders to climb up into the car. The front half got pushed back up, and there was a solid "thunk" of something locking. My Playland colleague then yanked down on the front with some force to double check, and he was on to the next car. I was studying carefully when I heard tires skidding on asphalt as an approaching electric engine suddenly shut down. My head snapped reflexively to see what it was.

Stopped just off to my right was a green golf cart carrying the oddest-looking twosome I had ever seen. Not that either man, by themselves, was odd, but the pairing – it wasn't one you were going to see on any country club fairway in this neck of Delmarva. The passenger, a pale middle-aged male in blue coveralls, looked like he just stepped off the rickety front porch of some rural general store. Wearing a generic blue and white feed cap, and also a pinched expression on his clean-shaven face, I couldn't tell if he was smiling or scowling. But there was something about him – maybe it was my previous summer living below the Mason Dixon line – that told me that his voice would have more than a touch of South in it.

"Weeeelllll..." he said, raising the middle of the word up a whole tone or two while throwing in more "e's" and "l's" than Webster's would ever allow.

"Moon, we got a new man on the job tonight!"

Moon was the driver. A coal-hued man of indeterminate age, he wore a short-sleeved light blue work shirt over sturdy arms that had clearly spent a lifetime working heavy machinery. With his face shaded by a blue grease-stained "Goodyear" hat, and his eyes as well as his wrinkles hiding behind mirror sunglasses, he might have been 45 or 65, I really couldn't tell. Moon smiled under his thin trimmed mustache, nodding a raspy affirmative "um-huh" as an unlit Winston dangled from the corner of his mouth.

"I'm Melvin, this is Moon," continued the passenger. "We're the park mechanics. When things break, we fix 'em. If you have a problem –"

Melvin paused, looked at Moon, and both men started to laugh. While I knew I wasn't in on the joke, I was sure that I was part of it. Moon took the cigarette from his mouth and continued chuckling as Melvin's composure returned.

"Well...you really can't have much of a problem with those things," he said while motioning his right arm at my meager three-car lineup. "But if you do, let us know. Anyway, good luck tonight."

Melvin barely got the period attached to his sentence before Moon hit the accelerator, and off they went toward the front of the park, a trail of laughter evaporating behind them

I was still trying to shake the "huh?" off my face when the jangly two-chord opening of The Pretender's "Brass in Pocket" echoed loudly throughout the park.

It was 6:00 pm. We were open for business.

Chapter Five

Who's Afraid of a Five-Year-Old?

An outstanding KIDDIELAND with a world of entertainment for youngsters . . . On a number of the rides even Mommy and Daddy can ride along.

I could see people starting to spread out from the front gate of the park. Once they paid their admission they could do anything, including play a round of miniature golf on the elaborate circus-themed course that sat on a significant piece of real estate in front of the Hurricane. The running of the ride, at least the part of making the cars go around the track, that wasn't going to be all that hard. Yet I was nervous, really nervous...about the kids.

For someone like me, who was an only child, who never baby-sat, and whose friends seemed to be only children or the last sibling of a brood, young kids were like the aliens from the *Star Wars* Cantina – strange exotic life forms that I'd just as soon stay away from. Other than my first girlfriend's little brother, from a relationship five years in my past, I had virtually *zero* experience with the population I was going to be dealing with tonight, that being kids under the age of ten.

Surely they would see right through me and know immediately that I didn't know how to talk with them or deal with them, or project even a hint of "adult" authority. I was just a guy from Pennsylvania who wanted to live at the beach. Maybe I was better off hiding in the weeds at Phillips.

Standing in front of my cars and the expanse of the ride...I felt so exposed. Completely out in the open, on my own, with only a vague idea of how things would happen, of my "script," as it were. It was like I had a page full of directions without any dialogue. What would I say to the kids? I couldn't just stand there mute. I had to say something, I had to interact with them. Really, who would be intimated by a bunch of little kids? The answer was easy – me.

Just like the Pretender's distinctive female singer I was now using my imagination, trying desperately to look relaxed and at ease in front of my ride. In observing the growing activity around me – oh that's right, we have a Sky Ride – I noticed a family of four on the midway continue past the umbrella rides and head my way. They split up as they got closer with the two brothers starting up the ramp to my ride while mom and dad took up positions at the picket fence next to the entrance. I moved over to let them in and heard myself say "Hi guys" as they displayed right hands with red stamps. As I re-clipped the chain they moved down to the first car and were now looking at me, expectantly it seemed. The older one, seven maybe, wearing dark shorts and a gray pullover sweatshirt with "Ocean City, Maryland" in black on the front, followed me with his eyes as I got closer to the car. I smiled – I couldn't help it to be honest – and reached inside to undo the restraining straps in the front and back seats. He was still looking at me before I said anything more...and looking down into his wide blue eyes my nervousness evaporated on the easterly breeze flowing through the park.

What I'd forgotten from my own days of being a young and eager rider of rides was this: thanks to my yellow Playland shirt I had instant authority. As the operator of this ride, I was one of the coolest people in all of Ocean City, at least to most kids this age. So I didn't have to say anything or do anything special. I just had to get them on the ride, smile, and make sure they were strapped in properly. With this realization, I relaxed and found someone inside me whom I didn't know existed – someone who seemed to enjoy being around little kids.

They didn't need any help climbing in and had no problem in deciding the seating arrangement, with little brother in the front and big brother in the back, both with a steering wheel in hand. Their distinctively similar faces were all smiles, huge smiles, like this was the best night of their lives. I could feel their energy, their positivity, their innocence...it was all so stark and honest. And stunningly unexpected, for me anyway. This was a giant chunk of life and reality that I'd never been exposed to before, and to be honest, a chunk that I'd never even contemplated. If you talked to me earlier in the day, hell, maybe even 30 minutes ago, I probably would have expressed my cynicism for the concept of "childlike innocence." But at this moment, standing beside the car holding the front support post, it was all laid out before me, just three feet away.

Feeding off of their incredible vibe, I wanted to do all I could to help them have a great time, a great time on *my* ride. I wanted to be the person who got their night off to a great start.

"Are you ready, guys?" I asked enthusiastically after clipping in their restraint straps. I couldn't help myself. They just shook their heads and smiled some more.

"Okay, here we go...get those wheels turning!"

And off I pushed them until their car came to life. There was a happy squeal from the younger one when the headlights came on and the car started moving on its own. I looked back to see if there were any other kids in line, and for the moment there weren't. So I walked across the track onto the ride's gravel interior to watch the boys as their car continued forward. All was well as both steering wheels went back and forth, the little guy in the front with the navy sweatshirt not seeming to notice the gearshift.

As I moved toward the final turn of the ride I looked at the parents, dad in sunglasses with a huge smile, and mom with her entire face – eyes, cheeks, and mouth – stretched into an upturned look of joy...the glow and warmth of this smile seemingly coming from every atom of her being. When the car swooped through the extended teardrop turn adjacent to the loading area, both boys were fully visible thanks to the right-sided steering wheels.

"Are you driving Jack? Are you keeping it on the road?" mom asked excitedly. The younger one looked over, smiled and waved, keeping his left hand on the wheel. The older boy waved too, his right arm almost looking like it was signaling for a turn, remaining upright and pointing to the sky as the car headed away from the loading area. With a few more steps I was positioned exactly where Lindsay stood, on the outside of the track at the final turn of the ride. Jack and his brother were still working their steering wheels as the car slowed just about to a stop, and I pushed it in the final few yards to rest against the next car.

"How was that?" I asked, reaching in to unclip Jack in the front.

"That was great!!" came the answer from Mr. Ocean City in the back seat. Jack was smiling still holding the wheel, while his brother started to undo his own clip.

"David...David!" said the mom, "Let the man undo the strap."

"He's okay, he knows what he's doing," I said. "Thanks, David."

I was stunned on two counts here: first being called a "man," and second, at my instantaneous and enthusiastic ad-lib with David. How did I do that?

David was out and waiting at the exit while Jack remained sitting in the car. He clearly didn't want to get off.

"Come on, Jack, you need to get off," said mom.

"Yeah, come on Jack, your brother's waiting," added dad. Surely Jack had heard that line before.

"That was fun, wasn't it?" I asked, sticking my head into the ride while keeping my distance. Jack shook his head "yes," but still didn't say a word. "Well, maybe you can drive the car again. But you'll have to get off and ask your parents first. What do you think?"

Jack looked at me, didn't say yes or no, but began sliding across the seat to get out. I backed out of the car and started walking to the gate to let the brothers out of the ride.

"Thank you," said the mom. "Thanks for coaxing him out. Jack, David – tell the man 'thank you.'"

"Yeah, tell the man 'thank you,'" added dad. Again, I was totally not used to this "man" thing.

David looked over as he opened the exit gate, offering a quickly shouted, "Thank you!" Jack mumbled his "thank you" as he rushed through the opening toward mom. A family huddle ensued, with Jack quickly returning to the entrance chain just ahead of an older boy wearing an Orioles cap, whose mom and dad took seats on the benches lining the outside of the ride's picket fence. I opened the chain and let them both on, with Jack purposefully heading down to the green car at the front of the line. The older and taller boy followed, then looked confused, like he wasn't sure if he was supposed to climb in with Jack.

"It's okay, you can have your own car. Climb in the red one there," I said, as a smile replaced the look of uncertainty on his face. I moved forward and reached in to clip Jack's restraint strap. He was already holding the steering wheel, a smile filling his face.

"Back so soon?" I asked. "That was nice of mom and dad, wasn't it?"

I backed out of the car and began pushing it along the track until the engine came on, and off Jack went.

Quickly moving back to the red car, I strapped my new rider into his seat. He was giving the gearshift a workout as we waited for Jack's car to go under the monorail ramp. Once I saw Jack's smile coming back toward me I pushed the red car along the track until the engine and headlights came on, and now I had two riders out on the track. I gave the empty blue car a shove forward as I walked toward the final turn to catch Jack's car. It looked like I might have another customer, as there was a family in a discussion not far from the entrance, but I was going to get my two cars exited before taking on someone else. It wouldn't be that long a wait – as long as Jack got right off.

Uh-oh.

A little flush of nerves went through me, contemplating how to negotiate with Jack and catch the second car. It wasn't quite a Phillips kitchen scenario, but it was clear that even my "simple" ride had the potential for complications. So I stood there feeling a little less exhilarated than I had a few minutes ago. But looking at the cars, the kids were having a blast.

Jack's car approached, and I moved to catch it while it still had some juice flowing in the engine, pushing it through the turn and to the rear bumper of the car in the loading area. I took a quick glance to see the other car still working its way into the final 180° turn, so there was no rush. As long a Jack didn't need coaxing.

"How's that drive the second time – just as much fun?" I said unclipping Jack's restraint strap. A smile and a nod were my answer.

"Are you ready…"

He'd already started sliding out of the seat and brushed by me as I tried to get out of his way. I barely got a step toward to exit before Jack scooted through the gate and rejoined his family.

"Bye," I said, waving at the boys.

"Thank you, again," said the mom. There might have been a conversation in the offing, but I needed to do my job, so I turned and quickstepped back toward the final turn. My Orioles' rider was just about at a stop, and I grabbed his car and guided it in.

"Good ride?" I said, watching him unclip the restraint on his own.

"Yep," came the reply as he moved across the seat and stepped out of the car. Out the gate he went to catch up with his strolling parents.

With my entrance ramp still unoccupied, I took a moment to catch my breath and put my thoughts about running the ride in some kind of order. It was far from a thoughtless exercise, although the basic steps of the on-and-off part would become routine. Hopefully. And the fact that the cars could come to a stop all by themselves, the most "major" issue would be having a loose kid wandering around the loading area. So as long as they were strapped in, and stayed strapped in, I would be okay.

"Nice job," said a voice from just over the fence. I had to spin completely around to see that it was Lindsey. I had no idea that she was anywhere nearby. Not that it would have mattered, I had enough going on. And it was all new.

"You're a natural, the kids like you."

"I'm as surprised as you are. But they're having such a good time. It's easy – sort of."

"Yeah, it is. As long as you can see them having a good time. Not everybody does."

"Really? How much more obvious can it be?"

"Some people, I think, just don't want to see it. It makes them think. Anyway, keep it up. I'll be back for your break."

"Okay. Thanks, Lindsay."

A parent with a toddler was now in my line, as were two brothers and a sister. Everyone was all smiles, everyone was ready to have a good time. They were at the beach, at an amusement park on a beautiful night, with hardly a care in the world. The toddler's eyes were dilated saucers as he walked hand in hand with mom to the front car. With mom's help, he could just about get his hands on the steering wheel, but there was no question he knew what it was for. His mouth had been open the entire time, frozen in a half smile that somehow captured and underplayed his excitement at the same time. Dressed in a white zip-up hooded sweatshirt, brown shorts, and a pair of those strange yet iconic unisex toddler sandals with a buckle, he was...I had to admit, cute. Especially with curly brown hair that seemed almost perfectly disheveled. As I clipped in their restraint, my thoughts were still stuck on what Lindsay just said.

How could anyone not see this?

Chapter Six

Spilling the Beans

It had been a wondrous night, and I was trying to get it all down in a letter to my girlfriend.

> Sitting here, there are really a lot of things that I want to say. If a single shift of work can change your life, maybe you'll understand this letter. I hope so. Anyway, what happened tonight had a profound effect on me.

I had really gotten in a groove after my conversation with Lindsay, loading the kids on and off like a pro, continuing to interact with them and their parents. The job was fun. I was completely relaxed and feeding on the positive vibe that everyone brought to the park. It was changing me by the minute, chopping the legs out from under the cynical bastard I'd become by the end of last summer when I hated my job, and hated the tourists – on the road, on the beach, in the lineup, in the supermarket, in the long line waiting to get into the restaurant. They were always in my way in *my* Ocean City.

> They put me on a ride that was a popular one, but it was popular with little kids! I was operating these antique cars that kids get in and pretend they're driving. It runs on a rail, but the cars have steering wheels and gearshifts. The kids love the ride. Some of them kept getting off and running to the end of the line!

But tonight, and being out in the fresh air certainly helped, I "got it." I was reminded why people came to Ocean City. I was reminded of my own history here and of my family's deep generational connections to the early days of the town. And watching the kids, I was reminded of myself, the eight-year-old who loved riding rides, and who dreamed of growing up to run rides in Ocean City.

Needless to say, I saw more little kids in one night than I've seen in my entire life. It was definitely a different experience for me. What really got me was the look on some of the kids' faces when they came around the last turn and I had to get them off. You would look at them and their eyes would be saying, "wow," especially the smaller ones. They would want to ride around again and I had to coax them off the ride.

I put down my blue ink Bic Banana and looked over at the television. Owing to the rather intimate dimensions of our condo it wasn't far away, sitting just two steps across the room on top of the mini-fridge. It was only a portable RCA 12-incher, but it was color, and we did have a rent-included connection to Eastern Shore Cable. So instead of a ghostly and rolling Rabbit ear UHF feed from Salisbury, we had a clear picture. Which mattered little as I tried to follow the bizarre sport unfolding on the screen. At first, I thought it was rugby, then a man wearing a white lab coat and matching fedora jumped out onto the enormous oval field, making a shooting gesture with his index fingers. A score flashed up over the action:

North Melbourne   9 7 51
Richmond   13 9 76

I picked up my pen. This new 24-hour sports network thing really wasn't all that it was cracked up to be.

I could see the kids were having such a good time, and the parents would either watch or get on too, and they were enjoying the fact that the kids were enjoying themselves. Watching the kids' reaction when they are on the ride is incredible – the younger ones are priceless. I can't believe how much I enjoy the kids. They see things in such a different way from the rest of us. I had a great time watching them. They really are cute.

Getting louder in the parking lot was the distinctive clicking of a coasting bicycle derailleur. That would be my roommate Greg coming home from his shift at Phillip's Seafood House on 141st Street. It was my suggestion that landed him there, as I had worked a number of substitute shifts at the Seafood House during the previous summer because they were always in need of help. Greg's brake pads groaned briefly against the metal rims of his Schwinn 10-speed, then I could hear his pedals continue to rotate forward as he picked up the bike to carry it up the stairs. With us being in 1-G, a bottom floor corner unit facing eastward on Assawoman Drive, Greg only had four wooden steps to navigate before having the full run of the metal railing outside our door. The railing pinged and hummed as Greg secured the lock on his bike, then I heard his keys jangle near the doorknob.

"It's open," I said, studying our oddly colored front door. It was pale green with a hint of yellow, attempting to tie in with the color accents of the thick shag carpet, a once white object that had toned gray through use and contained a beach worth of sand under its matted piles. Fortunately, thanks to the air conditioner, it didn't stink and wasn't gross to walk on. At least not yet.

Greg pushed in the door, which just cleared our lime green vinyl couch and round-tabled dinette set with inches to spare. I was purposely seated in the chair on the far side of the table. That way I didn't have to get up to let Greg get in – or have to smell him from close proximity.

Upon shutting the door, Greg unleashed a pungent gust of an all too familiar peppery yet sweet aroma – that of Old Bay crab spice. It clung to him like a cheap wetsuit, not that he could help it, as it was the default fragrance of every Phillips' kitchen. About the only thing the restaurant didn't put the Baltimore-made concoction on was desserts (and maybe salads). Once a half dozen 30-gallon crab barrels got steaming simultaneously on a busy Friday or Saturday night you could smell Phillips from blocks away. Even up on the boardwalk. It was a "Pavlov's Bell" for people who loved eating crabs. And it permeated every piece of clothing you wore on a shift, even your underwear.

Greg took off his brimmed University of Delaware cap and put it on the table, letting the smiling caricatured "Blue Hen" face on the front stare directly at me. Greg was looking at me too. Expectantly.

"How was it?" he said in an enthusiastic tone that was louder than his normal voice.

"It was...amazing, really, amazing," I said with a big smile. "It wasn't even like work. Hell, I punched out at 10:15!"

"Aw, man, no shit!" Greg began pulling out the yellow vinyl dinette chair across from me, then glanced over at the television. "What the hell is that?"

"Something Australian I think, at least that's the accent of the announcers."

"Wow...ESPN kind of sucks, doesn't it?"

"I thought you were into the Caribbean fastpitch softball?"

Greg shot me a half lid look, his mouth going flat in a smirk.

"The job, man, the job. Tell me about Playland."

"Don't you want to shower?" Greg always headed right for the shower after he came in. The fact that he bothered to sit down showed how intently he wanted the details of my night.

"Nah, it can wait."

"Well, at least put your shoes on the balcony. You're going to ruin those Brookses."

Shoes took the biggest beating at Phillips. Because of leakage from the steamer pots, there was often an Old Bay slurry coating the floor by the end of the night, inundating whatever you had on your feet. During the previous summer, I'd lost my favorite Adidas and a totally new pair of Nike waffles to this Old Bay onslaught.

Greg got up and walked down the hallway to the back door, which was in my bedroom. That and the bathroom were the only true designated spaces in the place. This room was the habitation equivalent of a Swiss Army knife. Besides the television and the couch, which pulled out to be Greg's bed, an entire compact kitchenette – cupboard, stove, sink, and under counter half fridge – was within arm's length behind me. Spilling out of a broom closet just beyond my reach was our resident "pet," a five-foot-tall avocado colored Skinny-Mini washer-dryer contraption that tried to walk down the hall every time we used it. The most prominent piece of furniture, a white Formica dinette table, was where I sat. Centered under an immense globe-shaped 100-watt bulb whose retina-burning properties rivaled a solar eclipse, the table took up almost half of our floor space. From it, we ate, drank, talked, watched television, watched the tourists on the stairs, read the newspaper, wrote letters, listened to music (from a pair of Bose speakers pointed directly at the table), de-seeded our weed...and passed the bong. It was the center of our summertime universe.

Greg returned barefooted and grabbed a can of Tab out of the minifridge under the television. A loud "pssst" filled the air as Greg popped the pull-tab, letting the pull ring and its curly metal tail dangle off his little finger as he returned to the chair across from me.

"How do you drink that stuff?" I asked, already knowing the "why" of him drinking this thoroughly gag-inducing saccharin-sweetened diet soda.

"Ah, you don't even taste it after a while," he said patiently.

"Right now, it probably tastes like Old Bay."

Greg didn't acknowledge my weak attempt at humor, tilting the can up for substantial swig. For Greg, a reformed cigarette smoker, the Tab routine was better than grabbing a beer or a real soda with sugar. Because in addition to casting off his nicotine habit he'd dropped a serious chunk of weight during the previous year, even taking up running to do it. These were significant feats of discipline for a 19-year-old, and I really admired him for it. He was now applying this discipline to his tan, having already worked down into the single-digit SPF oils of Hawaiian Tropic's Dark Tanning line. Such a pursuit, for many people, could be rightly judged as excessive and vain. But in Greg...he was just excited about his first summer at the beach. Sincerely excited. And he wanted to go back to school looking like he'd spent the summer at the beach – or as tan and as blonde as possible. I was rooting for him. I'd had the same ambitions the previous summer.

Greg put his can down on the table and looked over at my letter.

"Come on, you're already writing about it. Enough stalling...spill the beans!"

"Okay, okay. It was really crazy. I don't even know where to start."

"The beginning would nice."

"Yeah, well, Mark the manager guy is really cool. He came over at the end of the night to tell me how well I did and that he was glad he hired me."

"What were you doing?"

"I ran one of the kiddie rides, the Antique Cars. They run on a track with an electric rail. I got the kids on and off and strapped them in."

"They drive the cars?"

"No, no, no. The steering wheels turn and there's a gearshift they can play with, but they don't do anything. I had to make sure the cars were spaced out on the track so they wouldn't run into each other at the end."

"They just let you figure out how to do that?"

"No, one of the supervisors showed me before the park opened. A woman named Lindsay. She was really cool too. But you want to know the really crazy part?"

"What?"

"It was fun, I really enjoyed the kids. They were so excited to be on the ride, you should have seen their faces when the ride was over."

"Kids?!! Did you just hear what you said?"

"Yeah, I know. But I mean, the whole vibe of the park...everybody just seemed happy to be there. Including all the other workers. Crazy, right?"

"Well, maybe. Actually, it sounds kind of good."

"I know what *was* good. All I have to do is punch in, go to my ride – Mark said I'd have the cars again tomorrow – and turn it on. Then when we close at the end of the night, all I have to do is turn the ride off and punch out. No cleanup, no inspections. When you're done, you're done."

"Ah man, that sounds fantastic," said Greg, picking up his Tab for another long swig. "I tried to get our cleaning started early tonight, but we were still there 45 minutes after closing."

"Uh-huh. And the employee meal was yummy, was it not?"

"Puh – all it was good for was helping me keep the weight off. I cut my break short and went back to the kitchen to clean."

"I walked around the park on my break. The sun had just gone down and all the rides had their lights on. I had no idea they'd stuffed a Rotor back by the coaster. That thing is almost as tall as the Sky Ride. And I hope I get to run the Monster Mouse. It has a really mean first drop."

For the moment I drifted out of the conversation, staring across the room at the wall...did this night really happen?

"Is that all?" Greg asked with a smile and a dose of sarcasm. I looked back over at him and continued my Playland recap.

"The Spider ride was right across from me, and it's wild looking at night, all covered in green and yellow lights. When the arms move and the cars spin it looks like a 3-D work of art. Art that makes you barf."

I almost got a spit take out of Greg with my final line. He'd just put the can up to his mouth, then quickly put it down, swallowing hard on the little bit of Tab he'd manage to ingest. He was smiling as a dribble of bubbling brown liquid ran down his chin.

"You bastard," he said in a strained voice, "I almost choked on this crap. That'd be a hell of a way to go."

"And still smelling like Old Bay, too. They'd have to cremate you."

Greg laughed some more shaking his head back and forth. Although we'd known each other for almost two years, this was our first try at being roommates. It didn't seem like there would be any problems, Greg was good company. We saw the world in the same way and could talk about anything and everything. One of the things I appreciated most about Greg was that he wasn't fixated on girls' body parts or carnal conquest. Not that he didn't like girls – he would probably attract his share of attention this summer, especially with his new beach bod and naturally bleaching blonde hair. But it was just as likely he would attract attention from the opposite sex because he was simply a nice guy. Funny and considerate, too.

"Just one last question before I hit the shower."

"Yeah, what's that?"

"Do you think Mark would hire me?"

"We can find out tomorrow."

Chapter Seven

Dorchester Street

Whenn my aunt sold her West Ocean City trailer in the late 1960s, it was an enormous shock. How could she just get rid of it after we'd spent just about every summer weekend there? And nobody asked me what I thought about it...not that a seven-year-old should really be part of any adult decision-making process. But suddenly my special place, a place that I assumed would always be there, was gone. Just like that. Ocean City's role as a focal point in my young life was over. The loss I felt during the following summers was very real. Weekends and weeks at the beach were a given, an entrenched part of the family routine, at least that's what I had been led to believe, thanks to the trailer. And now they weren't – nor would they ever be again. Betrayal. It was probably the first time I ever experienced it. Certainly, the first time from somebody close. Something special had been taken from me, and there wasn't a thing I could do about it. It just wasn't fair.

The reasons for the trailer's demise were always vague. Maybe I was told but didn't understand, or maybe I didn't want to understand. It did revolve around a great aunt who owned the trailer next to us. In 1967 she moved her trailer to a newer and more scenic waterfront lot in Delaware. Why we didn't follow her was never explained, although this new location was miles away from Ocean City, and a 30-minute ride from the ocean. So things would have been very different there. Ocean City would have been far from nearby. But why couldn't we have remained in West Ocean City without my great aunt? That was the mystery. The park didn't close, and for years afterward, we'd drive by on Route 50 and I'd look down the gravel entrance road thinking about what could have been. What should have been. But the trailer wasn't even there anymore. It was sitting all by itself, forlornly in my eyes, on the grassy northeast corner of Route 50 and Race Track Road. For years, it was my own personal symbol of distrust. Proof that you could never count on things – even from people close to you.

It was entirely possible the ground rent increased to some outrageous amount, or that maybe the park was changing in ways my younger eyes couldn't see. Like the new neighbor behind us, a man whose dusk-to-dawn routine included lung-rattling coughing fits between ash-glowing puffs on his cigarettes. Not only was it unsettling, it was unavoidable since no one in the park had air conditioning. And perhaps coughing was the least of the ills and strangeness happening within the park's confines. Old family photos clearly showed that, at least to my now older eyes, the park was rough around the edges. But I've still never had an adult discussion about the trailer. I'm sure my feelings of loss, which were genuine and intense, would come as a surprise to my family. After all, I was "just a little kid."

With the trailer gone Ocean City was essentially erased from my life, especially in the years we didn't take a summer vacation there. Our default lodgings when we did visit were the Ocracoke Cottages on Dorchester Street, which sat bayside about a half block east of the Marina docks and restaurant. These were actually old family stomping grounds, tracing back to my great-grandmother renting rooms from Ocean City matriarch Annie Bunting before the inlet was cut in 1933. There were also dozens of black and white photos from the 1940s and 1950s chronicling the youth of my aunt and my father as they spent summer weeks and even summer months on Dorchester Street, pretty much becoming extended members of the Bunting family. Most striking were the photos of my father and Jay Bunting (Annie's youngest son) as they mugged and fooled around for the camera looking very much like brothers, my father appearing all the part of the doting, protective older brother. Like the trailer's demise, these scenes had never been fully explained to me. But through the laughter and smiles frozen in those photos, it was easy to see there were serious bonds between the two families.

Which explained why an unwavering part of the trailer "routine" included dropping off my great-grandmother to spend the evening talking with Mrs. Bunting while the rest of us went to the Boardwalk.

"Come in, come in children," was Mrs. Bunting's trademark greeting, always in a pleasant yet raspy voice that still carried its distinctively southern Outer Banks delivery.

Mrs. Bunting arrived in Ocean City in 1917 as an uncertain 20-year-old named Annie Spencer. The Ocracoke native had never ventured more than a ferry crossing from her Carolina barrier island home, and now she was hundreds of miles away embarking on an entirely new life. After moving in with her brother Tom, who'd already left the meager life options of Ocracoke behind to become an Ocean City policeman, Annie found work as a maid at the Mervue Hotel. She was soon engaged to U.S. Coast Guardsman Levin J. Bunting, and within five months of arriving in Ocean City, she was Mrs. Bunting. While Lev, or "dad" as she called him, watched the ocean, including patrolling for German subs during WW II, she, like many other Ocean City women, became an innkeeper, renting the rooms of their cedar-shake two-story Cape Cod to tourists during the summer months.

Those rooms expanded to five apartments by the 1950s, with a pair of two-story buildings overtaking the entire backyard of 205 Dorchester Street. In addition to the expanding business, Mrs. Bunting became something of a force of nature through the decades, helping with the fire company, and knowing everyone and everything that went on in Ocean City. And despite being born in the previous century, she still held court nightly from a padded recliner on her intimate screened-in front porch, the tiny red lights of a nearby police scanner flickering from frequency-to-frequency in search of the latest Ocean City news.

"Come in, children, come in – there's plenty of room."

Of course, we would all tumble inside, spilling into the doorway connecting the house and into the area on the porch behind her chair. No one was ever allowed to stay outside on the three gray stone steps up to the house. It didn't matter if the current party consisted of two people or ten, everyone had to come inside. That's because one of Mrs. Bunting's gifts was "taking stock" – of growth spurts, school achievements, husbands, wives, girlfriends, boyfriends, or what you were up to for the evening. She would make a fuss about everyone, effortlessly recalling something distinctive about that person from the previous week, month, or year, and then weave it into a personal greeting that always flattered and usually got a laugh.

"Oh, my, my, my, why he's the spitting image of his father at that age, towhead and everything. And growing too, why they just don't stop, do they?"

I was always squirmy during these early evening look-ins. I had things to do – there were rides to ride, Skee-Ball to throw, and caramel popcorn to eat. But Mrs. Bunting could always calm me and make my ears go red by comparing me with my father. I liked when she did that. I also liked what she didn't do – the kiss-and-hug thing. She was more of the handshake and hand-holder type, which was fine by me. Few adults ever made me feel as welcome and as special as Mrs. Bunting did.

"It's a beautiful evening tonight. How many rides are you going to ride tonight?"

I was always hard-pressed for an answer, usually resorting to a shrug.

"You're not going shy on me now, are you? Goodness, you used to run around here in diapers," she'd say, letting out a deep stuttering laugh that somehow seemed to carry a high and low tone at the same time.

Her laugh and her speech weren't her only distinguishing features. She was perhaps the "youngest" old person I'd ever known. And I knew what old looked like, having spent extended time with my 90-year-old great-grandmother, as well as great uncles and aunts who were in their 60s and 70s. Like my grandmother, who was already in her 50s yet still rode the rides and often spent the entire day with me in the ocean, Mrs. Bunting seemed ageless. Not that she didn't have gray hair and wrinkles. But somehow through all the years spent in a seaside environment, her wrinkles were organized, like glassy ocean swells lined up in a light off-shore wind, enhancing her prominent cheekbones and still tanned and taut skin. Throw in her boundless energy, which engulfed anyone and everyone who set foot on the property, and "old" was just never a term I associated with Mrs. Bunting.

Especially when we returned from the boardwalk hours later to find my great-grandmother and Mrs. Bunting still absorbed in conversation.

In fact, Mrs. Bunting seemed energized when we all piled back into the porch, like it was the start of Act II, wanting to know exactly what I did, how crowded it was or wasn't, and whether we ran into anybody we knew.

"The Ferris wheel, the boats – the ones in and out of the water – the airplanes, and...the whip," I'd answer, too tired to have any self-conscious reservations about talking.

"The big Ferris wheel or the one inside?" Mrs. Bunting would query.

"Inside. Oh, and the merry-go-round. And the cups and saucers and the Tilt-A-Whirl!"

"Good for you! You'll be up there hanging onto that mouse ride pretty soon."

While I was always squirmy during the initial look in, I was never in a hurry at this point in the evening, content to curl up on my mom's or my grandmother's lap and listen to the adults talk. Ocean City was my favorite place in the world, so of course, I wanted to hear about it, even if I didn't always understand the things the adults were talking about. And Mrs. Bunting told the best stories...I'd never met anyone who could tell one like she did. I didn't even realize adults were allowed to tell stories to other adults, at least in the animated and captivating way Mrs. Bunting did. It was only something my school teachers did at reading time, wasn't it?

Apparently not.

And being at Mrs. Bunting's meant we were still in Ocean City. The night wasn't yet over. Not that there was anything exciting left for us to do. But as long as we were in Ocean City, all was well with the world. It's likely I felt this because on the final day of our stays at the trailer we always went home by going west on Route 50, meaning that my last and lasting view of Ocean City would take place the night before.

After saying our goodbyes – and these always fell into the category of "extended" – Dorchester Street was usually quiet as we removed ourselves from Mrs. Bunting's aura and stepped onto the concrete sidewalk. Looking to the right, eastward through the darkness up toward the boardwalk, sporadic traffic zoomed southward just a half block away on Philadelphia Avenue. A block further east was the northbound traffic of Baltimore Avenue, and beyond you could see people walking across the Dorchester Street "opening" of the boardwalk. A half a block to our left Dorchester Street ended, meeting the bay at the Ocean City Marina, a brightly lit area where mirrored pairs of charter boats bobbed gently up and down along the branch-like docks that stretched out into the indigo water.

Once back into the car we'd usually take the "back way" to get onto the Route 50 Bridge. This entailed making a right at the Marina parking lot and driving north on St. Louis Avenue past the Marlin Club and Paul's Tackle Shop before looping around the bridge's concrete foundation and under the bridge deck to get to the outbound lanes of Route 50. With the road running right against the bay and through the first set of bridge pilings, there was always a strong salty smell lingering in this confined area. Usually, it was a pleasant odor, but it occasionally contained a sharp fishiness that made you shudder. Either way was an authentic and final beach farewell to the evening.

After a pair of right turns the car would be on the bridge, climbing quickly toward the metal drawbridge section that made the tires hum and vibrated the car. This was my signal to turn around and look out at the back window. Downtown Ocean City was lit up like a museum diorama.

Right below the bridge dozens of sport fishing boats were clustered around the Talbot, Dorchester, and Somerset Street docks, their distinctive sharp-bowed silhouettes darkening the floodlit water while the shadowy outlines of their outriggers and fish spotting towers formed a ghostly thicket of fiberglass and metal that soared high above a floating city of ship's cabins. Interspersed at the ends of each dock were tall lighted signs carrying gasoline logos, the nearest a torch-bisected red-white-and-blue oval with "AMERICAN" through the center. At the far end of the same dock, blue block letters spelled out "GULF" inside a glowing orange circle. And one dock south at Dorchester Street, there was a recognizable red Texaco star, its overlapping "T" and "TEXACO" set against a bright white round background.

From here my eyes moved a block inward, where three giant neon red letters seemed suspended in the night sky, spelling out "I-C-E" over the black shingled roof of the Ocean City Ice Company. The Ice House, as it was more commonly known, was a landmark because it had the coolest 24-hour vending machine I'd ever seen attached to the front of it. Not only did it dispense ice, but also frozen bait. Boxes of squid, shiners, or mullet, keeping you fishing even when the tackle shops were closed.

Looming a couple of blocks to the right of the Ice House was Ocean City's most prominent nighttime landmark, the giant aqua-colored water tower with its enormous floodlit "Welcome to Ocean City" message on the front.

The car would now be up to speed, and the bridge's light poles passed by quickly, aligned with the regular rhythmic clicking of tires over expansion joints. So I'd move my eyes to my favorite part of Ocean City's receding skyline, the otherworldly white glow of the Wild Mouse ride and the large roof-mounted orange letters at the south end of the boardwalk.

"Trimper's RIDES"

Just to the right of the sign I could get my final glimpse of Trimper's Ferris wheel, its white fluorescent interior star design turning counterclockwise against a black ocean night sky. And if we weren't too far across the bridge yet, I could sometimes see the Loop-O-Plane in motion, thanks to the fluorescent blue, red, yellow, orange, and white lights outlining its long and pivoting arms.

There was always a point of no return on these westward crossings, a place where the roadway flattened out, putting the bridge's concrete sidewalls and metal railing directly into my sight line. And though I might have been barely aware of geography or geometry, I knew that the further across the bridge we drove, the further south I could see, and the last thing I would see before Ocean City disappeared from view was the immense neon "M-O-T-E-L" sign on the roof of the Oceanic Motel. The Oceanic was the southernmost building in all of Ocean City, sitting right at the corner of the inlet and the bay. And the letters of its sign were the size of cars, easy to see, even from the far side of the bridge. Often it was this final "snapshot" that carried me through until our first Ocean City visit the following year, an image that rotated routinely through my memory during the chilly months of winter.

Chapter Eight

Morning

Consciousness arrived before my eyes fully opened, yet I could already feel the sunlight being deflected into the room by the thick curtains hanging across the oversized sliding window on the condo's east-facing wall. Opening my eyes while rolling my head rightward on the pillow, it was a relief to see that the narrow strips of light escaping the curtain edges were an intense yellow, meaning it was still early, which was important on a Saturday morning. After untangling my right arm from the sheets, I put my wrist up in front of my face to look at my watch and...damn, the thing was hard to read first thing in the morning. That's because the turnable bezel on my economy diver's watch was overrun with tiny city names, and tiny numbers demarking all 60 seconds. This attempt to make the watch look expensive made it overly busy for just opening eyes, but the dark blue dial looked really cool against the backdrop of my navy colored Velcro watch band, a subtle yet essential fashion accessory that helped mark me as a real surfer. Or viewed more cynically, the Velcro band simply meant that I knew what a real surfer *should* look like. And any real surfer would be getting ready to do the same thing I was about to do right now.

Get up out of bed and check the waves.

I gave up on my watch, using an elbow to prop myself up on the bed's Electric blue sheets. Despite their bachelor-pad innuendo they had been an innocent Clearance Bin purchase at the Mill Outlet the previous summer. My motivation was sticker shock, not romance, as they were the cheapest coverings I could find for the condo's large and luxurious queen size bed – a bed that remained completely unshared during my time at Phillips. Not that I carried a hint of disappointment over this detail. It still had been the summer of my life. So far, at least.

Across the room on top of the plastic turntable lid was my unset electric alarm clock. The bold black hands and numbers on its cream-colored face told me that it was only 7:20 am – perfect timing for Saturday morning. It was always better to be in the water sooner rather than later on a Saturday, getting a jump on the weekend warrior surfers from Baltimore and D.C., as well as the weekend beachgoers, who always managed to clutter up the sand and sea at a much earlier hour than they did on summertime weekdays. By 9:30 am, a full 30 minutes before the lifeguards came on duty, there would be enough tourists floating in the water to make surfing a less than fun proposition. A dangerous one too, at least for the swimmers. But they seemed to have no clue. It never failed...if you were out surfing, by yourself or even with a group of surfers, and there were no other surfers around for, say for a block in each direction, invariably a family would waltz out in the water right behind you. And this family always seemed to be an extended one, including sons, daughters, aunts, uncles, cousins, nephews, and the in-laws. It was almost like there was some kind of unwritten tourist rule forcing them to swim in our shadows.

A beach rule that was written down and unconditionally enforced was that all surfers had to get out of the water when the lifeguards mounted their chairs at 10:00 am. The exception was if you happened to be at one of the dedicated Ocean City surfing beaches. By pure luck and chance, one was just four blocks down the beach at 118th Street. This flexibility to keep surfing past "curfew" was priceless and had come in handy numerous times over the last two summers. (In fact, my first ever wave was ridden at 118th Street during a low tide June afternoon.) But due to the crowds, the surfing beaches weren't a very appealing weekend option – unless the waves were really firing.

Which I knew they weren't today. Actually, I was pretty sure there weren't any waves at all, but living just a half a block from the beach, you had to take a look. Always. There was no slacking on a surf check because you never knew when your persistence was going to be rewarded.

With my shirtless back now up against the headboard – an all-white stomach-high rectangle outlined by a wide avocado colored racing stripe – I finally tuned into the drone of the air conditioner, and looked over at the partially shut folding door that divided my bedroom from the rest of the condo. That's right, Greg was up late watching television. ESPN of course. There was just something about that channel, it was like a car accident (and by coincidence, Greg was watching auto racing when my eyes finally shut). Maybe ESPN was on to something after all.

I swiveled my feet out on the left side of the bed, planting them firmly in the carpet's overgrown grass texture before grabbing my sand-colored Sundancer sweatshirt off the closet doorknob. Finally standing up, I stumbled toward an image of Australian pro surfer Mark Richards doing an impossible-to-imagine backside bottom turn on a massive three-story wave at Pipeline. This *Surfing* magazine poster was already pinned to the wall when I did my first-ever walk-through of the place in February of 1979. Even though I couldn't surf yet, I took it as a sign that I'd found the perfect summer rental. (Surfers had lived here, maybe I could absorb some of the karma they left behind.) The poster remained on the wall when my lease ran out last September – I felt like it was my duty to pass the surf karma on – and it was still up when Greg and I moved in this year. Obviously, the owner never stepped foot in the place during the offseason. Hell, he didn't even bother to send back my security deposit, which worked out okay because I just rolled it over for this summer. Without a doubt, Mark Richards was my summertime talisman. I was happy to see him each morning. Even when there weren't any waves.

Collapsed onto the floor next to my Rainbows were my brown OP shorts, so I pulled them on, slid my feet into the leather straps, grabbed my keys off the dresser, and...hmm, where were my sunglasses? After sifting through the clutter on the dresser – Coppertone 6, Zoggs Board Wax, hairbrush, hairdryer, Quicksilver trunks – it hit me. I took them to work. They were in my backpack, which happened to be leaning against the side of the dresser. I unzipped the back pocket and pulled out the case, taking out my glasses before wedging the case between the Coppertone bottle and the hairdryer. With glasses still in hand I glanced into the dresser mirror to gauge whether it was a "hat" or "hair" morning, but an obvious answer didn't reflect back from the torso length white plastic frame. Picking up the brush, I made a few quick strokes on both sides of my head. Good enough – a hair day. I pivoted quickly to my right and headed for the back door.

Upright in the corner next to the door were my surfboards, a pair of Wave Riding Vehicles that proudly displayed the company's eye-catching "ring of dolphins" logo. Both boards were "clear," or white in color, meaning they didn't have any pigment in their fiberglass finish. All of their visible colors came from the hand-shaped white foam blank underneath the fiberglass. I bought the 6'2" – a single fin with micro-grooves in the tail – from the Clearlight Surf Shop in Fenwick last July. Its nose needed to be rebuilt after I drove it into the sand on a funky drained-out 56th Street wave just weeks after I wrote the check for the board. The queasiness I felt while looking at its flapping fiberglass front end...it was like someone had died. But the guys at the Sunshine House did a nice fix on it. Not that it ever looked like new again, but it still worked just fine and was my favorite. My other WRV was a thick 6'4" with a distinctive half inch stringer down the middle. My plan when I bought it in October was that it would be my winter board, having the extra thickness and length to counteract the extra weight of a full wetsuit. But at the moment, I was struggling with the reality of this being the first board I'd owned that I didn't fall immediately in love with – a struggle made worse by the fact that the board was bought during a carefully planned pilgrimage to the WRV factory in Virginia Beach. Maybe things would change, but so far, it just didn't feel "right" under my feet. On the plus side, Greg had a board to use. Hopefully, he'd stand up and get the bug. It would be nice to have company in the water this summer.

Pulling the back door inward, I stepped out onto our sun-drenched balcony and into a soup of sticky stagnant air that instantly fogged over my sunglasses. This stillness meant that any swell in the water would be clean and glassy. A good thing, if there were actually any waves.

The sun sat just above the row of four-story townhouses lining the beach, looking like a glimmering orange softball that you could reach up and grab. Because of the early hour, I needed to negotiate the balcony railing as quietly as possible. Otherwise, our neighbors might think they were getting an unexpected visitor. With it being morning and the metal still cool, I was able to carefully position my hands and thighs without burning them, making a quick and confident vault over the waist-high rail to the narrow ledge on the other side. The final drop into the parking lot wasn't all that high, maybe 18 inches, but there had always been something about the distance and the slight slope of the lot that made the landing tricky. You expected to hit the ground sooner than you did – it was a perfect height for turning ankles. I took a deliberate pause and focused my still waking nervous system into "careful" mode before gently launching off the side. Keeping my toes up while letting my knees bend deeply to absorb the shock, I touched down without incident on the gravel below.

Okay. Time to check the waves.

Since our street rose slightly at the end to overlook the beach, I didn't need to reach the sand to see that the ocean was exactly as I expected – flat. There would be no surfing today. Always a bummer. But today wasn't as much of a bummer, as I was looking forward to work and seeing what my second day at Playland would bring. And this day might even bring Greg a job there – that would be a nice bonus. As these thoughts drifted away, I walked out onto the beach, letting my Rainbows flap cool sand up the back of my legs with each forward step.

Flat, yet I'm still drawn to the water. The mornings of the previous summer conditioned me to love this time of day, even when I wasn't surfing. Of course, I wasn't alone today. There was already Saturday morning beach traffic, mostly walkers with the intermittent runner thrown in, even though Ocean City's soft sand was difficult to run on. It was an open question as to whether you were better off running on the beach in shoes or bare feet. Greg and I avoided the question completely by doing our running on the streets.

Looking to the south, down to 118th Street, there was nobody in the water – which was a relief. Nobody beat me to the waves. It was always easy to see exactly where 118th Street was because that's where the Caine house sat out on dozens of wooden pilings well beyond the dune line. Besides sitting right on the ocean, it was a stunning house with a massive outdoor deck that surrounded the entire living area. It even had an elevated wooden driveway and a two-car garage on its south-facing side. And when you were on the beach walking towards the house, it looked like a ship, thanks to the rounded forward living area and the sloping 45° angle of the decorative white paneled façade covering up the pilings underneath. Together they looked like a ship's cabin and bow

getting ready to launch into the Atlantic. That probably wasn't an accident, as I was sure the view through the large oceanfront windows made
it feel like you were on a ship. I'd heard that the city despised the house
and wanted to get rid of it, even hearing speculation that the surfing
beach had been put there on purpose to spite the Caine family. I didn't
know much about Ocean City politics, but this did make sense because
all of the other permanent surfing beaches were in front of vacant lots.
It was like the city said, "okay, you can keep your house on the beach,
but dammit, you'll be looking at and dealing with surfers all summer
long." Whatever the circumstances for the two being paired together,
the surfing beach and the Caine house were happy landmarks for me. I
rode my very first wave there, and I'd improved dramatically while surfing in its front yard. It was one of the better low tide breaks in all of
Ocean City.

But it wasn't breaking now. So it was back to the condo to figure out
what was next for this day. I was already sweating when I mounted the
railing to get onto the balcony, and it really hit me how sticky the air
already was when I opened the door and stepped back into the air-conditioning of my bedroom. I sat on the bed – because it was the only thing
in the room to sit on – and considered my options. Was I awake, as in,
awake, awake? Awake enough to stay up? Some coffee would help, but
Greg was still asleep and probably would be for a while. I'd have to go
out and get some coffee. I could get some breakfast too...maybe down at
Layton's on 92nd Street. It was still early enough to be doable on a Saturday morning, there wouldn't be a line yet. Or I could just get coffee,
donuts, and a newspaper and enjoy the rising sun. Oh, right, we still
hadn't bought those chairs for the deck yet.

Maybe I should lay down for a few minutes and think about it some
more.

It felt good to shut my eyes. I fought it at first, blinking hard to keep
focused on the textured ceiling, then just let them close.

Scenes from last night ran on a loop in my head...the sun just dipping
into the western horizon, bathing the sky and glistening bay in colors
that went from butterscotch, to amber, to finally a deep orange before
disappearing behind a narrow dark strip of mainland on the far side of
the bay...how the hundreds of white bulbs outlining the Hurricane appeared to "move" around the ride's perimeter as they flashed in a fitful
and fluctuating sequence...the spinning skeletal steel circumference of

the Airborne ride, angled gracefully upward at 45°, each of its chairs swinging through the sky beneath a mesh "parachute" ringed in colorful tiny lights...shadowy flares of upward shining floodlights making the Monster Mouse's sparse framing look taller and even more intimidating...the park's sun-faded monorail actually looking regal and inviting against the glowing sunset sky.

Could real life be better than your dreams?

The park slowly faded, merging into the gnarled letters and barely legible lines of my lefty-afflicted penmanship. Yes, I needed to finish that letter to my girlfriend. Then I could drop it in the mailbox on the way to work. Today was my first full shift, so I needed to be at the park by 12:45 pm. Where did I leave off? The kids, that's right, the kids were amazing...

It seemed like just a few moments, but as the warbled and chiming melody crescendoed, I knew otherwise.

"Doo-do-di-do-do-do-di-do. Doo-do-di-do-do-do-di-do..."

Oh, shit! The Mr. Softee truck! God, I didn't mean to fall asleep. Hopefully it was his first pass. That would mean it was just after 10:00 am.

Every synapse in my body fired simultaneously, sending a sharp involuntary jolt that opened my eyes and put me on my feet before I was aware that I was upright. Standing unsteadily in my now brightly illuminated bedroom my thoughts caught up. I had to wake up Greg. He wanted to go talk to Mark.

Chapter Nine

Instant Coffee

"**G**reg...Greg...come on man, it's time to wake up."
Greg stirred slightly on his square mattress, partially covered by a white sheet while fully blanketed in the daylight coming through the curtains over his pullout bed. Because the supporting metal framework of Greg's mattress expanded out from the couch for a jigsaw puzzle fit between the dinette set and the mini-fridge, I had no clear passage to the front door. But I could get to the kitchenette and get the kettle going on the stove. Coffee was just a few minutes away.

Greg's face twitched as he heard the drum-like reverberation of water hitting the bottom of the stainless-steel sink. The drumming sound let up as I aligned the kettle and the faucet, filling the kettle halfway before turning off the water. A short swing of my arm landed the kettle on the stove's circular metal burner.

"Greg...are you awake, yet?"

There was no answer as the outlines of three tourists trundled down the stairs outside our front window.

"I presume you want some coffee?"

I didn't wait for an answer, pulling the red-labeled Maxwell House Instant Coffee jar out of the playset-sized cupboard over the sink.

"Yeah, yeah, I'm awake. Did you go out this morning?"

"Nope, no waves. Then, shit, I came back and fell asleep until I heard the Mr. Softee truck roll by. Not what I planned for the morning."

Mr. Softee got Greg's attention. He picked up his head to scan the room.

"Man, what time is it?"

"It was only his first pass – it's 10:15."

I took our coffee mugs off the paper towel covering the drainage area next to the sink, using my "mom's eye" to assess their state of cleanliness. Not bad, they'd actually been rinsed yesterday. Because we didn't care for the looks of the grotty and mismatched dinnerware issued with the condo we were repurposing plastic margarine containers for coffee mugs. It wasn't a feeble stretch on our part as they were supposed to function as mugs. This multi-use feature was advertised on their packaging, and they even had a molded handle on the side. We had different colors so we wouldn't mix them up – Greg's was yellow, mine was light blue. We also had paper plates and cups for everything else we ate and drank. Disposable plastic forks, knives, and spoons too. Only a cycle through an industrial sterilizer would've convinced us to use the corroded flatware from the dusty crumb-filled drawer next to the sink.

Greg reached over and pulled out the volume knob to turn on the television. The channel selector was already set to channel 3, which was exactly where we wanted it. There was still time to catch the last half of ESPN's Sports Center.

"Did you hear if the Phils won before you turned the TV off last night?"

"Yeah, they won 6-5. They're only two games back of the Pirates now."

"How about the Orioles?"

"No, didn't hear that score. But we should soon," said Greg, pointing at the television.

I continued tending the kettle, scooping two teaspoons of brown powder into each of the plastic mugs. Greg pulled on a pair of blue gym shorts and pushed the mattress frame back into the sofa, sending a "kerthunk" and a "sprong" echoing through the room. He had just finished putting the vinyl sofa cushions back in place when he turned quickly around.

"Here you go..."

In Anaheim last night, the Orioles' Scott McGregor scattered four hits and allowed only one run in a complete game 6-1 victory over the Angels...

"At work last night Mark predicted the Orioles would win. He even wanted to bet on it."

"Betting with your boss? That doesn't sound quite right."

"Yeah, I don't think Mark was serious, he was just having fun with some of the guys who've been at the park for a while."

The kettle was huffing away at a sub-whistle, so I pulled it off the burner and began carefully pouring the steaming water into our mugs. Space was tight. Spilling coffee onto the shag carpet would be a nightmare.

"What was the wager?" Greg's curiosity was clearly taken by Mark willing to wager on the Orioles.

"If Mark lost the bet – the bet was an Orioles sweep – he was going to give the guy the weekend off, which the guy didn't want because they haven't been working all that many hours."

"And if Mark won?

"The guy had to work the monorail for a week."

"The monorail? For losing a bet? That doesn't sound like much of…"

"You should've seen it, the guy was like, 'Hell no!' He didn't want to even take the chance of having to work the monorail."

I paused to stir both coffees, then grabbed the paper cup we'd stuffed with sugar packets.

"You're taking it black, right?"

"Yeah, black. So, what's wrong with the monorail?"

"I'm not totally sure. The guy said it was a steaming fishbowl…or something like that. It is mostly windows, so if it doesn't have air-conditioning, it probably gets pretty hot in there. Like on a day like today, I guess."

I finished stirring Greg's coffee and placed the mug in front of him as he sat at the table in the chair nearest the door. I dumped two sugar packs into my mug, made a couple of quick stirs, and sat down across from Greg. He was already glued to Sports Center, where they had moved on to highlights from the College World Series Final between Arizona and Hawaii. ESPN had televised the game live the night before, but it was over well before I sat down to work on my letter to my girlfriend.

"Oh my god, look at those uniforms, they're worse than the Pirates," said Greg, referring to Hawaii's matching lime green jerseys and pants. "And those white shoes…only the A's can pull that look off."

"Yeah, I would've thought it was a softball team."

It turned out that Arizona won 5-3, although Greg and I really had no burning interest in college baseball. As Sports Center cut to a commercial, it hit me how hungry I was.

"Do you want an English muffin?" I asked Greg.

"Nah, think I'll just have some cereal in a bit," he answered, as I reached to grab the cellophane Thomas' package sitting on the toaster oven. The reason the toaster oven was on the dinette table was simple – it was the only place in the entire condo where it fit. We'd managed to stuff it up against the wall on the last quarter of the table, and used its stainless-steel top for storage. Putting food items on top of something that could heat up to 400° might not have seemed like the smartest thing we could do. But when you opened the oven's glass front door it popped into an angled position above the oven, spilling things – like say, bread bags, muffin packages, and Entenmann's donut boxes – off the back and onto the floor. We just had to remember to let the oven cool down before putting anything back on the top.

"Do you want me to call Mark, or do you want to do it?" I asked while trying to pull my muffin apart. Fork split my ass.

"I'll call him," answered Greg. "Do you think he's there yet?"

"Might be a little early for Saturday. But this is about when I called him yesterday," I said, finally wrestling my crumbling muffin apart and placing it on the toasting rack.

"Do you have the number?"

"Yeah, let me go get the employee handbook out of my backpack."

I closed the oven door and pushed down the black plastic "Start" lever on the front. With the heating elements glowing orange and toasting cycle underway I walked to my bedroom and pulled the Playland handbook out of my backpack, returning to lay the 45 rpm record sleeve-sized booklet in front of Greg.

"Damn, it's bright, isn't it?" said Greg while holding the almost-glowing yellow cover in front of his face. He took a moment to check out the park logo, which consisted of the "Playland Amusement Park," the park's address, and a half a dozen oversized dots that were supposed to be balloons.

"That's what's on the front of my shirt."

"How about the clown?" asked Greg, referring to a small clown face printed above the text.

"He's the mascot. You know, the big guy standing out in front of the park."

"I thought that was a pirate?"

"Jolly Roger still has a pirate. Playland gave their guy a makeover a few years ago. When was the last time you were there?"

"Probably junior high, six or seven years ago."

"Yeah, well, he's a jester now. Or a clown, or a genie. You'll have to tell me what you think when you see him."

Greg opened the manual and began scanning the pages for a phone number.

"Here it is, page nine. Can you believe that? Should be on the cover."

I couldn't argue. The number should have been on page one at the least.

"So, do you think Mark is there?"

"Can't hurt to try." Just then the oven popped, and since I was helping Greg, I hadn't gotten the margarine out. I made my move for the mini-fridge as Greg stood up from his chair, and we nearly had a mid-room collision.

"Go ahead, man," I said, with a laugh. "Good luck!"

"Thanks. It's weird, I'm already seeing myself at Playland. It would suck now if I have to stay at Phillips."

"Yeah, it would. Be sure to tell him you're my roommate. At least he'll know you have a ride to the park – and a phone."

"Phone?"

"Yeah, he was glad I had a phone. Sounds like people still go without them while working down here for the summer."

"You had one last year, right?"

"Yep. Just needed to deal with the phone company to get it on. Of course, they took a $50 deposit – which I got back. Anyway, good luck."

"Thanks," said Greg, disappearing down the hallway to my bedroom, where the phone sat on the nightstand between the back window and the bed.

I opened the mini-fridge, grabbing the margarine from the second shelf. This tub was orange and already half empty, so we'd soon have a "guest" coffee mug to add to our collection. As I dug my knife into the sunflower-colored spread, I tried not to listen in on Greg's voice, but I could tell from his confident tone that things were going well. On my knife's final scrape across my muffin's pitted surface, I heard Greg hang up the phone. He came back smiling.

"So?" I asked.

"I'll meet him at 12:15," said Greg.

"Do you want a ride?"

"No, I'm fine. I'll ride my bike. That way you can go in when you're supposed to."

"He knows you're my roommate?"

"Yep."

"Did you tell him you were working at Phillips?"

"Yep. He said he's thinking about doing a Phillips refugee program."

"Well, be sure to tell him that you're on to the monorail."

"Ah, I'll take anything. Besides, it can't be hotter than a Phillips kitchen."

"Probably not. And it definitely has a better view."

Greg picked up his coffee mug, making a swooping motion with it in my direction. I picked up my mug, and we "clacked" them together over the center of the table.

"To Playland," said Greg, "and the amusement park summer."

"It should be one for the books. Not that either one of us is ever going to write about it."

A Lot of Bull

"Greg...Greg, are you ready, man?'
It was almost 5:30 pm and we needed to get on the road. Of course, Greg had impressed Mark in the interview and was offered a job on the spot. Greg went into Phillips and told them that Sunday night's shift would be his last, so here we were on Monday evening with both of us heading to Playland. Greg came out of the bathroom, grabbed his backpack off the couch and pulled out a piece of Trident.

"No gum while running the ride – think that's rule number 78. It's somewhere there in the manual," I said.

"I'll get rid of it when we get to the park. I'm not sure what I'll be doing. Mark was really interested in what I did at the dining hall. He said we'd talk about it some more."

"Yeah, I didn't see your name on the schedule last night. Hell, I'm jealous, he gave you a shirt already. How'd he know you'd come back today?"

"Because of all the great things you told me about Playland."

"After one shift?"

"And now you've had three. Any doubts?"

"Nope."

"Then let's go."

We had no trouble driving to the park in the light Monday evening traffic, getting almost a straight shot after the usual stop-and-go sequence through the cluster of traffic lights fronting Condo Row and the Gold Coast Mall. As Capt. Bob's enormous sunglass-wearing bull came into view – the restaurant had also outfitted the fiberglass figure with a scaled-to-size chef's hat – I put my right turn signal on and got ready to turn into the Playland entrance. The park did have a sign, but the bull, just a block south at 64th Street, was easier to pick out of the commercial clutter lining the bayside lanes of Coastal Highway. A hat-wearing barnyard animal the size of a dinosaur will usually catch your eye. Greg eyed the bull closely as we made our turn.

"That's a cool bull. Maybe our oversized clown can take him for a walk," said Greg.

"In the parking lot?"

"How about down the boardwalk?"

Greg got the laugh he was looking for with that line.

"Yeah, that I'd like to see. And I have to say, I think the bull is a lot cooler than our, whatever he is."

"Well, at least he's got big balls – the ones he's juggling," said Greg with a smirking glance, once again looking for the laugh. I didn't want to touch the innuendo, although it was hard not to continue and speculate about whether Capt. Bob owned a bull or a steer – a steer being a bull without his balls. This anatomy tidbit I'd learned from Greg, who was an Ag major at Delaware. It took an extra second, but I found a way out.

"Maybe he and the bull can play fetch," I answered, getting a smile out of Greg.

We headed toward the group of employee cars spreading out from the go-kart fence and pulled into an empty space between a green VW beetle and a Chevy Vega with a Bondo-gray front end. Upon unraveling from my Sunbird's low-slung faux sports car bucket seat, I had a bird's-eye view of the glazed donut hue overtaking the red paint on my roof and trunk, as well as the rust bubbling out of the roof welds. My supposedly sporty yet economical little brother of the Pontiac Firebird had also eaten two clutches and multiple sets of front tires in the four years I'd owned it. So, I had plenty of GM-induced sympathy for the Vega owner.

"An accident or just an advanced case of General Motors rust?" I asked Greg, nodding toward the car behind him. He spun around, then disappeared as he ducked down between the two cars. He popped up quickly and looked over with an answer.

"Hard to tell. Might be a little of both. But those babies rust like crazy."

"They aren't the only ones," I said, looking down at a small but spreading crater of rust on the edge of my rear wheel well.

We walked up the access road and into the park, where Greg stopped to knock on Mark's office door.

"Catch up with you later, good luck!" I said, continuing my walk to the employee lounge.

"Should be fun – I'll find you on my break," said Greg.

I punched in, knowing that my name was already penciled in for the Antique Cars, but I still checked for Greg's name on the schedule hanging next to the punch clock. I didn't see it and headed out into the park to ready my ride for the evening.

I liked having my own ride to run, being responsible for it, and for essentially being my own boss. The downside was, I hadn't really met anybody yet. Lindsay and Calvin, the other relief supervisor, were the only people I'd had an actual conversation with. I'd been exchanging waves with the guys running the Spider, and made sure to say "Hi" to any employee who made eye contact. But since our breaks were staggered – the relief supervisors moved through the park ride-by-ride – there wasn't a dedicated break time, like the employee meals at Phillips. And you weren't supposed to talk to somebody while they were running a ride, not that I was going to saunter up to the guys running the Ghost Ship – a two-story "dark ride" through a sunken and haunted pirate ship – and start a conversation. Everybody seemed nice enough, there just hadn't been any chance to interact. People were either going or coming from their ride, going on or off break, or punching in or out.

Passing by the big brown bear that guarded the Antique Cars, I waved to the guys at the Spider, waved to the woman running the umbrella ride with the tubs, and climbed over my entrance chain to head for the power switch. After turning on the ride, I tested my three cars and then lined them back up in front of the entrance. It was hard to complain on my fourth night of work, but the Antique Cars were a little sedate, at least compared with the other ride-running possibilities in the park. At least I had the routine wired now. I'd just started looking for Greg when the golf cart carrying the park's dynamic fix-it duo gently rolled to a stop in front of me, with Moon and Melvin each wearing a Cheshire-like grin that made me nervous.

"We seen you pull that kid over yesterday – was he over the speed limit?" asked Melvin, as both he and Moon had a good chortle.

"Well, he climbed –"

"Yeah, we seen him. You were right to tell him," continued Melvin. "Things happen when you don't. You were damn right."

Moon shook his head in agreement, throwing in an emphatic "Umm-hmm" for good measure.

"Umm...okay, thanks," I said, trying to untie my tongue.

Melvin saluted me with his right hand, and off they went. Once again, they left me stunned. First, from the compliment – not at all what I expected when they pulled up. And how did they see what happened? Was there a hidden camera on my ride somewhere? There was hardly anyone in the park yesterday afternoon. The first time I saw Moon and Melvin drive by was right before my dinner break.

But they had seen me during the only moment of trouble I'd had on the ride. It happened not long after we opened at 1:00 pm. I'd sent two kids out in a car – one in the front, and one in the back – only to watch the kid in front undo the safety strap and climb out onto the running board to get into the back seat. I was shocked at first, not believing what I was seeing. I would have never...why would a kid do that? The parents had wandered off, so there was no help from them. Not wanting the rider to change his mind and climb back into the front, I ran after the car and caught up with it just as the kid settled into the back next to his friend. The climber was startled to see me running alongside the car, and with my adrenaline now pumping good I was about to offer a terse "What in the world are you doing" to the pair. But in looking in, there were big wide eyes – the kids were scared. In my hat, sunglasses, and official yellow shirt, I guess I was, as Melvin joked, the Playland police pulling them over.

"Please don't do that again," I finally said. "It's dangerous, ok?"

He shook his head, and it seemed I made my point. I broke off my chase and went back to the loading area to catch the car as it finished. The two boys didn't look at me or a say a word as they got off – and they never came back.

As Moon and Melvin weaved westward around my bear and headed off toward the fiberglass cow guarding the Tilt-A-Whirl, I resumed looking for Greg. I had a great vantage point from the Antique Cars because my entrance sat directly on the northern midway, just about at the midpoint of the park's rectangular stretch into the bay. When I faced out and scanned the park from left to right only the go-karts, bumper cars, and monorail were out of view – and the monorail was right at my back with its station looming over my ride. Otherwise, I had a full 180° view of the park, starting with the cluster of Kiddie Land rides directly to my left, then the Ferris wheel, the Spider, the games of "skill" directly across from me from on the southern midway, then the Sky Ride, the Dairy Queen, the Hurricane, the Rotor, Old Pro Circus golf, the Scrambler, the Airborne, the Monster Mouse, the Ghost Ship, finally ending directly on my right with the sputtering Hot Rods. Although some of the loading areas weren't visible, I was positive I was going to find Greg before the park opened...which happened when the PA system came to life with a thick bass note and simultaneous cymbal crash, followed by a pair of smooth electric piano chords. A nice touch, we were starting the night off with Ambrosia's "Biggest Part of Me." The song was on the sappy side, but I had a soft spot for the band, as their first album was a favorite of mine, especially Side 1. I felt like they'd paid their dues since then, and earned the right to have one of the most overplayed songs of 1980.

A very light stream of guests began coming into the park, and I soon had my first rider. Greg was nowhere to be found.

$20 Jackpot

By the time Calvin came to relieve me the western skyline had gone orange, and all the rides in the park had their lights on. I still hadn't seen Greg and was determined to find out where he ended up. I could see he wasn't working near me in Kiddie Land, so I set off down the northern midway toward the back of the park where most of the adult rides were located. On my immediate left was the Tilt-A-Whirl, which sat between the park's two midways next to the Sky Ride loading platform. Our version of the Tilt-A-Whirl carried the traditional color scheme – a large round blue base, six spinning red clamshell-shaped cars, backlit red and yellow plastic signage, and elevated pairs of long yellow and white fluorescent lights ringing the ride. It only took one person to run the ride, and Greg wasn't that person. Greg also wasn't handing out balls, putters, and scorecards in the bright yellow circus train-inspired mini-golf "clubhouse," which sat just beyond the Tilt-A-Whirl under the first tower of the Sky Ride.

On my right as I kept walking were the Hot Rods, Playland's original go-karts. These noisy gas-powered cars dated all the way back to 1965, the year the park opened. Making them Hot Rods and not just go-karts were the miniature open-top sports car bodies that covered each chassis. Modeled on the Chevrolet Corvette line of the late 1960s, their silver and smiling "grill teeth" front ends seemed just slightly less dated than the exterior radiators on my Antique Cars. Three Playland employees were doing the loading and unloading, but none of them was Greg.

Up next on the right was the warehouse-sized Ghost Ship, where a floodlit building-length roofline façade consisted of a splintered and sail-less wooden galleon being devoured by a giant crab with an eerie orange-eyed skeleton face that tilted back and forth all night long. As creepy things go, this worked, and the entire ride was an extended black light creep-fest full of aging mechanical gags – like a glowing ghoulish pirate whose disembodied head slid down a wire toward your car – that often needed fixing in the middle of a shift. A pair of Playland employees controlled the ride from the front corner of a porch-like extension that served as the loading area for the small electric powered two-seater "coffin" cars that methodically disappeared behind a set of wooden doors adorned with a smiling Casper-inspired ghost. I hadn't been at the park long, but I'd already learned that this was an "expert" level ride to run, especially since people would sometimes get out of the cars and wander around inside, throwing an unexpected human element into the building's two floors of terror. It was no surprise that Greg wasn't working there.

Looming straight ahead now was the shimmering Tinker Toy-like structure of the Monster Mouse, which towered above the monorail track and took up the entire northern bayside corner of the park. This was another ride that required two Playland workers, one loading and unloading, and a master controller who sent the individual mouse cars out on the track at carefully spaced intervals to prevent them from catching up with each other. All I needed was a quick glance to see that Greg wasn't part of the duo.

With the Monster Mouse up against the perimeter fence and the bay just beyond, I turned left at the corner of the mini-golf fence and started walking south toward the Hurricane. Hard along the perimeter fence on my right was the Airborne ride. It had just slowed to a stop in its ground level position, and the young woman working the ride was walking around its elevated loading platform unlatching the safety bars of each occupied swinging chair. Obviously, she was not Greg.

Spinning clockwise in front of the Airborne was the Scrambler, an angular ride that was constructed of mostly triangular silver framework, including an elongated pyramid of white fluorescent lights that extended upward from its slim and sci-fi alien rocket-shaped center support. At the waist-high control panel, entirely focused on the turning ride, was another young woman in a yellow Playland shirt. Rising over her left shoulder, stretching well above the perimeter fence and the monorail track, was the Rotor, or "hell hole." From the outside, you couldn't see what was going on in the ride's tall spinning cylinder, but I could see the Playland employee high up in the Rotor's elevated control booth who was overseeing the G-force hell transpiring in the hole. And it wasn't Greg.

Then looking straight ahead, up to the entrance ramp of the Hurricane...son of a bitch, there was Greg taking down the chain to let a line of people on the ride. How in the hell did he land the coaster on his very first night? Damn, I was jealous. He saw me down below, smiled and shrugged, then replaced the chain across the entrance and went over to supervise the passengers as they loaded into the coaster train. After checking the restraint bars, Greg gave a thumbs up to his partner, who was operating an oversized wooden handle protruding from the deck on the other side of the track. This guy had his back to the lift hill, and from my view, the handle was pulled to the right at a 45° angle. After Greg's signal the guy pushed the handle forward until it was 45° to the left, and you could hear the brakes release underneath the train. Greg then gave the back end of the train a good hard push, which sent it trundling onto the lift hill chain, making the distinctive wooden coaster "clack-clack-clack-clack" as it climbed upward along the flashing lights lining the outside railing of the track.

I'd started walking away from the coaster and had almost reached the end of its exit ramp before Greg came bounding over to the railing, looking down at me from under the long, backlit "ROLLER COASTER" sign.

"I'll catch up with you on break," he said, taking a peek as the coaster train moved off the lift hill and onto a slightly banked horseshoe turn that would take it towards its first drop.

"Okay. How'd you –"

"I have no idea."

"But it's good?"

"Yeah, it is fun."

"Good. Then get back to work. I was never here."

Greg turned and went back to the edge of the track to wait for the coaster to return to the loading area.

Things on the Antique Cars were pretty slow by the time Greg got his break. I was pacing slowly in front of my vacant cars as Greg came up the midway past the Hot Rods and the Tilt-A-Whirl.

"I found $20," Greg said before I had a chance to even think of anything to ask him.

"What?"

"Yeah, there was a $20 bill in one of the seats."

"What about who was sitting there?"

"It was an empty seat, nobody had been it for a couple of times around. Travis said if nobody comes back for it, it's mine."

"Wow...the only things the kids leave behind here are hats and gooey Lifesavers. Travis doesn't want half? That's the guy you're working with?"

"Nope, nothing. He said he's already found his fair share through the years."

"Okay, sounds good. Twenty dollars is a lot of money. I hope...well if they're still in the park, I hope the people come back for it."

"Yeah, we'll see. I gotta' get back. It's a great view from up there. You can see just about the whole park!"

"This looks like a 10 o'clock closing night," I said, gesturing over to the mostly empty and dormant Kiddie Land area. "Probably see you soon."

Greg waved and headed back to the coaster. I had three more riders and lots of free time before Lindsay showed up to shut me down at 9:50 pm. All I had to do was turn the power off, pick up my backpack and head over to the coaster, which was still lit up in all its white light flashing glory. This time I went directly across to the southern midway, making a right at the Dairy Queen to head toward the coaster, passing the still battling bumper cars on my left. They had been built into one of Playland's permanent cinder block structures and were enclosed on two sides. This created an echo chamber for the ceaseless metallic scraping of the car's electrical contacts against the wire ceiling and the occasional meaty "thump" of the cars colliding with each other. And from the ride's extended front opening onto the midway came the intense oily electrical smell that every bumper car ride in the world produced. Looking in, there were a handful of riders chasing each other counterclockwise around a long metal-bumpered center island. The Playland bumper cars, like the ones at Trimper's, functioned more as a race than as a continuous head-on free-for-all.

It was just a few more steps to the coaster, where I walked under the "Exit Only" sign and went up the wooden exit ramp to the loading platform, trying very hard to look like I belonged there. Being a Playland employee, I did technically belong there. And none of the riders would look twice, thanks to my yellow employee shirt. But also – technically – it wasn't my ride. So, I tried to make myself scarce, taking a quick step to my left to lean against a small section of railing that divided the exit ramp from a narrow ramp that led down onto the outer walkway of the coaster track. Greg had already loaded a batch of passengers, and he and

Travis were waiting for a foursome to come up the entrance ramp and finish things off.

"Our last run," said Greg, looking over to me as he ushered the late-arriving foursome to the coaster train. Greg checked all the restraint bars and signaled Travis, who pushed the long-handled brake lever forward. A loud "BRRUMPHHH" came from under the coaster train, and it slowly began to move forward. Greg then leaned into the back of the train, giving it a five-yard push before it rolled freely down to the lift chain. Once the train was on the lift hill, Greg turned and walked over with an ear-to-ear smile.

"Still have the $20," he said.

"Cool!! Pizza and beer at Pappy's?"

"You know it. It's still early enough to be dinnertime."

"You're okay breaking the diet?"

"Diet schmiet. I just spent the whole night pushing that damn thing onto the lift chain!"

"Just checking," I said with a laugh, watching the monorail pass behind the coaster at almost eye level. "And you're right – it is a great view from up here."

We punched out with big smiles and our adrenaline flowing. What a night. Greg got the coaster on his first night and found $20. Once in the car, we didn't even let the radio come on, as Greg had fished around in my cassette graveyard under the passenger seat and dug out something he swore was appropriate. As I pulled through the empty parking space in front of us, Greg pushed the cassette into the player, which readied to play with two sequential clicks. Through the car's newly-upgraded Pioneer speakers came a slightly distorted and aggressively-picked guitar note, which I knew from my own guitar noodling with the song was an open low-E. The note played for a couple of measures before the rest of the band kicked in with a half-kit drum roll and distorted ascending guitar chords – it was Molly Hatchet's "Flirtin' With Disaster." I looked over at Greg and smiled, nodding my head in full approval.

Chapter Eleven

Pizza and Beer

W e didn't even bother to change, driving straight to the Montego Bay Shopping Center where Pappy's sat in the northern corner against the 130th Street entrance to the Montego Bay trailer park. Just like Playland, the restaurant wasn't busy on a Monday night in early June. Maybe a third full, most of the people were seated in the dark wooden booths lining the walls rather than the sturdy country-style tables that filled out the rectangular center of the restaurant. A smiling blonde waitress waved us in, and Greg and I seated ourselves in an open booth about halfway back toward the kitchen, not far from one of the Tiffany-style hanging lamps with a stained-glass rim that said "Pappy's." We had just pulled the menus out from behind the napkin holder when a sandy-haired waitress came over, her slightly sun-reddened face peeking out from under the flat-topped W.C. Fields-style Styrofoam hat that the entire staff had to wear. In addition to the hat, which included a wide red paper band that said "Pappy's," she had on a red blouse whose prominent features included puffy short sleeves, and a black Colonel Sanders string bow tie hanging from an oversized white collar. On the right side of her blouse was a white plastic name tag with a narrow strip of black label-maker tape that said "Lynda" in raised white letters.

It was an elaborate get-up, even for an Ocean City restaurant, especially with the short black skirt and black canvas Keds. But with Greg and I sitting there in our nearly neon yellow Playland shirts and matching navy shorts, we had no room to judge – not that we would. We were all in the same boat, doing whatever we had to do to live at the beach for the summer. Something we all recognized as she looked down at us with what was probably her most sincere smile of the night. It was a pretty one, too.

"Guess you guys are doing well if you're already done for the evening," she said.

"Well, there's not a lot of pay in four hours of work, but we're not complaining. You're here for the duration?" I asked, meaning until "last call" at 2:00 am.

"We'll probably only be open until midnight. It's slowed a lot over the last hour. Can I get you some drinks?"

"He's buying, so it's all on him," I said, pointing across the table to Greg.

"We're pretty much ready?" said Greg, looking back at me.

"Yeah, we'd pretty much decided before we got in the car," I said with a laugh.

"Ok, we'll have a large No. 9 –"

"No. 9, a large spiced pepperoni pizza," said Lynda, confirming as she wrote it down on the check pad.

"And a pitcher of...let's splurge. A pitcher of Michelob," said Greg, looking up at Lynda from the menu. Lynda continued to write, then looked up from her pad.

"I'll need your ID's – no offense, I have to do it."

"Sure thing. Maryland's a bit strange, not that I'm complaining," I said, referring to Maryland's two-tiered drinking law. You could buy beer and wine at 18, but had to wait until 21 to buy the hard stuff – like you couldn't get drunk on beer and wine. Greg and I both fished into our back pockets and pulled out our wallets, with Greg getting his open first because I had to grapple with the Velcro flap on my nylon surf wallet. Lynda took Greg's wallet, looked at his driver's license, then handed it back. I handed her mine and she squinted hard at my Pennsylvania license for the birth date, as the state had stuffed it up against the upper edge with a bunch of other numbers. Lynda handed back my wallet, looked at me and smiled, then looked over at Greg.

"Funny, I thought you guys were brothers," she said.

"Huh – must be the mustaches," said Greg, looking at me with raised eyebrows and a wide grin that almost went to a laugh. We did both have growths over our upper lips. Mine was thicker, Greg's was much blonder.

"Partly...you guys just kind of look alike," said Lynda.

"It's probably the uniforms," I said, now noticing the "Pappy's" printed vertically in white on the two dangling pieces of Lynda's bow tie.

"Could be. You've got the same build, plus the blonde hair, the blue eyes...and the noses."

"Noses?" asked Greg, a bit defensively. The defensiveness was an act, he was going to have some fun with Lynda's comment.

"They look really similar."

"You mean big?" said Greg, again feigning defensiveness.

"No, no, they just look –" said Lynda, sounding a little flustered.

"You have to admit, Greg, they are...what's the right word...prominent," I said, speaking the truth while trying to reassure Lynda that we weren't serious in taking any offense.

"It's funny, I actually do have a brother, but I'd take him instead," said Greg, nodding at me.

"That wouldn't work. You and I get along," I said.

"For now," shot back Greg, now feigning sarcasm.

"Yeah, for now. You know, as long as you thought *he* was the older one," I said, pointing at Greg, who rolled his eyes and shook his head back and forth while looking up at Lynda.

She started laughing, so our banter had done its job. There was nothing wrong with her brotherly assumption. Or whatever she noticed about our noses.

"A large pepperoni and a pitcher of Michelob. I'll be back with some mugs," she said, heading off to put our order in at the uniquely open kitchen, which had a big glass window where you could watch your pizza being made. Lynda soon returned with our pitcher and one of the best things about Pappy's – frosted mugs. She offered to pour our first rounds, which we said wasn't necessary. After Greg filled both of our sweating mugs, he picked up his and proposed a toast.

"To the coaster."

"Yep, to the coaster," I said clicking my mug with his. Then I added, "Brother."

"That was wild, wasn't it?"

"Yeah, it was. Brothers...never crossed my mind before."

"Me neither," said Greg, as he took a quick sip from his beer.

The beer hit the spot, and we quickly drained our mugs before pacing our beer intake for the pizza. By the time the pizza arrived Lynda had learned about Greg's coaster find, and as we worked our way through all but one slice of a large No. 9, Greg and I learned that Lynda was from a Baltimore suburb called Parkville, and heading into her junior year at the University of Maryland. It was her first summer at the beach, although two of her other three roommates had worked in Ocean City the summer before. They were living on the bayside somewhere in the 140s.

Lynda already knew our names and where we worked, so Greg and I readily filled in the rest of the details – we were roommates on 122nd Street, Greg had quit Phillips last night, and this was my second summer working in Ocean City. Lynda was amazed that we could cover a full summer of rent with just the two of us. She'd never heard of anybody else who'd been able to pull off a double at the beach.

To the uninitiated, or to the people sitting in the next booth, this detailed swap of information might come off as flirting. But it really wasn't. Not saying that something romantic couldn't develop out of it – at least for Greg, anyway, I was already happily "committed" – but that wasn't the purpose of the conversation. It was a typical early summer information exchange between people who were excited, and yet at the same time, just a little nervous, about what the next three months would bring. I was new to it all last year, but I'd learned that it was natural to compare notes with others who'd packed up and headed off into the uncertainty of a summer on a narrow strip of sand that on a busy weekend night would be occupied by a quarter of a million people. We reassured each other of our choice to spend the summer at the beach and reaffirmed our hopes that this might be the summer of our lives. With one Ocean City summer already behind me, I could attest that, yes, an "all-time" summer was indeed possible. But it wasn't Frankie and Annette in *Beach Blanket Bingo*. One way or another we were all likely to work our asses off before Labor Day.

We said goodnight to Lynda wishing her a great summer and leaving her a $3.50 tip on top of our $9.00 tab. Unless we came back to Pappy's, we'd probably never see her again. No phone numbers had been exchanged, as was typical for this type of conversation. But if we did run into her, at say Castle's Pub, the Greene Turtle, or hell, even the laundromat, the A&P, or getting on the coaster, she'd be a welcome friendly face among the tens of thousands of faces Greg and I were going to see this summer. It would work the same way for her, too. We'd always be the brothers who weren't.

Chapter Twelve

On the Beach

I t had been a typical "living at the beach" day so far, which meant it was exponentially better than any summer day in my suburban Philadelphia hometown. There'd been some waves in the morning, nothing special, but worthwhile enough to keep my surfing skills moving forward. Some waves even qualified as memorable, as I maneuvered the board around on the wave face, linking sections together for longer rides than I ever would have gotten the summer before.

Surfing, I was discovering, was so much about time in the water. Being able to relax and trust your ability without your brain shouting commands like "STAND UP!" and "TURN NOW!" Things had slowed down in Year Two of my learning process. My goal last year, after I finally stood up, was simple – make the wave. ("Making" being defined as keeping ahead of the whitewater and riding parallel to shore on the unbroken part of the wave.) The catching and standing up parts were now as natural as walking, so when I got to my feet this year, it seemed like the entire wave was laid out before me. I didn't have to think, I just felt the wave under my feet, intuitively doing whatever it allowed me to do.

And yet, at the same time, surfing was very much a mental sport, offering up a diverse set of challenges that I was completely taken in by. While it might look like a bunch of guys sitting, relaxing, just floating around in the water, out in the lineup your brain spun like a penny-a-pull Vegas slot machine. Searching the horizon for approaching swells, looking toward shore to see if you were drifting up or down the beach, judging whether there was enough bubble space between you and the next surfer, and more importantly, whether you were the better surfer. That meant the next wave that came into the general vicinity was yours. This was happening more often this summer as I was now a better surfer than the average seasonal transplant – but you still had to carefully ID the locals, who you really didn't want to challenge. Without fail, I gave them first dibs, hopeful they'd accept this sign of respect and let me into the "rotation" as the waves came through. It usually worked...although for some locals, seasonal surfers were lower than crab shit. And that's how it always would be.

Another mental part of surfing was learning to deal with bigger waves. Convincing yourself to paddle into a wedging one-story wall of water was an act of faith, at least the first couple of times. Yet one of the significant big wave achievements took place before you even rode a single wave. That was simply making it out to where the waves were breaking.

Big waves broke further out than regular waves, so you always had a longer paddle. And that paddle was made even longer by the increased power contained in the waves. So, as you paddled into the impact zone, the area where the waves broke and turned into whitewater – in the case of big waves, roaring whitewater almost as tall as a person – you needed to get physically ready to push your board under wave after wave.

And even if you were physically ready for the non-stop paddling and your wave evading technique was strong – essentially doing a downward bench press with the board into the resistance of the water – you still needed to be mentally ready for not making much progress as your lungs began burning and your body moved into anaerobic overdrive thanks to dive after dive under the oncoming walls of ocean. If you didn't keep moving you'd be pushed all the way back to the beach, so you had to convince yourself that a lull would soon come, and you'd be able to coax your tiring body into a sprint for safety beyond this ungodly watery treadmill.

When you reached the point where your chest heaved like a punctured accordion and your arms flailed at the water like wet noodles, the already big waves seemed even bigger. You were never going to make it out. And then...there was an opening, a break in the continuous swells...come on arms, come on...keep paddling, keep paddling...keep going.

There was now just one more half-block long wall to negotiate. Harder and harder you worked your arms, sucking air like a just finished Olympic marathoner, moving upward towards a wave lip that had just started to peel over and blot out the sky. Now fully feeling the wave's momentum, you used it to your advantage, forcefully punching the board's pointed nose into the rising green surface, penetrating through the back to exit in midair, free-falling onto the now flattening backside of the wave. And then...you were sitting with the other surfers beyond where the waves are breaking.

If you were lucky. If not, you'd be back on the beach looking longingly at those who had enough skill to make it to the lineup.

And even if you did make it out, for at least the first couple of big wave sessions, there was a period of recovery when you sat on your board catching your breath, taking stock of what the heck just happened. The impact zone was a maelstrom, a violent place where you might have been pitched from your board, bounced off the bottom, and come up gasping as you frantically tried to start paddling before the next wave rolled through. Surfboard leashes made this a little less stressful because you knew that when you came up your board would only be six feet away (unless the leash broke). But it was still a jolting experience that pushed massive amounts of adrenaline into every cell of your body. Sometimes while sitting there waiting for your heartbeat to find a comfortable rhythm you'd question if you really wanted to be out...even after you worked so hard to make it out.

Part of these doubts came from knowing that, despite your effort, you weren't entirely out of harm's way. There would likely be "clean up" sets, which were groups of even larger waves that would show up randomly four, five, or maybe six times an hour, and break well beyond where you and the others were sitting. Some surfer usually made the traditional call – "Outside" – and everyone would start paddling for the rapidly vanishing horizon, hoping they could make it over the biggest waves of the entire day. If you didn't make it, you knew you were in for a beating, as this wave would likely rip the board right out of your hands as you tried to push through it. It was such a helpless and stomach dropping feeling to be so far from shore as a rogue wall of whitewater came barreling at you, with what you swore was malicious intent. The underwater pummeling was no fun, but the real danger came in how many surfers had to dodge this wave and whether all of them – or any of them – held onto their surfboards. If not, there were soft-bodied surfers and hard-shelled fiberglass surfboards – now underwater projectiles with protruding sharp-edged fins – mixing around in a wash cycle that could drag you over 10-yards of ocean bottom at what seemed like warp factor five.

Today, fortunately, had been nothing like that. It had been a sunny, mellow morning with clean waist high waves, and maybe ten guys scattered between 120th Street and the Caine house at 118th Street. This included Greg, who made it out about a half hour after I did. He definitely got full marks for effort, even though he floated around for most of the next 45 minutes without catching anything. He tried on a couple of waves but just didn't have the paddling speed to get his board into the wave. Not being much of a morning person, the pre-lifeguard shift wasn't Greg's favorite time to be out in the water. So, I gave him a lot of credit today, it was always nice to have someone to shoot the breeze with while waiting for sets. Hopefully, he'd stand up soon. If he didn't, I knew he'd lose interest. It was a scenario I watched play out with several guys the summer before.

We had come back from surfing and gotten some coffee, a little bit of food, and then Greg oiled up and headed back to the beach to bake in the sun. I was going to drag my towel up to the sand a little later, more for the social than the sun worship aspect, as a favorite pastime of ours was making fun of the crappy music on WKHI. We still got a big kick out of hearing "Funky Town," a song we'd never heard before until our second night in the condo. It came on the radio just past midnight after we'd given up on the television and bubbled ourselves a minor buzz from Greg's ice-filled bong. The giggles came as soon as the electronic bass line began its disco octave bounce, and each time the synthy flute hook wove in and out the vocals, Greg and I laughed harder. Wanting to get a closer "look," I'd gotten down in front of our right speaker to figure out what the song was about. My knee hit the shag piles just as the bass modulated downward into the percussive pause before the chorus. Then the bass started back up, and in came the fat, quick-hit guitar chord:

"Oh, won't you take me...to Funky Town!"

Laughter convulsed through me so violently that I fell over on my side in the hallway. I could barely speak, my arms wrapped around my vibrating stomach, only able to utter "Funky Town!?" as my breath came back. Greg doubled over and fell off his chair, laughing on all fours with his face in the carpet, an undisputed indicator of just how genuine his reaction was to the song – neither of us would voluntarily put our face in that carpet. The giggles didn't subside until the song was long over, and our sides hurt from the extended session of laughter. But we enjoyed every second. And it probably would have happened even if there wasn't the sweet scent of weed in the air.

One of the major reasons Greg and I got along so well was music. We were music geeks, and truth be told, we were kind of music snobs, always on the lookout for new bands. Other than meals in the dining halls, we never listened to Top 40 music, bouncing our radio dials between the Philadelphia FM rock stations WMMR and WYSP. Greg had turned me on to the Police, as he had their first album blasting out of his dorm room just days after it came out during our freshman year. He also exposed me to The Clash and The B-52's, although I was struggling to "get" Devo. Greg had just picked up their latest album before coming to the beach – for better or for worse, I was sometimes out in the surf with "Whip-It" stuck in my head. (Thanks, Greg.)

Since my U of D dorm room faced west I could sometimes pick up 98 Rock out of Baltimore, whose playlist differed from the Philadelphia stations. This allowed me to return the favor and turn Greg on to AC/DC. We were both blown away when their singer Bon Scott died in February. Neither of us had listened to *Highway to Hell* very much since then.

So, while the turntable on top of my dresser spun Rush's *Permanent Waves*, Black Sabbath's *Heaven and Hell* (we knew it was sacrilege, but we were really digging Ronnie James Dio as their new vocalist), Flash and the Pan's *Lights in the Night*, and *Duke* by Genesis, we got our fill of popular music on the beach listening to Greg's radio. We also got it at Playland. Sometimes the park had WKHI playing, but most of the time it was the feed from our own Top 40 Club, an indoor space on the park's southern midway with picnic tables and a longtime Playland employee in a DJ booth playing songs from the Billboard Top 40 chart. Greg and I were still wondering why it was called the Top 40 Club because from the outside it looked like a barn, vertically paneled with wood and painted barn red, complete with the doors and windows thickly outlined in white. The barn theme carried over to the inside too, where there were faux hay bales and a small wooden stage to augment the picnic tables. On hot days guests could duck in out of the sun to cool off, eat, and relax – as long as they enjoyed hearing songs from the Top 40.

Greg and I weren't total pricks with our musical taste, we didn't think the Top 40 was all bad. There were just some songs that we never needed to hear again. Ever. But "Funky Town" still made us laugh – and probably always would.

"What's KHI been up to?" I asked, spreading my oversized blue towel on the sand, anchoring two of the ends with my flip-flops.

"The usual – Elton John, Bob Seger, and Blondie," Greg answered, turning his head to face me from his back-toward-the-sun prone position.

"'Little Jeannie,' 'Against the Wind,' and 'Call Me?'"

"Yep."

"That's not too bad," I said, sitting down on my towel.

"Maybe. The park is kind of heavy on 'Little Jeannie' these days."

"I hadn't really noticed. I mean I know we hear it every night..."

"Three times last night. You're busy on your ride. I'm so close to the Top 40 Club right now, it's hard to ignore."

Once Mark learned the details of Greg's extensive food service experience – he'd been the assistant student manager at one of the campus dining halls – Greg's ride running days were over. He was now the manager of Playland's Dairy Queen, which sat directly across from the Top 40 Club. It was one of the park's main food outlet, so Greg had landed an important position. And for me, so far, it meant free cheeseburgers and banana milkshakes.

"Yeah, guess it is. Wouldn't you rather be running rides?"

"Nah, this is low key. Plus, I'm the boss. You're not complaining, are you?"

"Nope. You make a killer milkshake."

"Damn right. I guarantee you'll be disappointed on the nights I'm off. And be sure to pay for it then."

"Think on those nights I'll just pay for a Sprite and move on."

Greg smiled and put his head back down on the pillow he'd made with his T-shirt. I started squeezing Coppertone into my hand as KHI continued its string of commercials.

Ponzetti's pizzas aren't cheesy and doughy. Ponzetti's pizzas are crispy and delicious!

It was time to relax and soak up some rays.

Chapter Thirteen

Grades

K eeping Greg company on the beach was hard work sometimes, and today's midday shift on the sand had me feeling overheated and parched. So, I'd excused myself and come back to the condo to get a Coke out of the fridge and check the mail. As I walked toward Coastal Highway in the welcoming shade created by the elevated two-story section of our building that lined 122nd Street, I wondered how much mail got delivered to the Mirabella condo. We appeared to be the only seasonal unit in the entire building – I'd never run into anyone else at the mailboxes other than the mailman. Making a sharp right turn at the building's last exposed support post, I moved into the shaded corridor where the mailboxes were located, sliding the key to our box between my thumb and forefinger with its teeth pointing downward. On the wall to my right was a two-by-two array of metal mailboxes, each with a row of ten silver doors that hinged out from the right. Our box, 1G, was easy to find, sitting just below eye level in the middle of the top left row. It was also easy to find because I had written our names on a small strip of paper and put it in the narrow rectangular slot that sat over the stenciled 1G.

I pushed the key in the lock and turned it to the right, opening a tall expanse that dwarfed the two envelopes sitting upright in the bottom. The outward facing envelope had a Calvin B. Taylor logo – it was the monthly statement from the Ocean City bank where I had a summertime checking account. The other envelope, I could see, was from my parents. I was pretty sure of what was inside. My stomach instantly flopped, and my heart started racing like I was far, far from shore staring down the biggest cleanup set of my life. I knew that this wave was going to do far more than knock me off my board and drag me across the bottom. It was going to change my life.

Instantly, officially, and permanently.

Feeling around the edges of the envelope, yep, there was something inside that wasn't a letter. It was rectangular with thick ends...the U of

D's teletype grade printout. One of those things you had to tear at the end and then pull back the mimeograph cover sheet to glimpse the smudgy and sterile assessment of your academic toil. I was yet to have a great set of grades or at least a set that I'd looked forward to seeing. All I'd done for the last year and a half was hang on by my fingertips to delusions of becoming a marine scientist. Delaware didn't offer any type of undergrad marine degree, so I was a biology major. A very naïve biology major, at least when I started, as I had no idea that Delaware's undergraduate biology program was pre-med oriented, and set up to weed out the lesser students well before graduation.

Somehow, I still hadn't gotten the hint by last fall, scraping by with a C in Ecology and a C in Organic Chemistry. Thanks to this "success" I continued onward into Organic Chem II and General Physiology, a pair of classes that whooped my ass good throughout the spring. Nothing in either one really clicked or stuck, and by mid-April, I was struggling to not flunk them both. Physiology class met on Tuesdays and Thursdays for 90 excruciating minutes, with every lecture consisting of the professor's monotone narration of the scientific hieroglyphics on his faded and yellowing overhead transparencies. And there was absolutely no variation to this routine. He'd come in, pull the retractable movie screen down in front of the blackboard, fire up the overhead projector...and drone on. After a while, all it took was the hum of the projector's cooling fan to make my eyes close and my head bob.

It got so bad that on Honors Day, a day when the class was pushed back an hour to allow the Honors Students to be honored, I used this newly freed up 60 minutes to sneak into the unoccupied classroom and attach a *Playboy* centerfold to the movie screen. Part of my inspiration came from Harpo Marx, who hung a pinup girl on an anatomy chart during a chaotic classroom scene in *Horse Feathers*. But most of my motivation came from the Honors Day celebration itself, which I was several grade galaxies away from being part of. I'd never forgotten the previous year when a dozen or so Biology Honors' Students – who weren't slumming it with us regular Biology schlubs in a 400-seat lecture hall – paraded themselves in front of us, trading flowers, gifts and laughs with a professor who I'd had a last row relationship with since the first day of class.

This callous display of academic privilege totally pissed me off – weren't they fucking special? Not only did they know the professor in a way that wasn't open to me, they were also in a setting where the professor would actually be concerned if they began to struggle with the material. More importantly, the professor would approach their struggles with the powerful presumption that they were capable of learning the material, not the jaundiced eye that those of us who occupied the nosebleed seats seemed to receive whenever we bothered to descend through the exiting throngs to ask an after-class question, or when we gathered the courage to go knock on a door during office hours. So it was a bitter mix of doubt and hopelessness that had me firmly securing the Playmate of the Month with double-sided poster tape. After carefully guiding the screen back up into its case, I exited to the empty hallway and hurried for a stairwell, feeling like Bluto as he made his paranoid-chipmunk scamper across a midnight-hour Faber campus in *Animal House*.

My usual seat was in the back of the room, so I sat in the last row with my heart jumping out of my chest, trying to hold an innocent look on my face as the professor walked in. There were about 40 people in the class, so while I wasn't completely anonymous, I hadn't said a whole lot as each test sucked my Jacque Cousteau dreams into the depths of the Marianas Trench. Thanks to my nearly faceless persona I felt pretty safe, yet at the same time, part of me didn't really care. I'd only come up with the prank because I felt I had nothing to lose at this point. Or so I told myself. But if that was the case, why was I feeling lightheaded, kind of wishing that I hadn't liberated this Miss April from her staples?

When the professor pulled down the screen he wasn't even looking at it, which meant the classroom-wide laugh – and it was loud enough to make any comedian proud – took him by surprise. It also let me know that my comedic timing had been just about perfect. His forehead wrinkled as he continued looking out at us, unaware of the suggestive unfolded nakedness over his left shoulder. Then a small smile crept onto his bearded face, and he turned toward the screen. Gently nodding his head as he sized up Miss April, he took it all in stride, turning back to the class with half a smile and saying dryly, "Well, now that we're done with the anatomy lesson, the owner can come claim it."

A great comeback on his part, but unlike brave Harpo, I had no plans to raise my hand and admit my guilt. I just looked left, then right, trying to make it obvious that the person who did this was surely somewhere else in the room.

As the professor removed Miss April from the screen I already knew it was an empty triumph. I had a plan, it worked to perfection, and it got a better reaction from the class than I'd dreamed. Yet it wasn't going to focus my less than laser sharp French-accented marine science fantasies. And it wasn't going to prevent me from getting drummed out of biology...as the students being celebrated on this day moved ever onward with academic success that I could only dream about. So, what exactly had I been trying to prove?

Walking back to the condo, my head clicked through other academic moments from the last two years. Could I have changed anything? Could today have been different? My life was about to veer dramatically from the direction I hoped it might go. You could argue that I had been headed in this alternate direction for quite some time now, but my denial, as I bumped along with steady C's in science, was massive.

Until now.

I ripped open the envelope's flap as I went up the steps, but waited until I got inside to pull out the grades. I had to give my parents credit, they hadn't taken a peek before forwarding them on to me. I wouldn't have been mad. They were, after all, footing the bill for my academic mediocrity. And it would've saved me a phone call. But maybe they knew what they were doing by letting me deal directly with the fallout on my own. The evidence of their parenting acumen was on display in my shaking hands, my rib-rattling heartbeat, and the desire to be anywhere else on my life timeline than at this moment.

My left hand slid the mailer out while my right hand tore the white perpendicular strip off its right edge, and then made a quick yank on the black mimeograph cover sheet. It wasn't a clean tear, but my grades were there for me to see, fully exposed in the bright sunlight coming through our large sliding window.

Scanning down the column of letters...my hopeful eyes didn't find any miracles. And now it was official, all there in black and white. Seven credits worth of D. Physiology accounted for four of those credits, while Organic swept up the other three. And when added together, they expanded out to almost half of my entire credit load. Trying to balance this Titanic-like pull toward academic probation was a C in Personality, a B in Intro Philosophy, and somehow, in a final ass-kick of fate, a one-credit B in Organic Lab. That landed my semester grade point average at a thoroughly Delta house 1.78, with an overall grade point average of 2.12. An ugly number that few departments at Delaware would be willing to take on. Hell, you needed a 2.75 to transfer into the business program...not that I had the slightest interest in business.

I continued staring at the grades as I set the sheet down on the table. There could be no more denial. The bottom line was, I had failed at college so far. Even though I hadn't literally flunked, I had failed. I couldn't cut it in biology. That was a fact. It wasn't that I didn't try, or didn't want to do well. I flat out couldn't cut it. I wasn't good enough or smart enough to make a go of it. So halfway through my four years – shit, I might now need more than four years – I had no major, and a grade point average just above the academic Mendoza line. Thank God I wasn't on probation.

But the shit was real now, and life was real. Oh man, things had to be different when I got back to campus in the fall. There was no more time for fucking around...not that I had been fucking around. The final month of the semester was a painful, depressing time. Since the Delaware biology weeding out process was never-ending, of course, the Organic and Physiology finals were on the same day. Just hours apart, lasting three hours apiece, each being a session where I knew I was finished with science. I was toast. But the tests weren't totally meaningless. I had to try and get some result on the finals, as to fail the tests and fail the classes would have been disastrous. I just couldn't sign my name on the page and turn in a blank test a few minutes later. That was unthinkable.

Yet at the same time, I knew it was wholly possible that I could wring myself inside out for six hours and still end up failing both classes. So it was hard to make myself give a shit and truly focus. Those finals ranked up there as the hardest things I'd ever done. Perhaps physically, I'd done more challenging things, but the pressure I felt that day...my academic future at Delaware was on the line. It was the first time I'd ever felt *so* desperate. The only way out was to finish both tests because the difference between seven credits of F and seven credits of D was massive. However pathetic it sounded, I was relieved to see the D's. Not that I was proud of them, but in a weird way, I kind of was. I gave my all on finals day to land them. Putting up a good fight in a hopeless cause.

But life was more real now. My margin for error moving forward would be much, much smaller. Whatever came next at Delaware, I had to succeed. And whatever major I picked – or whatever major would have me – there would be a lot of catching up to do.

There was also that phone call to my parents. Fortunately, they knew. I hadn't hidden anything from them. My academic struggles weren't a secret – unlike Miss April.

Chapter Fourteen

A Dorchester Morning

A Dorchester Street vacation morning of my childhood could start in a couple of different ways. It all depended on whether it was a mom and dad trip, or a trip with my aunt, grandmother, great-grandmother and great uncle – all relatives from my father's side. Of course, there were stays at Mrs. Bunting's when everyone was along, but often my dad was missing. Not that there was any type of break up, or that he didn't want to be there. Sometimes he just wasn't available. And strangely, I really didn't mind.

For my dad, learning was like breathing – it was something he could never stop doing. So after a humble start on the assembly line of a local water cooler factory, he'd become a professor at a southeastern Pennsylvania college. Learning, as my dad viewed it, not only expanded horizons, it was a means toward better things. Through his undergrad degree – the first in the family – he stepped off the generational blue-collar path his life was destined for after high school (something I now understood and admired despite my own academic struggles). And this passion for learning set quite an example, as I grew up watching my dad earn advanced degrees and multiple academic summer residencies, including an entire summer traveling Europe in 1969. I also came to understand that "better things," in my dad's definition, didn't have to mean wealth or material possessions – Exhibit A being the five-room one-story Cape Cod with a used Volkswagen in the driveway that we lived in until I was 14. But by then I'd ridden the Tube to Piccadilly, eaten steak frites on the Eiffel Tower, chilled my fingers in the waters of Loch Ness, viewed Rembrandts in Amsterdam, looked directly into the eyes of the *Mona Lisa*, and received a cricket primer from two proper English boys while sitting in a Greek temple-inspired colonnade at the University College London.

Yet none of these overseas experiences could lessen my love for Ocean City. From the moment I woke up on Dorchester Street – our usual apartment was on the second floor of Mrs. Bunting's house – the day was full of potential. If it was a mom and dad trip, the day would usually start early, my dad and I gathering up our fishing poles and tackle box for the block and a half walk to Paul's Tackle Shop on Talbot Street. Paul's was a saltwater fishing wonderland, starting with its iconic red-lettered sign that spanned the entire front roofline of the cedar-shake building. Under the sign, forming the front wall of the shop, were two large glass windows, each holding a hanging forest of stout fishing rods and long-handled landing nets. Bisecting the windows was a wooden screen door that, once opened, led to multi-tiered glass display counters full of gleaming new reels, over which dangled the long sparkling fluorescent tails of the big-eyed trolling lures used for marlin offshore. Just beyond a doorway in the back of the shop were bubbling tanks of live and wriggling sea life – for the fishermen who wanted a challenge when baiting their hooks.

My favorite part of the shop was on the floor in the front, where it looked like someone had turned a wooden bookcase on its side and partitioned it into a dozen or so squares, then filled each compartment to the brim with a different lead sinker. Not only did Paul's have sequential weights of the standard bowling pin-shaped sinkers, but they also had pyramid-shaped sinkers, torpedo-shaped sinkers, and sinkers heavy enough to bend my pole over without a fish on the end. I might not have known what each of them was for, but I did know that they were the most affordable items in the store. So for the price of a soda I could pick up an intriguing looking sinker – that I might never use. But it would look cool sitting in the tackle box. I'd be ever-ready for that time when the "big ones" were biting. Once my mind settled down from the fishing fantasies inspired by everything in the shop, especially the deep-sea reels that were the size of my head, the visit ended in the usual way.

"A box of shiners, please."

This request could be greeted with a grunt, or a full rundown on what the morning might hold, depending on whether the person behind the counter had gotten their coffee yet. Although it must have been hard to fully inhabit the role of a crochety Captain Quint after a blonde, pompadoured nine-year-old laid a $0.25 piece of lead on the counter like it was a rare Egyptian artifact.

With our white cardboard box of frozen minnows in hand, we'd pick either the Talbot Street dock or Dorchester Street dock, leaning toward the one that had the least activity. The Talbot Street dock ended in a "T" that was usually vacant after the Capt. Bunting and Angler party boats pulled out at 7:00 am. The Dorchester Street dock stretched out into the bay with a final "L" section that didn't include any permanent boat slips, so it was open for fishing any time of day or night. From either dock, it was an easy cast to the deeper water of the boat channel, which is where the big fish hung out. For this reason, we never bothered with the shorter dock in the shadow of the bridge.

Occasionally we'd walk an extra block north and fish off the bridge, but I was always on edge up there with the cars from Route 50 whizzing by just inches away. Making a cast or dealing with a flopping fish could be tricky depending on the time of day. The traffic also seemed to accentuate my acrophobia, minor as it was, and alternating my worry between the speeding traffic and the height of the bridge left me pretty much hugging the metal railing for the duration of our session. Eventually, I learned to enjoy fishing from the bridge, but for the longest time, I didn't like being up there at all. Even with a fish on the line.

Walking out onto either of the docks was an exciting way to start the day, yet sometimes it was less of an *American Sportsman* experience than you'd hoped for. Depending on the wind, how many boats were still docked, or whether a boat had just taken on 100 gallons of Texaco Diesel Chief or Fire Chief, the fish odor embedded in the weather-worn planks could intermingle with the vapor of petroleum products in a gag-inducing way.

From my earliest memories of watching the sleek boats with tall outriggers go in and out of the inlet, I understood that fishing was part of

Ocean City's DNA. But what I didn't realize, was that this DNA had been created long before an unnamed 1933 hurricane cut the inlet to create the sport fishing economy that flourished at the docks. The resort didn't even have a name when the first guest house was built in 1869 to accommodate the adventurous and wealthy sport fishermen who could afford the train, stagecoach, and boat journey it took to reach Maryland's then wild and unspoiled coastline. After a new train line and the luxurious Atlantic Hotel opened a few years later, not only did more people come for the fishing, it was local fisherman who provided fish, crabs, and clams for the restaurant's seafood specialties. Demand for fishing guides and local seafood increased as new hotels and restaurants began dotting the growing seaside community during the late 1800s, and by the turn of the century, a new type of fishing had become a mainstay of the Ocean City economy. It was called pound fishing, a dangerous endeavor that involved launching wooden boats into the surf and rowing out to tend nets that could be a half mile or more offshore.

While dangerous, pound fishing was also very lucrative. So lucrative that at one point a dozen different companies had fish camps lining the beaches south of Ocean City. A new south-running train spur was built to service the camps, helping the companies – which now employed a large part of the local male population – get their fish barreled, iced, and swiftly sent by rail to Philadelphia, Baltimore, and Washington. Overfishing had the industry in decline by the time Mrs. Bunting arrived in 1917, yet she still had stories about how the men rowed out into all sorts of weather to bring up the nets and dump the day's catch into the boats. She claimed the real test of an Ocean City waterman came in maneuvering his catch-ladened and cumbersome craft back to the beach. Just like surfers they had to figure out which waves might be perfect for pushing their low-riding boats safely toward shore.

Although he didn't talk about it much, fishing seemed to be part of my dad's DNA, too. One of the things revealed to me during those late evening sessions on Mrs. Bunting's front porch was that my dad had spent countless hours with a line in the water during his many stays on Dorchester Street. This included boat time in the bay and the ocean thanks to Mr. Bunting's connections, as well as surf fishing on the then remote shores of Assateague for stripers, kingfish, and bluefish. He was masterful with an open-spooled bait-casting reel, his well-practiced left thumb always applying just the perfect pressure to his rapidly unspooling line during a cast. This same thumb guided line effortlessly back onto his reel, distributing the incoming yards of braided nylon evenly across the spool with machine-like precision. The only time his reel ever had a backlash – a "bird's nest" of tangled line – was when we swapped poles. A handoff that usually took place just after I'd put a bird's nest in my own reel.

While his meticulous and tightly wound reel was impressive, what I really admired were the distance and accuracy of his casts. Much of my admiration came from the physics-defying skill needed just to get a hook and sinker airborne with my dad's trusted stubby-and-stiff nearly-antique bamboo boat rod. There was absolutely no play, whip, or "feel" in the thing at all. Compared to my fiberglass rod, it was like fishing with a broomstick. Yet from all the years it had spent in his hands, he could cast a bait out beyond any breaker line, seemingly to within feet of where he was aiming. And fish always seemed to find his line. We could be standing side-by-side, using the same sinker, same hook, and same bait, and he would catch more fish. To me, he was the best fisherman I ever saw. Which meant I listened carefully to his lessons on how to rig a pole and bait a hook, watched and imitated as he tied knots in his line, looked hard at the dark and mysterious swirling water, trying to "see" what my dad was seeing, and worked diligently to train my left thumb to do some of the things his could do. What I wanted most of all was to be able to handle a bait-casting reel just like he did – casting over and over without a backlash, my line always taut and evenly distributed on the reel.

These lessons all came together during an early-1970s solo outing at Talbot Street. After picking up a box of shiners at Paul's, I sat under the "AMERICAN" sign casting northward toward the bridge and landed four forearm-length flounder in a magical 45-minute period. For a shining moment – and it was a glorious sunny morning – I was a grizzled "old salt," amazing anyone who strolled out onto the docks after breakfast at the Angler Restaurant. It was an impressive and heavy stringer that I carried back to Mrs. Bunting's for everyone to see.

Occasionally the fishing gear got packed for a trip with my aunt and my grandmother, but usually, it didn't. Logistics were part of the issue, as there was a minimum of five people in the car, including me. That meant there wasn't much room in the trunk for a pole and a tackle box (fishing gear could also carry a bit of an "ick" factor that not everybody wanted to deal with). Not that I minded. Even though my aunt didn't fish, in every other way, she was the definition of a "cool aunt." She was single, made good money, never drove a car that was more than a year old, kept her "gold-digging" boyfriends at arms-length...and spoiled me rotten. My grandmother was in on the spoiling thing too. As it stood, I was the only nephew and the only grandchild. So in addition to a bowl of Cocoa Krispies, breakfast on a trip with my aunt and my grandmother might include a Coke or Pepsi chaser. Nothing like a caffeine and sugar buzz to get the pre-adolescent juices flowing. A nutritional lineup that would never pass muster with mom and dad.

Maybe that's why those mornings are so vivid...almost jumping off the steps onto Mrs. Bunting's concrete driveway, standing out on the sidewalk of Dorchester Street waiting for my aunt to catch up, then moving up toward Philadelphia Avenue and circling the rectangular rental sign next to the towering yellow and white apartment building on the corner. Feeling the warmth of the sun as we scurried across the road's wide one-way expanse, looking south past the Ice House and the water tower toward the inlet where Philadelphia Avenue took a 90° left-hand turn at the Oceanic's "MOTEL" sign, turning eastward there to become 1st Street with its panoramic view of the now deserted and motionless outdoor rides at Trimper's. Once on the other side of Philadelphia Avenue my aunt and I would continue up Dorchester Street, walking by City Hall and the police station before hitting the extended all-windows storefront of S & S Hardware, a nearly floor-to-ceiling wall of glass that offered an X-ray view into the aisles of the store. Hanging in these windows like closely-spaced fence posts were fishing poles of every variety, from toy rigs with plastic hooks to towering surf rods for making long casts from the beach. Augmenting the hanging display were rubber hip waders, metal-handled landing nets, and crab nets, distinguished by their long wooden handles, shallow white twine netting, and thin coat hanger-like hoops that made them look like a budget basketball rim.

Along the bottom of the windows were blue-lidded Styrofoam coolers, heavy duty Coleman coolers, tackle boxes, live minnow holders, metal crab traps, oversized crab steamer pots...with even more fishing gear visible on the shelves inside. It was an impressive display that made it easy to forget that S & S was a hardware store, a detail that was fully reinforced when we took a right at the store's corner entrance to walk south on Baltimore Avenue. The windows facing out on the east side of the store were full of shovels, rakes, saws, mops, brooms, paint brushes, and other assorted hardware-type items.

We'd continue past Hall's Coffee Shop and its quartet of tall colonial columns, and past the multiple red brick pillars of the Corner News Variety Store, whose porch-like overhang sheltered a colorful outdoor display of inflatable surf mats, beach chairs, beach umbrellas, sand pails, and those miniature white Styrofoam "surfboards" with the smiling boy and the palm tree on the wrapper. From my own experience, I knew that these "sucker born every minute" items couldn't even float an overweight dachshund. And when you got the stupid thing in the ocean and tried to make it work – assuming, of course, that it didn't float because you were doing something wrong – the board broke into two pieces as soon as you put any pressure on the center. They were complete junk. Proof could be found in any late afternoon boardwalk trash can.

The Corner News' front door, which fittingly faced out at a 45° angle from the corner of the building, always drew my attention. That's because there was something next to it that I could only see in Ocean City – a tall black wire newspaper rack vertically displaying the front pages of the *Baltimore Sun*, the *Baltimore News American*, the *Washington Post*, the *Washington Star*, and the *Eastern Shore Times*. Seeing those names confirmed that I was on vacation.

Crossing Somerset Street immersed us in an invisible bacon-scented cloud, a mouth-watering aroma that had drifted across Baltimore Avenue from the Hungry Jack Pancake House. In addition to serving pancakes all day, the Hungry Jack was notable because the single-story building looked like an oversized log cabin. It caught your attention even without the bouquet of breakfast wafting out its front door. The aroma dissipated by the time we stopped at what appeared to be a vacant storefront just short of Elliot's Hardware. Yet a careful look through the glass front window revealed rows of bicycles lined up inside. Todd's Bikes on Caroline Street had long been the traditional starting point for early morning boardwalk bike rides, but for the moment we were favoring this new entry into the Ocean City bike rental world. The reason? They had Sting-Ray-style bicycles for rent – bikes with banana seats, sissy bars, and tall ape hanger handlebars. There was no way I wanted to hit the boardwalk with a dorky standard bicycle. I was almost 10-years-old. It was time to start looking "cool."

Chapter Fifteen

The Feed Bag

THE

FENWICK
FEED BAG
RESTAURANT

Greg swallowed the oddly pink-hued liquid in a single gulp, then put his shot glass on the table next to a second shot glass containing a turgid brown concoction. He stared at the glasses for a second, rapidly blinked his eyelids like he was trying to use them as windshield wipers, then trained his intense blue eyes on me.

"So what the hell are you going to do?" he said.

"I have no idea. I don't have a clue." I replied, shaking my head while breaking Greg's gaze to look down on my own pair of shot glasses. Both were filled with a milky liquid that looked like lemonade. But that's not what it was. My shots were Kamikazes. Greg had opted to mix and match a Watermelon and a Tootsie Roll. I took the sweating shot glass on the left into my left hand, then brought it up to my mouth and drained it clean, feeling the burn on the back of my throat as the mild fruitiness melted away. I hadn't even gotten my glass back onto the table before Greg barked out my next move.

"Now the other one..."

This rapid-fire shot sequence was Greg's way of cheering me up after an uneventful shift at Playland. His efforts to cheer also included picking up the evening's tab, not that he was in any danger of overextending himself. It was almost 11:30 pm and we were working on perhaps the best bargain buzz in all of Ocean City – Dollar Shooter Monday at the Fenwick Feed Bag. Kamikazes, Laser Beams, Watermelons, and Tootsie Rolls all for a $1.00 apiece. Technically, the Feed Bag wasn't in Ocean City, it was just blocks across the Delaware line, tucked in the back of the faux shantytown shopping center that was the Fenwick Village. This slightly out of the way location was a bonus, being off the radar of the mostly underage just-graduated high school "June Bugs" trying to get served this week in Ocean City. Not that we had any room to judge their efforts. I was still a few days shy of Delaware's legal drinking age, while Greg, with a November birthday, wasn't even close. Maybe it was just the early season, but the Feed Bag servers had yet to card us, or even take a second look.

I shifted my hand to the full glass but had yet to pick it up.

"C'mon...those go down easy," said Greg.

Kamikazes did go down easy, but that was part of their danger – you wouldn't fully feel the "hit" of the alcohol until five or ten minutes later. I finished the second glass with a quick tilt of the head, determined to let some significant time go by before the next round.

"So, your parents were okay with the grades?" asked Greg, referring to the phone call I'd made just after work to let my parents know that their greatest fears hadn't been realized. Not that my D+ grade point average made them feel optimistic in any way.

"I don't think 'okay' is the right description. They were supportive. Very supportive. My dad...it's like aliens took him over. If this had happened in high school, I'd probably been grounded and lost the car."

Greg's eyes narrowed as his head tilted slightly to the right, and I knew what was coming.

"Some of us managed to make it through high school just fine without having their own car."

"I know, I know...things would have been really ugly. That's all I was trying to say," I answered, defensively acknowledging the privilege of my privilege. My ears were going red, and it wasn't from the alcohol.

"I'm sorry. Really. You're in a shitty spot. I'm sorry. That was a cheap shot."

"Don't worry about it. I'm the one who put myself there."

"What's the difference with your dad?"

"We've talked a lot about my classes, the science ones. And he's been in my corner all the way."

"He's the department chair now?"

"Yeah, he can't wait to be finished with that. Such a pain in the ass. But he's been telling me all along he would never teach like that – the way my science courses were being taught."

"Wow..."

"Yeah, no shit. He's okay with things because he feels I gave it my best shot. Which I did. Any weekend I was home, I was in the books. Not just to impress him, I didn't have any friggin' choice."

Greg took a pause to look around the intimate and dimmer-switch ambiance of the Feed Bag's front section. There were eight tables total, all well-spaced four-tops that could be pushed together for larger parties. We were at a four-top in the back on the left, being tended to by a casually dressed waitress with dark hair and a blue apron. She had just delivered several towering toothpick-reinforced sandwiches to a table near the door, and a couple of the other tables in the half-filled room also had plates from the late-night menu. The food all looked really good – but that's not why we came to the Feed Bag.

A typical dollar shooter night in Ocean City involved sweaty and slurred-speech humanity packed four deep at a bar whose bartender was busier than a lifeguard during a hurricane swell, and drowning in the sloshing spillage on the floor surrounding the bar was probably the best way to get his attention. Dollar shooter night at the Feed Bag was...well, civilized. And in the calm and laid-back atmosphere, Greg and I could sit, relax, and have a conversation that didn't involve screaming into our cupped hands over the din of a distorted PA system. Not to mention that the Ocean City establishments having dollar shooter nights were religious about checking ID. Neither of us had a prayer of getting a dollar shooter in Ocean City until our 21st birthdays.

"I told Gary we'd be here..." Greg half mumbled, looking toward the front door. Gary had been at Phillip's with Greg, then quit Phillip's the day after Greg did to come work at Playland. It was unusual to find someone from Long Island working a summer job in Ocean City, but that's what Gary was doing. I presumed Gary had some type of business background because Mark put him in charge of Playland's games of chance. Greg's eyes moved back to the table, where he grabbed his Tootsie Roll and made the dark liquid disappear from his glass with a flick of the wrist.

"Man, my dad's all up my ass because I was five-tenths off the Dean's list," said Greg with more than a hint of exasperation about his father's exacting expectations. "You should come over to Ag. Put that biology background to use."

"Ag? What could I do in Ag? Drive a tractor, but that's about it."

"Hey – driving a tractor is harder than you think. Intimidating as hell, too. We did it first semester. The inside of the cab was like a spaceship. I could barely turn the damn thing on."

"Well, strike the tractor driving, then. They'd never let me in, anyway. Plus, those engineering and computer courses? No thanks. You guys lived at the computer center last semester."

"Yeah, they should build a dorm next to Smith Hall. So, tell me again – most majors have a transfer GPA?"

"Yep. I checked with the Business Department during finals week. They want a 2.75."

"And yours?"

"2.12"

"Shit."

"Yeah, exactly. Plus, I'm two years behind in required coursework. Playing catch up no matter who lets me in."

"How quickly could you get to 2.75? Like, take the easiest courses you could find next semester?"

"In figuring roughly, if I went full out 4.0 next semester – like that would ever happen – I'd still be a couple of tenths short. Not to mention another semester behind in the required stuff, and halfway through my Junior year without a major."

"Man..."

"And I'll be digging up new courses during the first week of class. After I drop the stupid science courses I'm signed up for, I'll pretty much have to grab any course with an opening. Not the ideal way to raise your GPA."

"Holy fuck."

Yeah, holy fuck. Laying things out here with Greg – of course, I'd been thinking about them all night long, I just hadn't said them out loud, not even to my parents – I felt worse now than I did when I first saw the grades. How was I ever going to fix this? Was I looking at three more years of college? A truly daunting thought, considering how much "fun" the first two years were. The Kamikazes probably didn't help, but my stomach slipped into the same rock-like sensation it had when I opened the mailbox this afternoon. Like I was hopelessly caught inside on a day so big that I'd never make it out. How could I be in Ocean City – my favorite place in the entire world – and feel so uncertain and unhappy? The only time I could ever remember being scared and unhappy in Ocean City was back in 1966 when little red bumps started appearing all over my body one morning in my aunt's trailer. When the fever hit, it was clear I had the chicken pox. My parents drove down that day and took me home – a blistering un-air-conditioned three-hour ride that I spent in near delirium while shivering under blankets in the back seat. Just the thought of it made me twitch.

"Hey – are you okay?" asked Greg.

"It just came to me."

"What?"

"What I'm going to do."

"Yeah?"

"Order another round."

Our server carefully set the quartet of shot glasses on the table. I got two more Kamikazes, while Greg opted to stay with Tootsie Rolls.

"Skol," I said to Greg, holding my glass up to offer a toast. Greg nodded, and we both finished our shots.

"To the summer," I offered, putting my glass back on the table.

"There's a lot of it left," said Greg.

"Yeah, I hope there are some waves tomorrow. I could really use some time in the water."

"The water is on the chilly side again."

"It did go cold, didn't it? It's that time of year. It can be anything. You don't know until you stick your toes in."

I looked down and reached for my other Kamikaze, grabbing it by the rim, lifting it ever so slightly off the table. Then I thought better of taking on this one so fast and put it back down.

"I'm so ready to get off the Antique Cars. I've already prodded Mark. I got a 'we'll see' from him. There's nothing wrong with them, but there's just so many other more fun looking options in the park," I said, looking over at Greg.

"Yeah, they are kind of tame. Mark will fix you up. Look at me, I'm thrilled at the Dairy Queen," said Greg.

"I hope so. I need the change. Did the Phils play tonight?"

"Yeah, they're in LA playing right now."

"And the O's?"

"They already beat the Angels. I saw the local news while you were on the phone."

I looked down to again consider my still full Kamikaze...and finally, the buzz I'd been waiting for since we first sat down was underway. Three shots, that was about right. Greg and I had played it safe during our first Feed Bag visit two weeks earlier, carefully gauging the effects of each round. We discovered that five was the magic number. Not too much for driving home, but enough to make the night enjoyable. More than five would be risky because I didn't need a DUI, and we knew they weren't wasting top-shelf liquor on dollar shooters. It seemed important to limit the potential for toxic off-gassing the next day. Few things were worse than being hungover on a morning when the surf was firing.

Not that I was overly worried about that at the moment. Thanks to that third Kamikaze, the dark curtain hanging over the day had started to rise. My birthday was Saturday, and both my girlfriend and family were coming down for the weekend. There could be some waves tomorrow, and maybe Mark would soon have me on a new ride, maybe the Monster Mouse, or the coaster. And there still was plenty of summer left. Over two months, then it was back to Delaware, where I'd pick up the pieces. With a new major, it would almost be like starting with a clean slate, other than the ball and chain that was my GPA. There was hope, but still...

"The thing is, I've failed or screwed up before, but usually there was a reason. I was lazy, I didn't try, I didn't care...my best friend from the Navy showed up the night before the exam. But that's not the case this time. I wasn't lazy, I did care, and I did try. But it wasn't enough."

Greg offered a tight smile, nodded his head slightly.

"Maybe look at things this way – since you don't know what you'll be doing in the fall, you don't even know what to worry about, right? So why worry at all?"

I had to admit, there was something, well, freeing, in Greg's logic.

"I did spend last summer dreading organic, and was ready to spend this one worrying about physics."

"And your calculus is already out of the way?"

"Yeah, over Winter Session."

"So, this will likely be the last 'free' summer you'll ever have."

"I like it, I like it..."

Greg picked up his Tootsie Roll, looked directly at me, and smiled.

"You got us the good jobs, it's going to be a good summer. You'll see."

"How can it not be – free cheeseburgers already."

"Yep. And dollar shooters," said Greg, before making sure he drained every penny of shooter number four.

Chapter Sixteen

A New Ride

"**W**ell...this is different."

"What's that?" asked Greg, as he pulled his time card out of the punch clock and moved it to the "IN" rack.

"I'm not on the Antique Cars."

"Congratulations – what did you get?"

We were both now staring at the chart on the wall in the employee lounge, where a name that wasn't mine had been penciled in for the Antique Cars. My eyes jumped to the ride list on the left, where I locked in on my favorites, then moved out to the column for Wednesday to see if my name was there. Monster Mouse, Hurricane, Spider, Airborne...nope, no luck with any of them. So I went back to the Wednesday column and ran my left index finger down from the top. Down, down, down...there I was, three off the bottom. Go-karts.

"Go-karts?" I blurted out, in a loud questioning tone that was total reflex.

"Go-karts?" repeated Greg, creating an almost perfect echo of my surprise.

"That wouldn't have been my first choice."

"Me neither, sorry to say. They're pretty noisy."

"Man..."

Greg waited for me as I grabbed my time card and punched in, then I followed him out of the employee lounge, splitting off when we reached the narrow corridor where we usually entered the park.

"Guess I'll keep going this way," I said to Greg, nodding my head in the direction of the access road.

"Okay – good luck."

"Thanks."

How in the world did I end up on the go-karts? I'd said nothing about them to Mark and barely noticed the track at this point, even though I walked past it every day on my way in and out of the park. The track was really more part of the parking lot than the park, so I hadn't paid much attention to how the go-karts worked or even who ran them, unlike all the other rides within the park that I'd been watching closely since day one. On some nights the lawn mower engine growl of the go-karts would drift over to the Antique Cars, but I really didn't know that much about them. Other than the commercials for "Ocean City's largest go-kart track!" that ran on WKHI once an hour.

And it wasn't like I was just going to dip my toes into go-kart running during a standard four-hour evening shift. Even though it was Wednesday, we had a full day and night ahead of us, starting with a company picnic for a large local chicken processor whose CEO was nationally known for his catchphrase "it takes a tough man to make a tender chicken." The employees and their families were already gathering in the parking lot and would stream through the gates as soon as we opened at 1:00 pm. It was a beautiful day for their outing. The sun was up full and bright, sharing the vibrantly blue sky with long brush strokes of wispy clouds. Fortunately, the breeze was onshore, blowing off what the goosebumps under my board shorts this morning told me was a 68° ocean.

I made a left at Mark's office, walking under the monorail track and past the giant smiling jester visage painted on the yellow wall that faced out from the park. A trio of head-high evergreen shrubs prevented me from getting a full view of the go-karts, but I could see a yellow shirted-figure moving slowly along the perimeter chain link fence that enclosed the track. The ride's chain link front gate was wide open, so I walked in and onto the smooth asphalt that put me at the top of the track's distinctive "L" shape. An old picnic bench and three silent karts were on the ground to my right, in what appeared to be the pit area, and the air carried a noticeable blend of gasoline and sun-warmed tires. The yellow-shirted figure was off to my left just around the track's first turn, maybe 20 yards away but obscured from my view by a 90° corner that gave me two layers of chain link fence to look through. I couldn't see exactly what my Playland colleague was doing, but he stopped, walked out into the center of the track, and took a hard look at me. His face immediately squinched up so tight that his eyes appeared shut – I could almost see the focus ring in his head turning desperately as he tried to identify what he was seeing. Because obviously, I wasn't what he expected.

He began walking up the straightaway toward where I stood, while at the same time, I started walking down the track towards him – it just seemed like the proper thing to do. His continued squint let me know that I still was an absolute riddle, although he did look a little familiar to me. I'd passed him in the park a few times, even though I had no idea what ride he ran. But clearly, I was a total surprise to him. There would be no reveal by my eyes, as they were hidden by sunglasses and the brim of my Montego Bay Hardware hat. The lightly tinted prescription aviator glasses of my new acquaintance, however, revealed all.

"Earl Shores," I said, sticking out my hand.

My back was starting to sweat under my backpack, partly from the sun, and partly from nerves, as it was easy to see that this guy didn't know what to make of me.

"Pat...Pat Hodges," came the answer. And a question. "Is this your first day?"

"No, I've been on the Antique Cars for the last week and a half."

"Oh, okay. Mark put you here?"

"I guess so. My name was in the go-kart slot today. That's all I know."

"Oh...okay."

Pat couldn't hide his skepticism over my presence. I had no idea why I was here, either, and maybe I really didn't want to know. Maybe Pat really liked his last partner and Mark was breaking them up, or maybe they didn't get along and Pat was promised somebody new, but that somebody wasn't me.

Although Pat was clearly younger, I grasped right away that he was the boss here at the go-karts. And I had no problem with that. Really, I didn't. There was a range of people working at Phillip's, with some having years of experience despite only being in high school. These younger guys knew the ins and outs of the restaurant and had a full bag of tricks to make a shift run smoothly. Me and the other "green" college hires would have been fools not to take advantage of their knowledge, hard-earned on summer nights when Ocean City's busiest restaurant had lines out the door and around the block. Old or young, respect in the kitchen came from being able to do your job. And respect was also earned by giving it, too. These lessons I soaked up quickly at Phillip's, and they were now a built-in part of my approach to any job. Pat knew nothing about my background, and obviously nothing about me. For all he knew, Mark had poached me from the go-karts at Jolly Roger, or maybe the go-kart place over the bridge in West Ocean City. I was older, with a full mustache, and a threat to Pat's top-dog status on the karts.

In reading the uncertainty etched all over Pat – not only in the still skeptical squint, but also in the sloped-shoulders, tightly crossed arms, and the distance he left between us – I knew that I was going to have to work hard to earn his trust. So, my main objective for the day was to do everything Pat instructed me to do. And do it *exactly* as he told me.

Pat turned away from me to look back out at the track, and I had my first assignment.

"We need to get the tires in order. They're all over the places after last night – they need to be put back in place along the edge of the track," said Pat.

"Sure, just let me stash my backpack away."

"You can put it by the bench. That's the hangout spot."

"Thanks," I said, before jogging over to the bench.

By the time I turned around Pat had disappeared into the bottom of the track's "L," so I hustled back down the straightaway to do whatever Pat needed me to do. He was almost knee deep in the tires lining the outer part of the track, trying to impose order on the multiple overlapping layers of round tread-less black rubber. It took me by surprise that Pat wasn't using his hands for the organizing. He was doing it with his feet – kicking and pushing the tires into place, making sure they were touching, but not over the painted white line on the outer edge of the track.

"Do you want me over there, or should I start on the tires lining the infield?" I asked, trying to squeeze initiative and consideration into a single question.

"Yeah, start on the infield."

And so I did.

My first kick was a revelation. The damn things were hard! Not that I'd hurt my foot, but its sudden stop sent a shock wave up through my leg's connective tissue that wasn't very pleasant. I wanted to shake it to make it feel normal again – and wouldn't have hesitated if Pat wasn't working fifteen feet away. But now just wasn't the time. Being only seconds into my first task, I couldn't hesitate or show any hint of indecision. I did grab a quick look at Pat in action before my second kick, noticing that he went with multiple lighter kicks rather than laying into the tires like he was kicking an extra point. Incorporating this technique into my next kick kept my myelin sheaths from screaming and made the task manageable. It also helped to first push the tires into position with the sole of my foot, then make the final alignment along the track's white line with a series of light kicks. As usual, I had no problem learning from someone younger.

It didn't take long to work up a significant sweat in the warm sunshine. I'd also worked myself ahead of Pat on the track's backstretch, being about 10 yards further along on the inside of the track than he was on the outside. Not that I was kicking my tires faster. The inside had the advantage of less distance and less kicking since there was only a single layer of tires to deal with. Pat had twice as many tires to reposition, with the double-decker layers being twice as heavy. He had a pretty good sweat going by the time he looked up to see a tall African American man in the pit area waving him over. The man was dressed from head-to-toe in blue, including a baseball cap that barely contained his bulging Afro. At his feet was another go-kart.

"Earl – can you work over here for now? I need to go talk to Dave. I'll be back."

"Sure...sure," I said, moving across the track to the outer layer of tires.

In starting over here...ooofff. The double tire layer was really heavy. I was almost within eavesdropping range for Pat and Dave, but then Dave reached down and pulled the new kart's starter rope, bringing its stubbornly sputtering engine to life. His hands moved up and down in front of his torso as he explained something to Pat – I presumed it was something he did to the kart. The conversation continued, and Pat nodded out in my direction, with Dave lifting his head to look out on the track. I snapped the brim of my hat downward while letting my eyes peer out of from the side of my sunglasses. Dave and Pat pulled on the starter ropes of the other three karts, getting them to a full roar before Dave moved swiftly through the gate and disappeared behind the evergreen shrubs.

I continued working on the tires as Pat walked down to me on the long straightaway that formed the backside of the track's "L." He was still squinting hard, but this time it was from his lack of hat or sunglasses.

"Come take a break. We'll have time to get the tires right during the afternoon," said Pat, in the most relaxed tone of voice I'd heard from him yet.

"Okay, thanks. Who's that?" I asked as we began walking up the track toward the pit area and the picnic bench.

"That's Dave, he's the go-kart mechanic."

"I'm not sure I've seen him before. He only does go-karts?"

"He helps Moon and Melvin when they need help. But the karts are his specialty."

"I see..."

"You've met Moon and Melvin?"

"Oh yes, they welcomed me on my first day."

"Yeah, they enjoy doing that. But they're good guys. Really, they are."

"I have no doubt. They don't miss much that goes on in the park, do they?"

"It's part of the job. They pretty much double as the park's safety patrol. Some of these rides will kill someone if they break."

We'd just about reached the pit area, where the two-by-two array of idling go-karts, at least for the moment, idled the conversation. I was about to sit down on the bench when Pat motioned me to follow him over to the ride's entrance.

"This is where people line up to get on," said Pat, pointing to a chain link door just beyond the evergreen bushes. Pat swung the door inward and pointed to a thick shoulder high red paint mark on the metal pole that served as the frame of the door.

"See this?" asked Pat.

I nodded in the affirmative.

"That's our height limit. No exceptions – they've got to be at least this tall. The sign says so," said Pat, now pointing to a wooden sign mounted on the outside of the fence explaining the 48" tall rule in bold red letters. "If anybody gives you crap about it today, let me know."

"Thanks – I will."

"We'll have some riders soon," said Pat, pointing the growing line of picnickers outside of Playland's front gate. "Then you can see how things work."

In a day that had already been full of surprises, I got one more as I sat down on the picnic bench and had it sway almost six inches to my right before one of the loose support bolts underneath "caught" and allowed me to stay upright. The bench and I were still seesawing for equilibrium as I glanced at my watch, noticing that it was after 1:00 pm. People were starting to enter the park, and...wait a minute, where was the music? My watch did run a few minutes fast, but the feed from the

Top 40 Club was usually "on the air" by now. Since Pat was still standing by the go-kart entrance, I decided to walk over, wanting to be a "team player." (Or at least appear to be a team player.) And over there I could make out the mid-tempo acoustic guitar and the slightly behind the beat baritone of Bob Seger, whose hit "Against the Wind" was filling the park's interior. Against the wind, Mr. Seger may have stood a chance. Against the mid-range rumble of Playland's go-kart quartet, he didn't have a prayer.

Besides the constant concert-decibel throb of the engines, it was strange being in the front of the park, or outside the park to be exact. Instead of being immersed in Playland, the way the Antique Cars were, this location felt isolated. Standing next to Pat, looking into the park, all I could see was the towering Playland jester, the monorail track, the Ferris Wheel, and our kiddie umbrella rides. If I turned around and looked eastward through the pit area, my view was the tire-outlined "L" of the go-kart track, the still filling parking lot, the blue municipal water tower at 66th Street, the man-made peak of the Slide N' Ride, and the back of the buildings lining Coastal Highway. The most obvious thing out here was the sun and its midday intensity. Somehow it felt harsher here than on the beach, like a set of personalized UV rays were assigned to the blacktop under my feet.

My team player instincts were telling me to go back and kick some tires, but then the first riders of the day appeared at our gate. Pat let the two teens and two adults in, sizing them up as they passed by the height mark on the pole, but saying nothing because they were all clearly tall enough to drive the karts. As the riders began squeezing themselves into the go-kart's low-riding red tubular frames, adjusting their bottoms and tugging on their shorts to cope with the sun-heated padding of the black vinyl seats, Pat motioned me with his right hand to take a position directly behind karts. Pat then moved to a position directly in front of them.

"Okay...the green pedal is the gas, and the red pedal is the brake," yelled Pat at the foursome. "These aren't bumper cars – there is no bumping or funny business out there. You'll lose your ride. Treat the karts like they were your own. Any questions?"

There weren't any, so Pat stepped out of the way and waved the cars off onto the track. He then waved me over to him.

"I'm going out into the middle of the track to watch them, you go over along the fence and watch from there," said Pat, pointing to the fence lining the park's access road. "I'll signal when there's a lap left – then you let the riders know. Just hold up your finger."

Pat held up his right index finger for good measure.

"Then when they come around again, get out on the track and wave them in. Got it?"

"Got it," I said.

Pat bounded out into the gray gravel of the infield, taking a position at the bottom of the "L" that offered him a panoramic view of the entire track. I did as Pat instructed, making my way over and through the double layer of tires along the straightaway next to the access road. About a third of the way down the fence I stopped, now having a clear view of the track, and also a view of Pat as he watched the karts. There was nothing but smiles on the riders' faces as they sped by and took the sharp clockwise turn in front of the pit area. I surmised that this was a family unit of mom, dad, sis, and brother. Brother and dad were in the front engaged in some good-natured jostling for the lead, trading off the top spot as they moved around the track. Then junior went in a little too hard into the corner on the far side of the track, clattering into the back of his father with a loud metallic "THWAK!" This happened to be the corner closest to Pat, and he was immediately up on the tires wagging his index figure at the young man, yelling "No more!" as the two karts struggled to regain the speed scrubbed off by the collision. Mom and sis had just about caught up and probably could have overtaken "the boys" if they wanted. But the accident and Pat's scolding had taken the life out of the session. They finished the remaining laps in an orderly and less than full-speed four kart convoy, almost like they were following an imaginary pace car.

Pat signaled to me with his finger, and I cautiously positioned my left foot onto the outside of the track while extending my left arm and my left index finger to make sure the approaching riders saw my one lap left signal. Pat jogged out of the infield, waving me out onto the track as he continued on to the front of the pit area.

The family rounded the final turn of the backstretch and began heading my way. I was now standing in the middle of the straightaway, instinctively pumping both hands downward to make them get on their brakes. As they slowed down – thank goodness – I switched to a waving motion to guide them into the two lanes of the pit area. They divided themselves unevenly as they pulled up to Pat, with dad, sis, and mom going into the lane nearest me, while brother ended up being the lone kart in the lane next to our picnic bench. Pat had both arms out in front of him at this point, with his hands tilted forward at a 45˚ angle, adding a "freeze" to the stop he was asking for. I wasn't exactly sure why he did this until he turned his hands over, palms facing the sky, and lifted them upward, like a preacher commanding the flock to rise up as one. He wanted everybody to remain seated until the cars were at a complete stop.

It was something I wouldn't have given any thought to before working on the Antique Cars. But it had become clear during my brief time in the park that the most dangerous scenario for a ride operator was having somebody try to get off while the ride was still moving. The go-karts offered a unique challenge because the riders controlled the ride. They weren't strapped in and waiting for Pat to come around and undo the restraint bar.

On Pat's signal, the family got up out of their cars, heading to the exit gate and the park beyond. About a dozen picnickers were gathered around our entrance, but since they had yet to congeal into a line, I walked over to where Pat stood at the front of the cars.

"Did it all make sense?" asked Pat.

"Yep, it did."

"Every group is different – you'll see. But it's important to keep them seated until all the karts are pitted and stopped. Once people park their kart, it's like an instinct, they want to stand up. If somebody plows into their back bumper while they're trying to stand..."

"Oh, man..."

"There can be serious carnage."

"I'm sure."

Pat walked over to open the entrance gate, encouraging those loitering just beyond to come in a ride.

"You can send this group off if you want."

"I'm in no hurry, Pat. I'll just keep watching and learning. Plus, I've still got tires to kick."

Chapter Seventeen

My Patch of Soul

The afternoon went by in a numbing blur of uncounted laps and walks between the pit area and my personal observation point among the tires on the final straightaway. Our steady stream of riders consisted mostly of the chicken man's employees, and to their credit, and my relief, they were respectful and mellow on the track. They were also polite and deferential about the height limit. An "I'm sorry" from Pat was always a good enough answer, and I was thoroughly impressed by how well he handled the parents who approached the height limit mark saying "I don't think he/she is tall enough, but I told them we'd see." What a no-win situation that was. It put the ride operator completely on the spot, making us the bad guys, not mom or dad.

"I'm really sorry," Pat would say, looking directly into the child's eyes with a warm smile as he delivered the disappointing news. "You're really close, next year for sure."

Pat seemed sincere…and I guess he was sincere. I took notes, mental ones, knowing that Pat's polished and polite height limit etiquette could come in handy on a lot of other rides in Playland.

We spent most of the time on our feet, moving around through the shimmering waves of midday heat emanating from the asphalt. At different times we changed up, with me taking the lead observation spot out in the infield. I spent these laps trying hard not to look like the total fraud I felt I was, praying there wasn't a serious incident. And somehow, the go-kart gods listened. Although I did get to see over and over how people wanted to stand up as soon as they parked their kart. It was an instinct that Pat kept under wraps with each cycle of riders.

Through the monotony of watching the go-karts pass by hour after hour, I began to notice things that weren't obvious to me when the shift first started. Far from shiny and new, the karts were actually on the worn side, with the red paint on their chassis tubular framework heavily chipped, and in some places, rubbed off from repeated human contact. The engines carried a noticeable film of grime, with the darkest spots being just below the muffler and around any areas where fluid could leak or spill. Randomized on the sturdy comb-width metal bumpers that encircled the cars were long scuff marks and irregular indentations from G-force collisions that I didn't care to imagine. And while none of our wheels actually wobbled, there were dimples and dark marks on the silver rims that made the miniature slick tires look less than wholly round as they rolled over the track. Not that I thought Playland didn't take care of its go-karts. The wear and tear from doing hundreds, or perhaps even a thousand laps a day, was extreme. That was obvious from the few uneventful hours I'd spent on the ride.

With the Perdue crowd starting to dissipate, we got a welcome breather just before 4:00 pm. I wasn't sure what Pat meant when he said that it was almost time for a gas check, but as we caught our breaths on the ever-undulating picnic bench, Dave opened the exit gate and began pushing a new kart toward the pit area. A squat round red gas can was tucked under its sharply angled steering column.

"For the evening rush," said Dave. "I've got one more coming."

He left the kart by the picnic bench and went out the gate to retrieve the other kart.

"Gas check. Every three hours we take a look in the tanks," said Pat. "It's a bitch when the karts run out on the track."

"Dangerous?"

"Yeah, plus you've got to push the thing all the way back to the pits."

Pat grabbed the two-gallon metal can by its center handle, and carefully lifted it out of the kart's triangle-shaped steering framework. He then carried the awkwardly sloshing container to the back of the pit area, setting it down just behind the second and last kart in the lane next to the picnic bench. Pat reached his right hand over to the kart's vibrating gas tank and quickly spun the cap off the cylindrical black shape that sat above the engine just behind the seat. Now peering down into the dark circular void left by the unscrewed cap, Pat grabbed the upper edge of the seat's black padding with his left hand and shook the kart back and forth. Upon seeing what he expected to see, Pat reached down and pulled the plug out of the sideways rubber "J" protruding from the top of the red metal can. He then picked up the can, twisted its flexible spout down into the hole in the tank, and started pouring gas into the still-rumbling engine. A quizzical look must have run across my face.

"Yep, we just leave them running. Can you open up the rest of the tanks?"

I did as Pat instructed, holding on to the other three gas caps because I couldn't find a solid place on the quivering engines to leave them. I took my cue from Pat, who was still holding onto the cap from the kart he was filling. Pat had moved on to filling the kart in the next lane when Dave pushed our sixth and latest addition through the gate, steering it around to the back of our pit area.

"That's enough?" asked Dave

"Yeah, we'll be good. It's a Wednesday," said Pat.

"And gas?"

"I think this might be enough. Things should slow down after the next fill."

"No problem. Just let me know," said Dave, who then looked over to me. "Hey man, I like your soul patch."

While I was flattered to have Dave acknowledge me, I had no idea what he was talking about. Soul patch? What the hell was a soul patch? And damn, he was giving me a compliment, but how did I respond? Pretend I knew what he meant...and risk making a total ass of myself? Or just admit right up front that I wasn't as "hip" as he thought I was? Considering the impression my response was going to create – not only for Dave but also for Pat – the moment had gone from innocent to uneasy in the blink of an eye. And it wasn't far from falling into the "monumental" category, because the next words out of my mouth might define me, at least within the park, for the rest of the summer. Was I unhip, yet honest? Or a blowhard bull-shitter who might pretend to know things that I really didn't?

The decision wasn't all that hard.

"Soul patch?" I asked, as smoothly as I could.

"Yeah, soul patch. This thing," said Dave, while smiling and stroking the group of dark whiskers growing down from his bottom lip.

"Oh, yeah. That..." I said, with a laugh and much relief. "Thanks!"

Dave smiled at Pat and wandered out the gate without saying another word. Pat had moved on to the filling up the karts in the first row, and he was smiling too.

"You're doing something right. Dave doesn't waste words on too many people," said Pat with a chuckle.

Greg slid the white paper plate with my cheeseburger across the counter. It was a dessert-sized plate which the roll of burger filled quite nicely, a perfectly centered brown island within a uniform ring of white. An orange slice of American cheese was conforming to the dark outline of the patty, gently melting into the bumpy charred edges that extended beyond the roll's perimeter. Either it was the most beautiful burger I'd ever seen, or I'd been out in the sun too long inhaling go-kart exhaust.

"Man, that looks so good. I'm absolutely starving," I said to Greg while grabbing the burger plate and the red-logoed Dairy Queen cup sitting next to it. I'd opted for a Coke with ice instead of a milkshake, owing to Coke's superior thirst-quenching capabilities.

"I've got a few minutes, I'll meet you at the table," said Greg, referring to the yellow picnic table that resided next to the Dairy Queen. I sat down facing the Top 40 Club, while Greg sat across from me facing the Sky Ride loading platform. Our conversation hadn't even started when Bruce Cockburn began wondering where the lions were.

"You smell like a gas station," Greg said without hesitation.

"Yeah, I guess that's not a surprise – I hadn't noticed. Sure you don't mean a lawn mower repair shop?"

"I guess if you wanted to get picky about it. You still smell like gasoline."

I brought the juicy burger to my mouth and took a bite. A strong whiff of gas came with it.

"Ewww...I just got it. It's on my hands. Has to be from the gas caps," I mumbled while chewing on my burger.

"Besides the smell, how is it?" asked Greg.

"Intense. There's no downtime. You're always watching the karts to make sure the drivers behave themselves."

"Have you thrown anybody off yet?"

"Who me? Nah, we haven't thrown anybody off today."

"How's the guy you're working with?"

"Pat? He's okay so far. He's definitely *the* kart guy."

"Do you like it?"

"You know, I don't know yet. There is one good thing about being out there," I said, pointing toward the park entrance with the hamburger in my left hand.

"Yeah, what's that?"

"You can't hear the Top 40 Club."

Greg offered a weak laugh as he got up to return to his post at the Dairy Queen.

Things were more demanding after the dinner break. From 6:00 pm on there was a steady line, and with two extra karts on the track, it was six in, six out, over and over and over. The evening crowd was on the aggressive side, being skewed male, with both the teen and pre-teen variety heavily represented. Nobody came close to actually getting thrown off, but Pat was issuing warnings on nearly every run. Not that he was being a dick or overbearing, he was just trying to keep order. That meant we had to be laser-focused on every group that hit the track, unlike our floodlights, whose diffuse yellow glow generated hundreds of moving shadows that put my head on a swivel while looking out for imaginary go-karts.

The rest of the park melted away as darkness fully set in, with Pat and I overseeing an eerily illuminated island of motion and noise in Playland's parking lot. If the afternoon had been a blur, the evening was a full-on whirlwind, like I'd wandered into a time-warp twilight zone where things could be in slow motion and fast forward at the same time. Nothing seemed to exist beyond the boundaries of our fence. Even when I propped my sagging legs against the fence lining the access road, there was only a lifeless lane of gravel and the deserted Ocean City Municipal garages beyond it. Yet the karts continued to go around and around within our chain link confines, weaving in and out of shadows that I still found disconcerting.

It wasn't until after 9:30 pm that our line dissipated and we had runs with less than six cars. I'd been putting Pat off all night about doing the send-off spiel, but finally I gave in, seeking out a final coaching session before letting the four lined-up riders through the gate. I was relieved to see that they all easily exceeded the height limit.

"I should say exactly what you say? I asked.

"As long they get the info, I don't care how you say it," said Pat.

"You want me to bring them in at the end, too?"

"Yep, this all yours. You're in charge."

"You're sure about this?"

"Yep, can't finish the night without you sending them out."

I walked over and opened the gate, letting the riders in, then took my place at the front of go-karts, where Pat had been standing all day. This was a completely different look. To see faces and not backs – it was like I was the conductor of some weird gas-powered quartet. They got situated quickly and were now all looking at me. In checking something I nervously forgot to do when they entered, I could see admission stamps on the left hands of all four riders. I looked up to Pat, who was in my usual position behind the karts, and he nodded in the affirmative. We were all set – there was no time like the present then.

"Umm...the green pedal is the gas, the green one on your right. And uh...the red pedal, the red one on the left is the break," I sputtered with little conviction. Pat turned his head slightly to the right and cupped his ear. Guess I needed to say it again.

"The green is the gas, the red is the brake!" I shouted, to which Pat nodded in approval. Now I had to figure out the rest of my words.

"Please keep your eyes open and your hands on the steering wheel at all times," I continued...hey, that wasn't bad. And Pat was smiling. "Please treat the karts with respect. Bumping or messing around will end your ride early – any questions?"

There weren't any, so I again looked at Pat, who once again, nodded his head up and down. I stepped aside, like a matador evading a charging bull, and waved them off. Pat and I instinctively moved to our positions, with me on the lead in the infield, while Pat took up the secondary post along the final straightaway. The four karts spaced out quickly on the track, with everyone leaving a kart length or more of room between each other, seemingly intent on nothing but driving. Things were going so well that I let them go several laps beyond the usual ten, finally nodding at Pat on lap twelve to start wrapping things up.

Before coming out to watch the karts, Pat had moved our pair of unused karts up to the front of each pit lane. So I now had these two empty and idling karts serving as a buffer between me and the incoming riders. Pat was still out on the track, forcefully urging the riders to slow down, even yelling "brake, brake, brake" as they approached him. Things were going smoothly as the first three riders came in and remained seated, obeying the hand signals that I borrowed from Pat. We were waiting on the last rider, who had just driven by Pat and was coming into the pits. He wasn't going overly fast, but he wasn't slowing down either. Why wasn't he? His foot was on the brake...but, shit, his left foot was still on the gas! I could hear Pat yelling "Let off the gas! Let off the gas!" as the rider headed into the pit lane on my left, which already had two occupied karts lined up behind the empty one in the front.

A collision was coming, and all Pat and I could do was watch.

It happened so quickly, yet somehow, I saw it with the same razor-sharp slow-motion clarity that I experienced while riding a wave. And I'll swear the initial "THWACK!!" was spelled out in white on an orange background, like a campy comic book caption from a fight scene in a *Batman* rerun. The offending rider's torso snapped forward, his arms stiffening against the steering wheel to brace his body, while his unsupported head bobbed forward like a top-hatted drinky bird looking for a water glass. Simultaneously the head of the next rider snapped backward over his seat, and as his head started recoiling forward, a second "Thwack!" filled the night air, sending the lead rider's head over the back of his seat. As his head started forward, I heard the third "thwack!" – and realized that this live-action Executive Ball Clicker had propelled the empty front kart directly at my ankles.

Without a driver to weigh it down or work the brake, the runaway kart had plenty of ligament-damaging momentum. While it wasn't a situation that I'd ever anticipated being in, I had two things in my favor: 1) the accident already had my adrenaline flowing, and; 2) I'd been a 20-foot long jumper in high school. I didn't have a thought as I leaped to my right, watching the kart drift by me onto the first straightaway of the track. After getting my bearings I instinctively chased the kart, grabbing its steering wheel to slow it down, turning the kart into the tires lining the infield. They did the job, bringing me and the kart to a quick stop.

"Are you okay?" asked a just arriving Pat, who was slightly flushed.

"Yeah, I'm okay. Thanks." I said, now feeling a little shaky as the rush of the moment subsided.

"Good, good...you did good."

"Yeah, thanks."

"I'll take care of these guys. Why don't drive the kart around to the pits as a reward for catching it?"

"Sure...sure..."

Pat turned around to jog back to the pit area, leaving me to pull the kart out of the tires and onto the track. I collapsed into the seat with a deep breath, hearing Pat yell "Is everyone okay" as I placed my hands on the steering wheel and put my foot firmly on the kart's worn green gas pedal. The kart got underway as the engine revved higher, leaving the answers to Pat's question obliterated by distance and the roar of the piston-powered five and a half horses sitting behind my seat.

Chapter Eighteen

A Bike Ride

Bicycles in hand, my aunt and I walked across Baltimore Avenue, then crossed Wicomico Street, using its south sidewalk to get to the boardwalk. Billy's Sub Shop was already open and offering its $0.49 Bike Rider's Special Breakfast, a fast-served "two eggs, toast, grits or home fries" bargain that helped Billy's compete with the slower and traditional sit-down service of the nearby Hungry Jack. Once past Billy's we continued pushing our bikes up Wicomico Street's sloping sidewalk, past the closed doors of the Cork Bar and toward the Pier Building, a looming two-story block long structure that dominated the horizon. Painted entirely white, the side facing us was shadowed gray because a still-rising sun was beating on the building's opposite side. The Pier Building had been a boardwalk landmark for decades, with this version, according to Mrs. Bunting, dating all the way back to 1926.

As a prominent piece of Ocean City architecture that I looked at least 100 times a day, its first floor, with businesses like Thrasher's French Fries and Kohr Brothers Custard, wasn't much of a mystery. But its towering second floor, lined by tall column-framed windows and housing a high-ceilinged ballroom that I'd never had the opportunity to see, was a true Ocean City mystery. A mystery only enhanced by the unfamiliar yet enticing rock music I'd hear escaping through those open windows, and the silhouettes of people in the Ballroom who flashed past the window frames like nighttime apparitions in an abandoned house. I was never exactly sure what was going on up there. But I was confident that one day when I was old enough, the mystery of the Pier Ballroom would be solved.

Once we reached the rows of empty benches that filled the area between the Alaska Stand and Dolle's, I was allowed to mount my bike and cautiously turn right onto the boardwalk to ride south toward the inlet. "Boardwalk" was a misnomer in this part of Ocean City, because what our bike tires were smoothly moving over as we pedaled south in the warm sunshine was actually concrete. And that was the way it had been for as long as I could remember.

As we picked up speed, I set my sights on the skeletal steel frame of the Coast Guard lookout tower. This was another long-standing Ocean City landmark that sat at the southern end of the boardwalk, just a stone seawall and two lanes of asphalt from the current-driven waters of the inlet. The structure soared above the inlet parking lot, its compact white observation shack seeming to have eyes thanks to a small pair of windows facing out from the side of the building. Our approaching angle brought these "eyes" to life, as they were framed by a set of sky-reaching radio antennas that gave the tower a mantis-like appearance.

The pedaling was easy as my aunt and I approached Trimper's outdoor rides, where the Tilt-A-Whirl, Loop-O-Plane, Zipper, and Ferris Wheel all sat deserted and dormant off to our right. Then just past the Tilt-A-Whirl things changed. The boardwalk became a boardwalk, taking the ride from smooth to bumpy as our bike tires chattered over narrow wooden boards that had been laid out like closely spaced railroad ties. Up through the wheels came a stuttering vibration that made our legs work harder as we negotiated the ramp-like incline up to the football-field-length southern terminus of the boardwalk.

Lining both sides of this elevated section were long benches, which in addition to providing places to sit, also served as fencing to keep boardwalk bikers and pedestrians from plunging off into the parking lot. Because of the view, this was one of the most popular spots in all of Ocean City, a place that my family would stroll to at least twice a day. Once in the mid-morning before it got too hot, and again in the evening after things had cooled off and I was busy on the rides. Even when the benches were full, it was a pleasant place. There always seemed to be a breeze thanks to water exposure from the ocean, inlet, and bay, and it was easy to distract yourself, as there was usually some variety of boat working its way out to sea. And on mornings like this one, there were boats with casting fishermen bobbing along the extended rock jetty lining the far side of the inlet. Beyond the jetty, stretching south as far as you could see, were the unoccupied beaches of Assateague. The strange thing was, you didn't mind if the beaches were occupied. In fact, you were thrilled when they were. That's because the occupiers weren't human – they were the island's wild ponies.

There was just something magical about the south end of the boardwalk. Whatever hustle and bustle you survived to get there, it all melted away after a few minutes in the breeze. "Peaceful" was how I always thought of it.

Although it was a little less peaceful right now, being busy with a steady parade of bike riders. There were three different ways to take in the view while on a morning ride. The first was to pick an empty spot next to the benches and stop completely, either putting both feet down or balancing one foot on the knee-high benches. This was definitely the best option when bike traffic was sparse. Just take your time and enjoy the view. But the downside to this type of stop was getting hemmed in by a family of bikers doing the exact same thing you were. Navigating out through pedals, handlebars, and elbows could be tricky. You usually had to wait for everyone to leave before getting your ride started again.

The second and quickest way to take in the view was to make a slow looping left-hand turn while swiveling your head to pan across the scene like a movie camera. This method got you immediately back on your ride, although it left you vulnerable to collisions with bikers who were using the same method but looping in the opposite direction. A final compromise option was to stay on your bike and walk it through the turn. This gave you a little more time to see the sights and more control when dodging the other cyclist.

But on a morning like this one, watching a twin-boomed West Ocean City trawler named "Les-B-H" clear the red channel buoy directly out from us as the sun's water-reflected glare fixed our eyes into paper-thin slits, there was no "wrong" way to experience this part of the boardwalk. What a glorious start to an Ocean City day, a day that was just revealing its promise. And that promise came into focus as my aunt and I turned our bikes and began pedaling toward the north end of the boardwalk.

On our left was the Inlet Lodge, an extended rectangular three-story hotel that now hid Trimper's entirely from our view. Running parallel to the inlet, this seafoam green building connected directly to the board-walk through the glass front doors of its Coffee Shop, over which hung a red-and-white sign reading "Sealtest Ice Cream." There was also a waist-high sandwich board sign outside its doors announcing that the Coffee Shop was "OPEN." I held my pedals in a coasting position as we rode by, wanting to get a good look inside because it was one of those Ocean City places that I'd yet to visit but hoped to in the future. The other thing I wanted to do was to stay in an Inlet Lodge room that over-looked Trimper's. How cool would it be to have the sights and sounds of the Zipper, Loop-O-Plane, and Ferris wheel coming through your window all night long?

Past the Inlet Lodge, I looked right, taking in the inlet parking lot's sea of silver twin-headed meters, all glistening in the sun waiting for the day's first feeding of quarters. Beyond the rows of empty angled parking spaces sat the still and silent rides of the pier, their order seeming to be purposely arranged by height, starting with the kiddie umbrella rides near the Pier Building, then ascending through the Tilt-A-Whirl, Scram-bler, and Loop-O-Plane before finishing up with the lofty Paratrooper. In their state of stillness, the rides seemed to be resting up from all the twisting and turning they had done the night before.

I picked up momentum heading down the short wooden slope to-ward the concrete part of the boardwalk, where my aunt and I pedaled past Souvenir City, an odd top-heavy green building on our right that looked like an elevated double-wide trailer. Another boardwalk land-mark was then immediately on our left, that being the demonic pterodactyl-sized black bat hanging off the façade of Trimper's Haunted House. Next up were the closed white doors of Trimper's carousel building, then South Division Street, where I turned my head to the left for a look down the block at the now tranquil Wild Mouse. Dayton's occupied the next corner, and even though it was closed, the scent of fried chicken still filled the air as we went by and pulled even with the closed doors of the Playland, an arcade that I'd be spending time and quarters in after we finished our bike ride.

We pedaled on, moving past a slower mother-daughter bike duo at Worcester Street, a street that I didn't need to look down because that was where the creepy mechanical Fun House lady swayed and cackled all day long. (She was quiet now. This was one Ocean City place that I didn't want to ever go into.) Sportland, my second favorite arcade, quickly went by, then at the unlit Dumser's sign, my aunt and I slowed down, getting ready for the human traffic that always filled the claustrophobic corridor next to the Pier Building. Even with Dolle's and Thrasher's closed the area was thick with people. When biking through this section you always had to be ready to stop. You never knew when a four-person human wall with a baby stroller would be coming your way.

I never understood why this area was so busy so early. What was open, at least in the Pier Building, was the Kohr Brothers stand, its garish light bulb outlined sign already lit and visible. I'd never acquired a taste for their mouth-coating custard, preferring hand-scooped Dumser's ice cream instead (vanilla milkshakes were my favorite). And who really wanted custard at 8:15 am in the morning? Also open in the Pier Building just beyond the gated pier entrance was a shop that seemed overrun with hanging and headless half-torso mannequins wearing every T-shirt variation of "I'm With Stupid" that had ever been created. And sitting just inside each of their front door openings was a tall black-and-white poster of a long-haired hippy guy sitting on a toilet – what the heck did "Phi Zappa Krappa" mean? Were people really looking for this kind of stuff right after breakfast? Now across from the Pier Building, there were no doubts as to why the "Since 1933" sign on top of Alaska's was already turning. The browning bacon aroma coming off their open-air grill told you all you needed to know.

We cleared the congestion unscathed, emerging back into the sunshine and onto a part of the boardwalk where things felt more relaxed. It was easier to follow boardwalk bike riding etiquette on these blocks – northbound traffic stayed to the right, while southbound traffic stayed left. And from here on, there would only be buildings lining the west side of the boardwalk. Buildings like the one that housed the brick storefronts on our left in front of the Atlantic Hotel. The shops were nice looking with fancy glass doors and air conditioning, yet the actual businesses were a strange mix of high and low ambitions – glass blowers and original oil paintings versus bootleg 8-tracks and a Candy Kitchen.

The next block also began with recently constructed brick storefronts, then as we moved closer to the familiar Dorchester Street area, turned over to what looked like two brick-fronted garages. The first "garage" housed Ponzetti's Pizza, while the corner garage, the one with the long unfurled green awning, housed the Boardwalk Department Store. This was a special place for me, as already in my young life I'd spent hours in there picking out just the right T-shirt iron-on designs from the thousands of iron-on choices lining their walls. And not only did I get to pick out the design, but I also got to pick out the T-shirt, too. The freedom involved in this two-step process...I was pretty much allowed to wander the store on my own and make my own choices about what I wanted to buy and wear. Essentially, be a mini adult. And I treasured every second of it.

Across Dorchester Street we pedaled past The Friendly Gift Shop (favored by my aunt for jewelry and watch browsing), the just opening Taylor Pork Roll stand, the closed Tastee Freeze, and one of my all-time Ocean City favorites – Fischer's Popcorn. This place was home of the best caramel popcorn I'd ever eaten. It was always still warm and slightly gooey when they handed you the box, and so delicious that it made Cracker Jack seem like sugarcoated cardboard.

We were even with the Irish House now, a place whose evening organ sing-a-longs drifted endearingly through its screened front openings and out onto the boardwalk. Then on to the multiple green awnings of the Maryland Inn, past the old Coast Guard Station, the Sporting Center arcade, and Heppe's Candy, the only store on the boardwalk my family would buy candy from. Just past Heppe's was another all-time Ocean City favorite, the Edwards 5 and 10. Edwards was special because my family was greeted by name whenever we stepped inside. It was also special because it was the only place I'd ever found packs of baseball cards from Topps' elusive 7th Series.

The Boardwalk Gift Shop was on the corner, and here I looked down North Division Street to check out the Showell Theatre marquis. I was also making sure the neon "DONUT" sign hanging over the entrance to Ernie's Donuts was lit and glowing red, signaling that the shop was open and doling out its round fried dough perfections. Few things in Ocean City were as thrilling as having a smiling and flour-covered Ernie reach into the display case, then gently hand across the counter his gift of a still warm melt-in-your-mouth glazed donut hole. Hopefully, there was a chance I'd get one before we hit Playland. Bringing my eyes back to the boardwalk I checked the time on the pole-mounted Esskay Meats clock, chuckling at the apron-clad cartoon butcher on the clock face.

Things changed at this point. The boardwalk turned into a boardwalk and narrowed from the wide concrete we'd been on since the inlet. And that wasn't the only change, as from here on things were much less familiar because my family hardly wandered, at least on foot anyway, much beyond the previous "Showell block." There wasn't much point. Everything we needed, including 24-hour bait, was within walking distance of Mrs. Bunting's apartments. That said, I was familiar with the next upcoming landmark, the sizable gray-shingled bell on top of the Plimhimmon Hotel. Since the hotel itself was bright yellow and four-stories tall, this thing was visible from all up and down the beach. And even without the bell, the Plimhimmon was distinctive, thanks to its block-long covered porch that fronted the boardwalk, and the green awnings that gave shade to every single window on the ocean facing side of the building.

As we rode on past the Plimhimmon things changed even more. Between the inlet and the Showell block the businesses, shops, and arcades were lined up side-by-side along every available inch of the boardwalk. And their counters, front doors, and display windows sat directly on the boardwalk – there just wasn't any empty and open space along these downtown Ocean City blocks. But once you started into the numbered streets, there were older hotels and apartment houses, with some dating all the way back to the 1920s. These older buildings were constructed mostly out of wood and came in all different shapes and sizes, with the apartment houses being slightly oversized two- and three-story houses, while the hotels were taller, boxy, rectangular buildings that either fronted or ran perpendicular to the boardwalk. When side by side, these varying-shaped structures gave the boardwalk a less than uniform and even jarring appearance, especially since most them were set back from the boardwalk, connecting to it with extended porches or fence-lined walkways. There were also fewer shops up here, especially after you passed Albright's Department Store and Lambros Beachwear. Just shaded verandas with rocking chairs at places like The Baltimorean, The Purnell, The Breakers, the Hampton House, and the Hotel Majestic.

The next familiar section of the boardwalk was the 9th Street area. We'd never spent much time up here, but somehow I still recognized the enormous striped storefront façades of the Boardwalk Galleries and the Hess Department store. There was also an "up the beach" branch of the Alaska Stand here, looking like a mini-version of the downtown location. And a few blocks above 9th Street the boardwalk landscape changed again, taking us out of Ocean City's past and into its future. Sitting on the boardwalk at 15th Street was the oceanfront Santa Maria, a block-long three-story concrete building that marked the beginning of "Motel Row." This was a stretch of boardwalk blocks that, not long ago, had been vacant sandy lots. But now they were filling in with multi-story oceanfront motels featuring modern masonry construction and names like the Sea Scape, Sandyhill, Stowaway, Surf and Sands, and Ocean Mecca. The last motel in this section was the Diplomat, which I knew because it was located a block before the boardwalk ended. When I saw the blue water of its oceanfront front pool, I knew it was just about time to turn our bikes around.

I always had a great sense of accomplishment during our ride south back to the inlet. And a great sense of anticipation, too. That's because I knew that even though our bike ride would soon be over, my day in Ocean City was just beginning.

Chapter Nineteen

Seamless Sea and Sky

A lthough the sun wasn't out I was still using the outstretched fingers of my right hand as a "brim" to get a better look at the waves rolling toward me. They were definitely in the fun category, both in size and shape, but the sketchy visibility made sizing them up a challenge. It was absolutely worthless for my brain to decide "yeah, that's a good one" when the nose of my board was already floating up the face of the wave in the opposite direction. Yet it was a challenge that I was more than happy to have. That's because it was one of my favorite kinds of summer beach days – overcast and rainy with good waves.

Not that I woke up every day hoping for some type of mid-Atlantic monsoon season. But because of the rain, the beach was something that it hardly ever was at 11:00 am on any June, July, or August day – empty. Well, almost empty, as there were a few hardy souls huddled under beach towels, trying to stay warm after a short dip in the ocean. They were better off in the water today than out, as the ocean temperature was quite comfortable. But any exposed body parts, like my arms and torso, needed coverage and insulation. The long-sleeved wetsuit jacket I was wearing did just that, repelling the rain while trapping my body heat within its neoprene layer.

Keeping an eye on us all were the rain gear-clad lifeguards, who were duty-bound to man their elevated wooden stands just in case the sun made a miraculous appearance between now and 5:30 pm. Rainy-day-empty-beach duties for a lifeguard were significantly less taxing than sunny-day-packed-with-tourist duties, although each wet and chilly hour up on the stand probably felt like a year. One of the duties they were "flexible" on was corralling us surfers into the single-block confines of the designated surfing beaches. On a day like today it was up to the guard's discretion. As long as no swimmers were around, and you showed respect by checking with the guard first – a lesson passed on by a former lifeguard I worked with at Phillips – you could pretty much surf anywhere you wanted. So after talking with the guard on the stand at 120th Street, I'd paddled out there rather than going down to the surfing beach at 118th, where there were already a half a dozen guys in the water.

Greg didn't yet see the point in days like this, so I was alone this morning. But that was okay, as it offered some time to reflect on what a birthday weekend it had been. There was the milestone of turning twenty – I was surely over the hill now – but I'd also gotten three days with my girlfriend Robin, spent time with my family and Mrs. Bunting, had a delicious birthday dinner at The Hobbit, and even had a fantastic surf session on Friday morning with Robin on the beach behind a telephoto lens firing away. There would be some great shots in that roll. The sun was out, the light was right, I was surfing well...the weight of my biology debacle didn't feel quite so heavy after that session. It was by far the best day I'd had since the grades arrived. I was so glad Robin braved the bus from Clemente's Cafeteria to come down on Thursday night. I picked her up after work, driving downtown to Ocean City's surprisingly busy bus terminal on 2nd Street to get her. That gave us all of Friday together, at least until my shift at Playland, and the entirety of Saturday, since that was my day off. I played brave when my parents came by on Sunday to drive her back to Wilmington, even though I completely felt sick as I let go of her hand when she got in the car. I was grateful that my parents would take her home and not bat an eye – at least that I could see – about her spending the weekend in the condo. Greg was really good about it all too. But our time was over much, much too soon. At least I knew that the slightly hollow feeling inside of me right now was not from grades. It was from missing Robin.

One of the things that made rainy day surfing good was that the wind was usually calm or offshore. This left the ocean with a velvety texture that was enticing to paddle into. And once you got your board on edge there was a patiently peeling wall that offered time to think and try out new maneuvers. For whatever reason, I found that rainy surfing days were a perfect canvas for expanding my surfing skills.

But they were far from perfect surf days. A calm and glassy ocean was also a perfect canvas for the millions of expanding bulls-eye circles created by the rain falling out of the sky. And it was often disorienting to be surrounded by acres of tiny splashes, especially when the splashes and raindrops merged together in the distance, blending the ocean's bubbling gray surface into the sky's ghostly shifting clouds to create a horizon without any discernable line. This seamless backdrop of sea and sky, when combined with the morning's leaden and shadowless light, obliterated the ocean's details. Only the biggest of waves approached me with any recognizable features or form – most waves just seemed to pop up out of nowhere. A "nowhere" effect was all the more pronounced by the rain beating off my forehead and running into my eyes, leaving me with little time to figure out if I was going over the wave, under the wave, taking the wave...or just taking it on the head.

And without fail, a flat light day could make you feel completely out at sea. It didn't matter if I was sitting on my board 15 yards or 40 yards offshore, peering through the rain across a mostly featureless ocean imparted a feeling of great distance. (The Caine house was surely setting sail today!) A final eerie scrap of the conditions was that despite the overwhelming grayness, there was a distinct layer of green just below the ocean's surface. It was visible around my knees as the rest of my legs went invisible while dangling into the marine murkiness below, a spooky sensation that had me wondering about what else might be keeping my toes company in the sand-infused pea soup under my board.

But then a juicy set of waves would show up, literally in my face, and all I would think about was how to catch one of those buggers and ride it for all it was worth. Yeah, there were a lot of challenges, but I really enjoyed surfing in these conditions. It might have been an illusion, but rides seemed longer. And I got an extra kick out of braving the weather, not that there was really that much to brave, at least in my thinking. I could never understand why there weren't more guys in the water on days like this. What's a little rain when you're surfing...and already wet from head to toe? And depending on how "floaty" your board was, you might be in the lineup waiting for waves while submerged from the waist down. If this were a sunny day with the same waves and, hypothetically, surfers were allowed to surf anywhere and all over in Ocean City – at 11:00 am no less – I'd have a lot more neighbors. We might not necessarily be elbow to elbow, but there would be surfers up and down the beach as far as the eye could see. Right now, the nearest surfers were about 25 yards off to my right. They'd just paddled out in the 119th Street block. I still had the entire 120th block all to myself.

I'd been in the water for just about two hours now and was looking for a final "perfect" wave to end my session. Fatigue had set in and, despite my wetsuit jacket, which had done its job thoroughly, a chill was setting in too. Actually, that was pretty much how most June sessions ended unless you stuffed yourself into a full suit, of which mine was the hooded variety. It was a great suit, a top-of-the-line O'Neill "O'riginal," but as something designed to keep you warm in December, it was total overkill for late June. Hot, heavy and constricting, it was like being encased in an oversized garden hose. It also carried a significant "dork factor," as no local would be caught dead surfing in a full suit in June. It just wasn't done – the "I am totally a tourist" alarm bells would sound from Assateague to Indian River. Although sometimes I did wonder about the wisdom of this unspoken rule as I sat in the lineup watching trunks-only locals shiver uncontrollably on brisk June days when they really should've known better. Not that they needed a full suit, but a jacket or a spring suit (long arms/short legs) certainly would have been a good idea. And made their time in the water much more enjoyable.

In checking out the sparse surfing congregation down at 118th street I could see that everybody was covered by some appropriate level of wetsuit, with spring suits being the preferred model. Beyond the surfers was one of the distinctive features of surfing in this part of town – an almost panoramic view of Ocean City's high-rise Condo Row. As these multiple structures climbed continually skyward through the early 1970s, turning the lonely sand dunes of North Ocean City into a mid-Atlantic Miami Beach, hopeful town officials and realtors nicknamed this stretch of beach the "Gold Coast." So far, it had turned out to be a decent name for a mall, but the glamor associated with, say, southeastern Florida's Gold Coast had yet to appear. Apparently conjuring up a playground for the rich and famous took more than just a name and six-figure penthouses. As Mrs. Bunting memorably said after her family treated her to dinner at The Wharf, a new and nautically themed "fancy" place on 128th Street where she was less than impressed with the food, the expense, and the full-size sailboat "anchored" in the parking lot: "It was nice and all, but you can't eat atmosphere."

Condo Row's northern end started right here at 118th Street, where the enormous rectangular block long Carousel condo building rose up through the mist like something out of a super deluxe Girder and Panel Building set (a Kenner toy that I loved playing with even though the finished structures always struck me as faceless and cold). I'd never bothered to count the floors, but it dwarfed the Caine house and was at least four times as tall as the original four-story Carousel Hotel, which still occupied the beachfront at 118th Street. The most distinguishing features of the Carousel's ocean-facing side were the dozens of uniform and precisely aligned balconies, whose white waist-high steel railings looked like teeth on a monster with a hundred mouths.

Next up was the smaller Fountainhead condo, another parallel to the beach concrete rectangle that was almost hidden from my view because it sat farther back from the waterline than the Carousel. Beyond the Fountainhead was the dramatic "V"-shaped Sea Watch condo, a building that actually had some variety in its construction, including unique balconies that rose upward like steps as the building came to a point on the beachfront. It was as tall as the Carousel and completely hid the High Point North building, but not the curving toward the ocean "C"-shape of High Point South.

High Point South would always be etched into my memory as the very first Ocean City condo building. It seemed to spring out of nowhere in 1970, an exotic multi-floored high-rise structure the likes of which Ocean City had never seen. I was in the back seat of my parent's brown VW Bug when it first came into view off in the distance, sitting all alone on the beach in the orange-tinged early evening light, looking for all the world like some displaced NASA rocket gantry. All I could do was stare as the car chugged ever closer, then look upward in awe as we passed by it on Coastal Highway. It was taller than anything in Ocean City, including the Ferris wheels, the roller coasters, and even the Coast Guard tower at the inlet. And it was taller than most of the buildings I'd seen in and around Philadelphia, too. I was only half grasping my parent's explanation of the differences between condominiums and apartments, but my overriding thought was, why would anyone want to stay there? So far up the beach, and really in the middle of nowhere. The boardwalk and the rides were miles away – it wasn't even that close to Playland at 65th Street. You'd have to get in the car and drive to ride bikes, play Skee-ball, eat French fries, or even go fishing. I just couldn't imagine people spending money to stay in such an out of the way location.

But little did I realize that the High Point was just the beginning. That it was setting the course for how Ocean City would evolve over the next decade. That eventually there would be more than a dozen high-rise buildings in a man-made concrete condo canyon that now stretched from 118th Street all the way down to 94th Street. And that by 1980 the High Point, the ground zero of Ocean City's condo boom, would be almost invisible and overshadowed by more ambitious condo neighbors.

Thanks to the rain all the condos lining the beach beyond the High Point blended into a long line of water-stained concrete, a series of Easter Island caliber monoliths, at least in terms of the empty and ominous thousand-yard stare that the unnaturally eyeless South Pacific statues contributed to the world. The Gold Coast always looked its best under midday summer light, when the twelve o'clock position of the sun all but bleached away the overwhelming shadows that this extended row of high rises cast onto Ocean City sand. In those few afternoon hours when the sun was high overhead, the canyon quality of the area evaporated, making some of buildings interesting, and almost cheerful. The most eye-catching was The Pyramid at 95th Street, because not only did it look like a pyramid, it was painted bright white and stood out from blocks away. From the surfing beach on 96th Street you could look directly into the building's jagged triangular front and see the honeycomb-like structure that the architects created.

Squinting hard through the dim light I could see a sliver of the Pyramid sloping out onto the sand. But that was only because I knew where to look, and how to find a bright white section of concrete that was a mere 24 blocks away. The amount of concrete along the shoreline between me and the Pyramid was beyond my comprehension...how wrong I'd been about people not wanting to stay in this end of town. I was here too, essentially part of the condo crowd, content with my walk to the beach, yet unfazed by having to use my car for everything else – to get to work, to go to the market, to pick up some surf wax. The Ocean City realtors, developers, and city fathers had certainly done their jobs selling the Gold Coast dream. And many of the dream buyers were currently up to their hubcaps in Coastal Highway runoff, negotiating bumper-to-bumper traffic in front of the Gold Coast Mall.

Chapter Twenty

Chase Kart

Pat and I got along well during our first week together on the go-karts. I'd come to understand that the go-karts were one of the most challenging things in the park to run, not that I was ready to trade places with the guys at the Ghost Ship, who occasionally had to chase a "runner" through a multi-story maze of booby-trapped black light darkness. It became a very dangerous game when Ghost Ship riders abandoned their miniature coffin-on-wheels for a more intimate tour of the dozens of haunted underwater scenes inside the building, as these dioramas were littered with moving cables and spinning parts that could inflict serious damage on a human body. There was also a high voltage electrical system that, after 15 years of use, was on the fragile side. We might not have had control of the riders on the karts, but at least we could see where they were and what they were doing at all times. And it turned out we had our own interesting way of dealing with people who didn't want to follow the rules.

The "Chase Kart" showed up on a Friday, which was no accident, as Friday was going to be the start of our busy season. Nobody told me that was the reason, but I knew from the previous summer that Ocean City crowds picked up dramatically after the schools let out and the calendar officially turned over to summer. That happened on the previous Saturday, June 21st, a date that I had an intimate relationship with because it was my birthday. This year, in addition to being my birthday, it marked the first opportunity for families with school-age children to take their annual weeklong Ocean City vacations. The serious season was here – there would be 11:00 pm park closings from now on.

The new addition was sitting by itself over against the fence lining the access road, pointing forward like it was ready for action. It looked pretty similar to our regular karts, at least on first glance, but it didn't take long to realize that it was something "other" from the still-silent karts lined up in the pit area. As I walked over for a closer look I could see that it was much more worn than the regular karts, with its pock-marked tubular frame being a 50/50 mix of red paint and exposed metal.

Along the outer seams of its seat were a series of ratty duct tape patches, which joined up with several long vertical duct tape strips down the center of the seat to give it a strange zebra-like appearance. There was something else different about it that I couldn't initially put my finger on, then after a quick look at the karts in pit row, I knew what it was – there was no protective bumper. It had thick tubular constructions on its front and rear ends to serve as bumpers, but there was nothing encircling the entire kart, like there was on our regular karts. That meant its tires were fully exposed. They could take a direct hit in an accident, or even cause an accident if they rubbed up against the exposed tires of another kart. Clearly this was a leftover from a previous generation of Playland go-karts.

Pat had been out working on the tires, but he'd made his way back to the front of the pit area by the time my examination of the kart was over.

"What is it," I yelled over to Pat, "a spare for tonight?"

"Nope," answered Pat with a grin that made me curious. Curious as to what he knew that I didn't.

"Is it for sale?" I continued to probe.

"Un-uh. It's something to have a little fun with."

This clue made no sense at all. Fun? On the go-karts? Pat had to be kidding.

"You're kidding, right?"

"Nope," said Pat again, smiling now from almost from ear-to-ear.

"Ok, I give – what is it?

"Our Chase Kart."

"Say what?"

"It's our Chase Kart. It's so we can go out and take care of the people who don't listen."

"You *are* kidding?"

"No, not at all."

"We're allowed to chase people down?"

"Well, yeah – this is a Playland issued kart."

"It doesn't look like it could catch anybody. Or even me if I was out running around the track."

"Looks aren't everything. And that's the beauty of it. There's nothing else like it in the park."

"Yeah, go on..."

"It has no governor. Dave disabled it."

I was familiar with what a governor did, even if I didn't know exactly what a governor mechanism was. The governor limited the revolutions on an engine, keeping your lawn mower under control and limiting the top speed that go-karts and minibikes could achieve. On our Playland go-karts you could feel the governor kick in by the time you reached the first turn. Even if you buried the gas pedal with a stiff leg and a firm heel, the kart would reach its preset top speed and go no faster. This was the governor in action, and it was set the same on all of Playland's go-karts. Some karts were a little faster than others, but they were all pretty much of equal speed. Something that allowed Pat and I to keep the ride safe and relatively under control.

"So that means?"

"It will go as fast as you can drive it. Makes the other karts look like they're standing still," answered Pat.

"What's its top speed?"

"Who knows. You can't even get it up to top speed on our track. But you'll never feel the engine back off like the other karts. When you hit the gas the speed just keeps building and building."

"Somebody thinks we'll need it tonight?"

"The park's just going to get busier from here on. The 4th of July is only a week away. We'll have the Chase Kart for backup from now on."

I looked back down at the kart, believing it was the fastest thing in the park, but not believing at the same time. It looked so worn out. The engine was the dirtiest one I'd seen so far, except for places where the grime had been rubbed away by a human hand making a repair. And I was half afraid that I'd get permanently stuck to the duct tape if I sat down. Pat took notice of my extended scrutiny of the kart.

"I'll show you later. Trust me, it'll be fun."

As expected, it was a hectic night. The busiest I'd seen at Playland, easily judged from the number of cars in the parking lot and the line waiting to get on our ride. We'd started with seven karts, and were now up to eight, which meant Pat and I had to be extra vigilant watching the traffic on each run. The karts could get really stretched out, with the faster and more experienced drivers lapping slower drivers. And there were kids who were obviously getting their first chance at driving the karts – we'd pulled several out of the tires already. They hadn't done anything wrong or had anything wrong done to them, they just lost control for a split second and panicked, driving straight into the tires. They just didn't have the experience to know what to do when things went wrong out on the track.

A feeling I could totally relate to. All it took was a quick glance down at the ping-pong ball-sized scar on the inside of my left knee, a maroon bordered area of light-colored flesh that still refused to tan a full eight years after I wiped out on Jolly Roger's sandy minibike track, discovering that my shorts offered no protection from the superheated exhaust pipe cover of a Suzuki Trailhopper. Not only was I covered in sand from the fall, I'd stalled the bike – one of the Jolly Roger guys had to come restart it. As a second-degree blister rose from my throbbing knee like a surface-breaking ocean volcano, the pain of embarrassment completely overwhelmed the very real distress signals my scorched skin was sending to my brain (be assured the pain was very real all night). I owned a minibike, but nothing like the orange-colored demon that the Suzuki seemed to be. Once I twisted the throttle and the Ocean City night air went whistling through my ears, I knew I was in over my head – and in trouble. All these years later, and after owning a Yamaha MX125, I still wondered who thought that sending inexperienced preteens out onto the rutted sand dunes in the back of Jolly Roger with no helmets and a three-speed gearbox was a good idea. I never stood a chance. And thinking about the guys who ran that ride, they probably knew the Ocean City ambulance crews quite well by the end of that summer.

The plus side of our busy night was that we reached 9:00 pm quickly, and without throwing anybody off the ride. There had been some niggling incidents and a few minor collisions, but nothing to get really worked up over. Nobody had yet stuck out as a "problem." I'd just sent a group out and was moving to the center of the infield to watch the eight riders make their way around the track. There was a guy in fourth place who seemed a bit impatient. Or maybe he stuck out because he was wearing sunglasses at night on our dimly-lit track, or maybe it was the cheesy "Disco Sucks" tank top, or maybe it was his forward-leaning over the steering wheel posture, whatever it was, my eye was drawn to him immediately. So whether he deserved it or not, he was getting extra scrutiny. And not just from me. As my eyes followed the karts around the track to where Pat stood along the final straightaway, he went wide-eyed and began pointing with his index finger as Mr. Disco went by.

The guy wasn't an asshole, at least a full-on one. He was just annoying. Trying to push the back bumpers of the riders in front of him rather than making his intent obvious and ramming them. It was kind of clever – he'd moved up to second place by the middle of his second lap, thanks to driver number two and number three not matching his aggressiveness. Instead of pinning him against the tires when he tried to weasel by in the corners they left enough room for him to go through. The lead driver was in his sights when Pat caught my eye. "I'm going out!" he yelled as he moved through the tires toward the pit area.

Pat got to the Chase Kart quickly and yanked the starter rope upward with a well-practiced pull. Being enveloped in the din of eight moving karts, I couldn't hear the Chase Kart come to life, but I did see the large plume of gray exhaust that came out of its engine, forcing Pat to cover his mouth and wave the choking smoke away with his other hand. Pat was still coughing as he jumped into the seat and hit the gas, zipping out of the pit area like a just green-lighted drag racer, moving past the other karts as promised – like they were standing still. And he didn't even need to take the shortest line around the track, this kart could simply stay wide and pass by everything and everybody. It took just over a lap for Pat to lock in on the back bumper of Mr. Disco, who was still trying to harass the lead driver into second place. I had no clue as to what Pat was going to do – go side-by-side and give a warning? Or just give him a good stiff whack with the Chase Kart?

Mr. Disco headed toward the hairpin right in front of the pits completely unaware that Pat was less than a foot from his bumper. They stayed aligned this way through the next straightaway and into the left turn that started the perpendicular bottom section of our "L." Pat was still inches away as both karts entered the sharp 180° right that turned onto the track's bottom straightaway, yet as Mr. Disco exited the turn, exposing the right corner of his back bumper to Pat, Pat hit the gas and smoothly bulls-eyed that corner. The leverage in the impact was just about perfect, and in the blink of an eye Mr. Disco was headfirst in the tires lining the infield, being spun so expertly that he was almost facing the wrong direction. Pat was long gone and in the next turn before Mr. Disco knew what hit him. I jogged down through the infield to do my job and get the disabled Mr. Disco out of the tires.

"What happened?" he asked, looking up at me through his faux-Ray Bans.

"Careless driver," I answered, desperately trying to keep a straight face as I reached down to grab the steering wheel and guide his kart back out onto the track. "I'll make sure he doesn't get on the ride again."

"Yeah – yeah, you need to do that."

"I will," I said, averting his glance, partly to maintain the pretense of "straightness" but also to check the still moving traffic before sending him on his way. "All clear. Be careful now."

Before I started kicking the worst of the tires displaced by Mr. Disco's spin, I looked back to the pit area and was surprised to see Pat walking through it. He was out of Chase Kart, having already parked the damn thing and shut it off. It was almost like what just happened never happened. The only telltale sign was Pat's enormous grin.

What a sly son of a bitch. Yeah, I liked him a lot.

Chapter Twenty-One

The 5th of July

W as that really a parking space in front of the uptown Layton's at just after 9:00 am on Saturday of the July 4th weekend? It was indeed. So after a quick glance in the rear-view mirror I moved to the far-right lane of northbound Coastal Highway and pushed in the clutch, gliding up against the curb to align my Sunbird's front bumper with the red-and-white "No Parking Here To Corner" sign that stuck up out of the sidewalk like a mutant metallic sunflower just short of 93rd Street. I was on my way back home after an abbreviated surf session at 52nd Street, a location I'd picked because I knew it would work with the morning's incoming tide. While that part of my decision making was sound, what I'd neglected to consider in my slightly stuporous pre-coffee state were the "side effects" of the three-day holiday weekend. This miscalculation left me scrambling for an early morning parking spot on one of the last empty and unbuilt blocks in all of Ocean City.

In addition to the tight parking the holiday announced itself in the surf too, as over a dozen guys were flailing around in the sunny yet totally sideshore conditions. That was way more than there should have been, but at least they had an excuse for enduring the substandard surf, as most of them would be landlocked in Baltimore or D.C. come Monday morning. My reason for driving 70 blocks to wallow with the weekend "riff-raff" was more primal – I *needed* to get in the water. Greg and I were scheduled for three ten-hour shifts over the weekend. Last night made it one down. With two still to go I woke up this morning desperate for a diversion.

Although when my feet splashed through the shallows and I discovered how significantly things had cooled off from earlier in the week – the opaque green water near shore had that unmistakable low-60s "skin-grabbing" quality to it – I'd had some second thoughts. This perception of coolness was enhanced by the morning's strong south wind, giving me a deep and immediate chill that I knew my long-sleeve wetsuit top was two neoprene legs and a neoprene torso away from neutralizing.

Which was probably just as well, as I out-paddled a couple of the weekend guys for the few decent set waves I saw before getting back to the beach just as my hands and bottom jaw started trembling from the cold. Mild hypothermia wasn't exactly what I was looking for, but I did feel a little of the usual surfing buzz as the warmth of my sweatshirt calmed my hands enough to let me strap the board back on the car. That empty space in front of Layton's was a sign – an extra reward for my morning efforts.

Layton's was bustling inside. All the tables and counter seats were full, with a healthy group of people huddled around the hostess stand waiting to be seated. At the register I ordered two large coffees, and also asked the young woman helping me to open the upright glass doors of the bright display case behind her and put two glazed and two chocolate-iced donuts into a bag.

"Do you want a carrier?" she asked, her slim, smooth face and pixyish dark hair looking out of place in Layton's dowdy uniform, which consisted of a brown short-sleeve polyester "waitress" dress and a frilly white waist apron.

"That would be great, thanks."

"Cream and sugar is on the counter – help yourself."

"Got it, thanks."

After telling her to keep the change I fixed my coffee with three sugars and a mini-moo of creamer, leaving Greg's cup untouched. Then I walked into Layton's adjoining beach store, where they sold beach chairs, sunscreen, beer, ice and more, grabbing a *Philadelphia Inquirer* off the floor after carefully situating my drink carrier on the narrow counter beside the register.

A more casually dressed young woman was working here, dressed in shorts and a yellow golf shirt with "Layton's Beach 'n Tennis" over a left side breast pocket. I handed over the paper and she studied the masthead for a moment.

"You do know that out of town papers are 40 cents?" she said, glancing up with a slightly wide-eyed look that seemed to be saying "don't blame me." With the list price on the paper being just 15 cents, I'm pretty sure she thought I'd put the paper back on the floor.

"Yep. Here you go," I said while handing her two quarters. "Keep the change."

"Oh, thank you! Have a good day...and don't forget your coffee!"

I appreciated the reminder, but there was no way I was going to forget the coffee. Or the donuts. There wasn't a better way to kill a Saturday morning. Especially a holiday weekend Saturday where the best thing Greg and I could do was stay inside and out of the way of the 200,000 tourists visiting Ocean City (of course we'd have our chance to "mingle" at Playland in just a few hours).

Traffic was bumper-to-bumper yet rolling through Condo Row, before coming to a standstill just south of the Gold Coast Mall, leaving my passenger window filled with the dome-covered glass-walled mushroom that was the indoor pool of The Irene condo. The stop-and-go pattern continued through the multiple traffic lights in front of the mall, with things finally opening up at the Greene Turtle.

Once past the Carousel's concrete parking garage at 119th Street there wasn't much lining the east side of Coastal Highway, just a two-story bungalow with a sandy pull off at 121st Street that served as my cue to slow down and put on my signal to make the turn at our building. Pulling up into the Mirabella lot I could see that my original shaded parking spot was still open, so I turned left into the angled space toward a pair of white storage closet doors labeled 1A and 1B. An involuntary and audible "alright" came out of me as I got out of the car and saw that our front curtains were open. This meant Greg was up – I could take the carrier with the coffee directly in through the front door instead of having to negotiate myself and two cups of steaming liquid over the back-porch railing.

My keys jangled as I pulled them out of my sweatshirt pocket giving Greg the chance to say "it's open" before I got anywhere near the doorknob. He was at the stove tending the kettle as I opened the front door with a "whoomph," a big smile coming over his face as he watched me place our Layton's bounty on the table.

"Talk about timing...spoiled like royalty, starting the morning off with real coffee!" said Greg. "Have to say, I really wasn't diggin' that jar of Taster's Choice."

"It was on sale. We'll have to pick up some Maxwell House next time at the market," I said, removing the cups from their slots and setting them on the table. Layton's plastic lids were vaguely transparent, so I pulled back the narrow drinking tab on the cup nearest me, pretty sure that I saw light brown liquid splattered up on its underside.

"This one's yours," I said, pushing the other cup over to Greg.

"Thanks!"

I sat down in the dinette chair nearest the door, pulling out the sports section while sliding the rest of the *Inquirer* to the middle of the table – an "offering" to Greg for grabbing the sports first. He'd removed the lid from his cup and seemed mesmerized by the steam rising off the coffee's black surface. Then the spell broke, and he sifted through the remaining parts of the newspaper, finally pulling out the section with the comics.

"The Phils lost yesterday, right?" he said, folding the paper back along the seam to have both pages of the comics exposed and facing outward.

"Yeah, 1-0 to the Cardinals. George Hendrick hit a home run in the bottom of the 10th," I said, skimming the *Inquirer's* recap of the game. In glancing at the rest of the page, Evonne Goolagong had beaten Chris Evert in the Wimbledon women's final, and under the headline "Brats," John McEnroe had defeated Jimmy Connors in the men's semi-final. Upon reading this story's opening sentence I flipped to an inside page to check out the television listings in the "Sports Calendar."

"Hey, turn on the TV – it's Breakfast at Wimbledon. Borg vs. McEnroe!" I blurted out in a more demanding tone than I meant. Fortunately, Greg was tuned into my excitement.

"Yeah, that works. It'll be nice to see some real sports in the morning, not those ESPN reruns. What channel?"

"Let's see...it's on Channel 3 at home. That's NBC, channel 11."

Greg twisted the channel selector up to 11 as he turned on the television, denying us the chance to see what minor league sport ESPN was running against a Wimbledon final. Not that we were the biggest tennis fans but having live professional sports on in the morning was a treat too good to pass up. I'd watched last year's Borg-Tanner Wimbledon final from this exact chair.

As the television warmed to its task we heard Bud Collins' distinctive voice before any image came up. And when the cathode rays in our picture tube finally aligned themselves, we could see that John McEnroe was already up 3-0 in the first set.

"You are working today?" Greg asked, as Bjorn Borg, a small white slash at the top of the screen, unleashed a blistering serve to start game four. Mark had been scheduling Saturdays as my regular off day, but I'd made a point to tell him that I wanted all the hours he could give me over the 4th of July weekend.

"Yeah, I told Mark I would. With this being a holiday, it didn't seem like a good time to be driving," I answered, with Greg knowing that "driving" meant going up to Newport and bringing Robin down for the weekend. As badly as I wanted to see her, I knew we'd be landlocked in the condo because of the crowds and the traffic. Not necessarily a bad thing, but even getting groceries or beer would be a hassle.

"I figured the weekend would go by the quickest with me in uniform and on the clock," I continued.

"Did you have any second thoughts last night? It was a long, busy day," said Greg.

"And hot, too. The busiest day so far, wasn't it?"

"I'll say. We went through 13 sleeves of cake cones by closing."

"What's the total on that?"

"Thirty cones per sleeve...do the math."

"I can't. Remember, I'm on academic probation this summer," I said, receiving a cock-eyed look from Greg.

"That's 390. And you did pass calculus. And you can instantly tell me how many games the Phillies are out of first place."

"I have the sports section. And one is one. The first number you learn."

"And the loneliest number..."

"I didn't say that. I prefer 'Mama Told Me Not to Come' if we're talking Three Dog Night."

"We're not, but that's a good song."

Greg went back to working on his coffee. I had one eye on the sports section and the other on the tennis. And I was still checking out the Major League box scores when McEnroe took the first set by a shocking 6-1 score.

"McEnroe might be an asshole, but he can sure play some tennis," said Greg.

"He's behaving himself today, at least for now," I said, sharing Greg's mixed feelings about the bushy-haired American. Although as a fellow lefty, I did have a soft spot for him – tantrums and all.

"Yeah, we'll see."

It had been a busy week at the park, with each day seeming to build to the crescendo of last night. Even though it was a Friday, we'd opened early because it was July 4th, and by the time Greg and I finally got into the car to come home, it was almost midnight. There was a line at the go-karts right up until closing, which didn't happen until after 11:00 pm. And even after the line was shut down Pat and I still sent out three more groups, leaving us pushing the go-karts back to their storage area at 11:45 pm. Greg and I had even missed most of *Fridays*, our favorite new television show that ABC's Baltimore affiliate aired in its intended 11:30 pm time slot. *Fridays* was just a late-night rumor in the Philadelphia area, not being shown until after Channel 6 ran their usually dated and lame *Million Dollar Movie*. What Greg and I liked about *Fridays* was that it seemed fresher and edgier than *Saturday Night Live*, which had gotten kind of hard to watch. (Did anybody really think Buck Henry was funny?)

Combining the busy week with the long Playland work day – not to mention our ruined television viewing – and it was definitely the kind of night of where we wouldn't have minded going out for a beer (or two or three) to wind down. But that was a proposition we never considered. We knew that in two more nights the claustrophobic holiday crowds would be gone, and it would still be Dollar Shooter Monday at the Fenwick Feed Bag.

While delayed gratification was the theme of last night, the Psych 201 concept wasn't in play this morning.

"You want a donut?" I asked Greg, reaching in to rescue one of the chocolate-iced donuts before too much of their brown goodness adhered to the inside of the wax coated bag.

"I'll get to it," said Greg, sounding a bit torn. I did feel bad about tempting him with something he might not want to eat. In making sure that there were enough donuts for both of us I was just trying to be a thoughtful roommate. But I also knew that the donuts wouldn't go to waste. Whatever Greg didn't eat, I would.

It didn't take long for my donut to disappear, and after it was gone, I handed the sports section over to Greg.

"Hungry, huh?" said Greg, looking at the yellow crumbs scattered on the napkin where the donut had been.

"They're really good!" I said, pointing to the Layton's bag. "And I earned it – that damn water was cold this morning. I came out with the shakes."

"Glad I didn't bother."

"Yeah, it was sideshore with a crowd. You didn't miss much. Didn't miss anything really."

I picked up the front page of the *Inquirer* but didn't find much to hold my interest. There wasn't anything more about the Selective Service proclamation that President Carter signed on Wednesday, an event that had both Greg and me more than a little unsettled. It made us all the more determined to follow the Republican and Democratic conventions closely when they took place this summer.

"You know, we're working Phillips-type hours this weekend," I said with half a laugh.

"But at least we're not working at Phillips," Greg reminded me with a bit of "touché" in his tone. "I mean, you're still good with the go-karts?"

"Yeah, last night was just busy. It was sort of a younger crowd, except at the end. We didn't even have to bring the chase car out. So, as nights on the karts go —"

"Could you see any fireworks out there?"

"No, not really. There were some flashes to the south, and we heard some booms, but that was it."

"Where do they shoot them off?"

"Down around the pier I think. Last year some of the guys were trying to get up on Phillips' roof to watch them."

"Actually climbing out onto the roof?"

"Well, the upper parts of the building — it's like a labyrinth because so many sections were added over time. I never actually made it up there, but I think there was a porch, or a deck, or something like that. A week later people were trying to get up there again to see Skylab come down."

"Oh Christ, I forgot about that. Where did that thing finally end up?"

"Somewhere in Australia, I think."

"Yeah, that sounds right. Kind of looks like Borg woke up," said Greg nodding at the television, where the score on the screen had the defending Wimbledon champion up 3-2 in the second set

"Yeah, they're going to be at it for a while," I said, draining the slightly bitter yet sickly-sweet bottom dregs of coffee, where all of my undissolved sugar had concentrated. "Man...that last bit was nasty."

"Drink it black and you'll never have that problem."

"But first there's the problem of drinking it black. Speaking of problems...shit, my wetsuit and towel are still in the back seat of the car. I'll be back," I said, getting up and turning around to open the front door.

After putting my surfboard and towel over the porch railing, I walked back to the foot shower, which hung off the exterior wall of our unit and faced out to 122nd Street. I turned on the water and held my wetsuit jacket under the warm spray, making sure the red nylon lining inside turned a saturated dark maroon before shutting off the water. Returning to the porch, I hung the wetsuit over the railing, then climbed over and grabbed a white plastic hanger off the clothesline, balancing the water-soaked jacket on the hanger's downward angled shoulders. I was about to take the dripping jacket inside to hang in the shower when I remembered that both Greg and I would be using the shower sooner rather than later because our Playland shift started at 1:00 pm. As I lifted the fully-loaded hanger back onto the clothesline, I made a mental note to bring the wetsuit back inside before we went to work.

Pushing in the back door, it was nice to feel the cool air produced by the humming air-conditioner mounted above the doorjamb. The unit was doing double-duty because the air-conditioner over the front door wasn't functional. It hadn't been functional last year either, but nobody was living in the front room like Greg was this summer. So far, we seemed to be doing fine with just the single unit. If things got too warm I'd call the realty company.

Walking back into the front room I could see that Greg, who was now working on the "Jumble," still hadn't touched the donut bag.

"You should do the crossword for a real challenge," I said, giving Greg a hard time for his "studious" summer ambitions.

"This is plenty friggin' challenging," he said, flipping the paper around so that I could read it. "What's this one?"

Greg had unscrambled "HOVEL" and "MIRTH" and was pointing to the third Jumble which contained the letters "YARBET." I worked on the letters in my head for a few seconds, then gave up.

"How the hell should I know?" I said with half a snort, but the words had barely made it out my mouth when a cluster of brain cells decided to fire in unison. "Oh, that's 'BETRAY.'"

"Of course, it is," said Greg with a fine-tuned layer of sarcasm. "Here, you finish the damn thing. I'm going to the beach."

"The beach will already be crowded. And remember, we don't have that much time."

"Yeah, I know. With this new Native Tan Royal Oil all need is an hour and I'm basting like a Thanksgiving turkey."

"Yeah, watch that...that's potent stuff. I'm staying inside to save my energy. I've got a whole afternoon of standing in the sun when we get to work."

Greg was up and heading for the door by the time I finished my sentence. His Gotcha trunks were already on, and he made a stop by the mini-fridge to slide into his flip-flops before gathering his towel, radio, and Native Tan bottle from a pile of beach gear beside the couch.

"You're going to be here, right?"

"Oh yeah, I'm not going on that road again until we leave," I said, pointing out the window toward Coastal Highway. Greg pulled open the door and stepped outside, leaving the door ajar as he peeked around the stairs for a live look at Coastal Highway.

"Damn, already a rolling backup heading toward the mall."

"Yep. We'll have to leave a little early."

"Sure thing. I'll be back in plenty of time."

Chapter Twenty-Two

Tie Breaker

As usual, Greg was good to his word, coming up the steps in front of the window right at noon. I'd spent the time puttering around inside, leaving the tennis on while turning down the sound to listen to my favorite side of the Genesis *Duke* album, finding the minor chords and longing lyrics of "Alone Tonight" and "Please Don't Ask" comforting as I worked on a letter to Robin. I'd hoped to get the letter in the afternoon mail, but was halfway into a second page and still hadn't wrapped things up (and we'd probably talk tomorrow night after work when AT&T's long-distance rates were the cheapest). I did manage to finish off my second donut, and the album had finished a while ago too, although the Tonearm was still suspended over the record because I had yet to tend to the turntable. Rather than change the record I'd turned up the volume on the television again, letting Bud Collins and Donald Dell fill the silence with their continuing call of the Wimbledon final.

"You're just in time," I said to Greg as he came in the door. "McEnroe has already saved two match points, and they just started the fourth set tiebreaker."

"Someone has to win by two points, right?" said Greg as he walked in front of me to the chair on the other side of the table, leaving a pungent coconut scent trail behind him.

"Yeah, once someone gets seven points," I said, observing Greg spread his towel over the chair to protect it from his body's shimmering layer of tanning oil.

From the very first serve Borg and McEnroe went at each other, hitting exquisite winner after winner to reach 5-5. Then, while on serve, Borg sent McEnroe scurrying for a sharply-angled volley that McEnroe couldn't return, despite disappearing from view.

"Match point?" asked Greg.

"I think so," I answered, right before Bud Collins caught his breath and confirmed that it was.

Borg's stinging forehand return of McEnroe's serve looked like a match winner until somehow McEnroe's fully outstretched racket delivered a devastating drop shot that left Borg stranded on the opposite side of the court. Greg and I exchanged appreciative glances. We might not have been the biggest tennis fans, but we were hardcore sports fans. And this was sport and more, the otherworldly creativity of the players being like the improvisational "call and response" between two virtuoso jazz musicians.

Borg made it 7-6 with an expertly placed backhand passing shot and had another chance to serve for the match. After the briefest of volleys, McEnroe hit his own stunning backhanded passing shot that had Greg, me, Bud Collins, and the Wimbledon crowd all reflexively gasping "OOHH!!" as a tumbling Borg hit the ball weakly into the net.

"That was nuts!" said Greg.

"Uh-huh. And it almost sounds like the crowd is rooting for McEnroe now."

But that shot turned out to be just a warm-up for McEnroe's next winner, an impossibly-angled on-the-run cross court tracer that left Borg waving at the air. This had McEnroe serving to win the set, but Borg would have none of it, getting his forehand on McEnroe's serve and driving the ball past the sprawling American. McEnroe was still on serve and quickly made it 9-8, earning another set point. But again, Borg wouldn't crack, evening up the score at 9 before the players switched sides. The switch put McEnroe on the bottom of our tiny screen, where he mishit a Borg serve out of play to make it match point once again. Or as Bud Collins pointed out, for the fifth time.

"I think McEnroe's done," said Greg. "It's all been amazing stuff, but he knows he's not going to make it out of the tiebreaker."

"Could be – but he is serving now," I said while running my left hand through my hair and noticing that it was still coarse from my earlier outing in the ocean.

After the television cameras caught Borg's girlfriend taking a deep breath, McEnroe grunted a leftward swinging serve that Borg backhanded weakly over the net judge to make it 10 all. The methodical Swede made up for that mistake by forcing a charging McEnroe to flub a shot into the net off the frame of his racquet. It was match point again, and the match appeared to be done and dusted when McEnroe backhanded a shot into the white band at the top of the net. Yet, somehow the ball hopped over to the other side leaving Borg stranded on the baseline and the score tied at 11. Still on serve, Borg ran McEnroe back and forth before earning another match point, number seven, as commentator David Dell rightly pointed out.

"Hell, I'm out of breath from just sitting in my chair – my heart is racing too," I said.

"I know, right? I feel like I had an extra cup of coffee, like a Big Gulp of coffee, maybe."

McEnroe tied things at 12 with another sharply angled cross-court winner and took a 13-12 lead after unloading a fierce forehand volley that caught Borg moving when he should have stayed put. This gave McEnroe another set point with Borg serving, which Borg used to reinforce his "Ice Man" nickname, coolly stroking an almost too long shot that McEnroe returned into the net. Once more they were tied, but the shocked gasp of the Wimbledon crowd said everything about how human Borg looked while plunking a simple backhand into the net despite overlooking a yawning chunk of empty court that McEnroe didn't have a prayer of reaching. Up 14-13 McEnroe was now on serve with set point number four. It took a few moments and a "Quiet Please" from the court announcer for the crowd to settle into silence, and after serving Borg entirely off the left side of the court, McEnroe – now overlooking his own yawning chunk of empty court – punched a basic forehand volley just wide of the right sideline. Another gasp came from the crowd, and also from Greg and me. It was all tied at 14.

A strange and fully played "let" interlude left McEnroe still on serve, and he made the most of the point's replay by producing a magical drop shot that Borg scrambled for but couldn't touch. This gave McEnroe a fifth set point, but his return of Borg's solid serve didn't stay in bounds. McEnroe then broke the 15-15 tie with a leaping forehand passing shot that brought Greg and me out of our chairs with a loud "OOHHH!!" that was a transatlantic echo of Bud Collins, Donald Dell, and the entire Wimbledon Centre Court crowd.

"That was *crazy*!" said Greg.

"But is it enough? Neither of them is giving an inch."

For the sixth time McEnroe had set point, and he seemed to have Borg on the run after a strong serve. But then he mishit what appeared to be a routine crosscourt backhand, and it was 16 all. Borg's return of McEnroe's serve would have been a winner...had it stayed in bounds. So it was set point number seven, with Borg serving. We almost didn't believe what we saw as Borg anticlimactically hit McEnroe's service return into the net, but that didn't stop both Greg and me from jumping out of our chairs and saying "YESSS!!!" in near unison, with Greg throwing in a fist pump for good measure.

"I think McEnroe's going to win the match!" he said enthusiastically.

"He might, he might. Wow – that was amazing, I feel like I was playing!" I said, finally taking a look at my watch. Greg saw my face change as the excitement of the tennis instantly drained away.

"What? What's the matter?"

"I don't believe it – it's 12:25, we're going to be late!"

"Oh shit, I'm still covered in oil. I can't go to work like some weird greasy tropical French fry."

"And I'm still covered in salt, my hair is like a Brillo Pad."

We stood there silently for a few long seconds, trying to size up how much mess we were actually in.

"Go ahead and get a shower," I told Greg. "I'll be fine, I always wear a hat anyway."

"Are you sure?"

"Yeah, absolutely. Do what you need to do. I'm going to grab my wetsuit off the clothesline."

"I'll be quick. I promise," said Greg, reaching into the Layton's bag to grab a big hunk of glazed donut.

As soon as the bathroom door closed I realized that my wetsuit top would have to stay outside since there was no way to hang it over the tub with Greg in the shower. That left me wandering back to the bedroom where I grabbed my Playland shirt off the floor, bringing it up to my nose for a quick body odor check. Faint, but distinct enough for me to fish my extra Playland shirt out of the dirty clothes pile for an armpit-to-armpit comparison. The "dirty" shirt won the day, although a double layer of Speed Stick was definitely in order. By the time Greg busted out of the bathroom shirtless and still dripping I was in full Playland attire and tying my shoes, watching him scurry down the hallway like a drowned rat.

That was my cue to finally grab my wetsuit, which I brought in and hung over the shower head. While in the still steamy bathroom it hit me that my toothbrush hadn't been used. So I squeezed a dab of toothpaste out and ran the brush around in my mouth, making my last spit into the sink just as a fully-dressed Greg returned to the bathroom for the exact same purpose.

"I'm ready once I do this," Greg said, turning sideways in the doorway to let me out.

"Okay. I need to get my hat and my backpack," I said, heading to my bedroom, where I grabbed both items then started for the front door. My hand was on the doorknob as Greg grabbed his backpack off the floor, then out we went, hustling down the front steps and over to the car.

"I think we set a new record, it's not even 12:40. Think we're going to make it," I said, sliding the key into the ignition.

"It's all up to the traffic. We only need to go 53 blocks," answered Greg.

"Yeah, I hate to do this," I said, letting the car coast into a brief opening in the northbound traffic. Then I let out the clutch and hit the gas, squealing the tires to get us into Coastal Highway's center median.

"Tourist. That's a dick move you know?" said Greg with a laugh.

"It is. But we need to get to work, right? Desperate times..." I said, now using the wide median as an extra southbound lane while looking for a break in traffic. I found a likely cut off victim in the form of a puttering VW bus and upped our speed to squeeze in without the driver laying on the horn. It was a relief to be underway.

Traffic wasn't all that promising through Condo Row but opened up just past Lombardi's, making the rest of the drive seem pretty normal. Then turning onto 65th Street, everything looked not normal. The employee section of the parking lot was much fuller than we were used to, and there were actually people lined up at the front gate waiting to get in the park. This had Greg and me out of the car quickly and jogging up the access road, where we took some flak from Pat.

"Hey, you guys are late!!" he said in a slightly loud and mock "supervisor" tone.

"No shit," was all I could say as I ran by.

Finally, Greg and I made it to the break room and grabbed our time cards.

At the sound of the "thunk," it was 12:55 pm.

Chapter Twenty-Three

Years of Experience

Because Greg needed to work on one of the ice cream machines we were walking through the park gates right around 12:30 pm. This was going to be a full shift, a hot one at that, with little solace that the sun and heat would keep the park relatively empty until late afternoon. Even with no one on the ride Pat and I would still have to man the picnic bench next to the always running go-karts, sucking in the pit area's concentrated exhaust fumes. On days like this, lucky riders often got a 20-lap outing because we were desperate not to have too much downtime. It was amusing to watch the enthusiasm for go-kart driving fade away as the riders grew bored from going round-and-round. But Pat and I didn't care. We'd do whatever we could do to make the shift feel like less of an eternity.

I'd waited until 12:40 pm to punch in, then headed down to the go-kart track. By this point in the summer, I hardly bothered to look at the ride schedule. Pat and I had become *the* go-kart guys. Mark told me himself that he was pleased with how well we worked together. That was nice and all, but not really what I signed up for. While it was still better than working at Phillips, a go-kart shift was more physical than what I did at Phillips – although carrying crab pots and multiple prep trays during a "runner shift" was pretty strenuous work. It was funny that those were the nights I liked best. In keeping the crabs, clams, and seafood stocked and supplied through the night, while not having to deal with the waitresses, I felt like I had control of what was going on. Unlike when Pat and I flooded the track with eight individually controlled go-karts during our always lined-up evening sessions. We just held our breaths and hoped for the best. But always on the ready for whatever stupidity might come.

In lining up the things that I didn't sign up for, I couldn't get over that, just like last year, I reeked at the end of the night. Sure, it was the nose hair singeing fragrance of spilled gasoline rather than Phillips' pungent "Eau de Old Bay," but I was starting to think I preferred the latter. I'd also, just like last summer, ruined an expensive pair of running shoes at Playland, with my gold colored Brooks going gray with black streaks from their daily contact with the tires lining the go-kart track.

A minor annoyance this summer was that Pat always beat me to the karts. Even on a day like today when Greg and I were early. The only time I was first was on Pat's day off. Today he already had most of the tires back in place and was having some fun with the Chase Kart, waving at me as he skidded through the turn by the pit area. I'd just placed my backpack on the picnic bench – which still swayed despite our pleas with Mark to fix it or get us a new one – when Dave pushed another kart through the gate.

Thanks to Pat I'd developed a good relationship with Dave. He was still frugal with his words, but I'd come to learn that behind the scenes he was a supporter of mine. In fact, I'd learned that he was likely the reason I'd been stuck on the karts all this time. Apparently, he'd told Mark that he wanted me working with Pat – it was nice to know that I was doing something right at Playland. One of the cool things about Dave, besides his understated sense of humor, was that he treated both Pat and me as adults. It was something I really appreciated. Yet somehow, I didn't feel adult enough to ask him why I was stuck on the karts. Maybe if it hadn't been my first summer at the park, or maybe if it were August and not July, I'd have the nerve to ask. For now, I just accepted it. In evaluating my current standing at Playland, that's just the way it had to be.

"Take this one out for a spin. I just replaced the points and condenser and want to see if it's ready," said Dave.

"Sure," I said, as Dave pulled the starter rope, bringing the kart to life.

I pulled out and buried my right heel against the green gas pedal, locking my entire leg into a straight position to make sure the kart ran full out through every section of the track. The way Dave had the karts set up, you could floor them through even our sharpest turns as long as you committed to a tight line and held firm on the steering wheel. They'd slow from friction but always carried more speed through the turns when running flat out, as opposed to feathering off the gas into the corner, then hitting it hard when you exited. This kart felt good, and since I now knew just about every inch of asphalt on the track, I locked into a comfortable driving rhythm that got more locked in as the laps went on.

Sitting behind the wheel of a go-kart was something that felt natural long before I arrived at Playland. That's because part of my aunt's "spoilage" of me was a go-kart for my ninth birthday. It was used but had once been a racing kart, complete with miniature Goodyear slick tires and a sleek 10-HP engine that we never managed to get started (we'd been told that racing engines needed to be pushed at speed to fire up). To the rescue came my great uncle, who ran a landscaping business and was savant-like in taking care of small engines. He custom ordered a 4-HP Tecumseh engine, built it up from parts, and mounted it where the old engine had been. Once the kart was functional I ran it in the large side yard of my grandmother's house, having a kart-worn dirt oval where I floored it through the turns, the steering and front wheels pointing left as my free-spinning back wheels created a dirt-spitting balance of force and friction that allowed the kart to slide clockwise at a 45 angle. Nobody ever taught me the technique, it was something I did, automatically it seemed, to keep the kart's momentum going. To me it was obvious, but when friends came over, they couldn't make the kart work the same way. They'd spin out, or slow down, so they didn't have to slide through the turn. I figured my advantage came from having more time in the kart than my friends did. But anytime I voiced that thought my great uncle would just smile and say that I took after my grandfather. Right down to being left-handed.

So it turned out that of all the rides in Playland, I was most qualified to run the go-karts. Not that Mark had any idea at all. It wasn't like I'd put "got a go-kart for my birthday" on my application, or if he'd asked whether I had any go-kart experience. But I did have quite a bit. Years, in fact.

I focused on keeping a tight line, staying inches or less from the tires in each turn while not letting the back-end of the kart skid out and lose momentum. With each lap I gained ground on Pat – surely he was just cruising in the Chase Kart, not even worried about what I was doing behind him. We'd probably gone 10 laps when Pat finally slowed down and pulled into the pit area. I pulled up short to allow him to get out and push the Chase Kart to its official parking spot next to the fence. Then I pulled into the pits, carefully aligning my kart behind the two karts next to the picnic bench. Dave was still there, so I got up to go tell him that the kart seemed fine. That in fact, it felt really good. But I wasn't quick enough on the draw.

"Damn! That was some driving. You made up ground on Pat," said Dave, in an enthusiastic tone that I'd not heard before.

"Did you set up this kart to go a little faster? It moved really well," I said.

"No, it's set just like all the rest. If anything, I thought it would be on the slow side."

"Ah, I had a go-kart growing up. Just a lot of time behind the wheel."

"Yeah, that would help, but there's more to it than that."

Pat was now standing with us – I noticed that he was in shorts today. Definitely a smart move on his part. He'd heard what Dave said, but wasn't offering anything to the conversation. He just stood there smiling with his arms crossed.

"Trust me, you've got something going on with your driving, you do," continued Dave, shaking his head up and down for emphasis. He then put his right hand up like he was making a "how" sign and started walking toward the exit gate. "I gotta' go. You two take it easy today. It's a hot one."

Pat was still smiling at me. There was no margin to blush in this heat, but Pat could see I wasn't sure what to make of Dave's assessment.

"Dave's not one to dish out praise. Take it, man."

"Yeah, I guess. They're just go-karts."

Chapter Twenty-Four

Fixed

"Hey, that's not bad," offered Gary after I'd successfully knocked over two of the open-mouthed acid trip faces on consecutive throws.

"Are those things supposed to be clowns or cats?" I asked, compelling Gary to turn around and contemplate the four rows of foot-shaped and fringe-outlined "things" that stood up like teeth on long blue beams at the back of a garage-like corridor that opened onto Playland's southern midway.

"Damned if I know. I never really gave them much thought."

"Does it matter?" said Greg, giving me an "Are you nuts?" squinty single-eyed Popeye smile.

"Nope. I was just looking for an official judgment," I said, smiling back as smugly as I could.

It was only 5:40 pm and Playland was mostly still and silent as the three of us stood in the "games" section just inside the front entrance of the park. Greg and I were receiving a guided games tour courtesy of Gary, who had been a partner in Greg's exodus from Phillips and ended up being the overseer of Playland's games.

"See if you can get the third...clown, or cat, or whatever it is," Gary continued, in a matter of fact tone that carried not a hint of challenge.

I picked up my last rubber-coated baseball out of the thin wooden molding that had been shaped into a triangle on the top of the game's knee-high barrier wall, feeling its unnatural sponginess as I rolled the smooth surface in my left hand until my index and middle fingers aligned with its artificial laces. On the upper right of the corridor, maybe 20-feet away, were a cluster of a half dozen still standing faces, a promising location because it felt natural to throw across my body from left to right, like I was pitching to a right-handed batter. I took aim, took a deep breath, then took a shortened step toward the barrier wall as I let the ball go with a firm snap of the wrist.

It had been four years since I stood on a Teener League mound and looked in on a hitter, but this "pitch" left my hand feeling like a strike. I knew the velocity was right, if the ball impacted the thinner upper half of the figure. That was the trick of the game. Hitting the bulbous bottom half of the stupid thing was no good because that part was amply padded to absorb the ball's impact. You couldn't "win" – have the figure fall over backward on its hinge – if the ball hit there. I was still feeling good as the ball sped toward the part of the figure I'd aimed for...unfortunately, my throwing judgment was rusty after four years of neglect. The ball went wide left, just brushing through the figure's fuzzy boa-like blue fringe.

"Aww, really close. Too bad," said Gary.

Greg, who already had a miss, wound up and threw his final ball. With a solid "thwock" he cleanly took down a figure in the bottom row.

"We should've worked together," said Greg, stepping back from the wall with a laugh.

"I can't let you try the water guns right now because things need to stay clean before we open," said Gary, referring to the boardwalk staple where you shot water into the mouth of a plastic clown, trying to be the first to inflate and pop a balloon that rose up behind his head. That was fine with me, as the game was never my favorite. The faces always struck me as creepy, and I'd never won while playing the game – ever.

So Gary guided us past this game and over to another boardwalk classic, the milk bottle game, where he hopped over the short wall and into a wide area that had a cartoonish farmyard scene painted on a hanging canvas background. In front of the background, as was typical for the game, were three short milking stools. Scattered on the ground were gleaming metal milk bottles that Gary picked up and arranged into three-bottle pyramids on each stool. He then came to the front of the game with four baseballs – two for Greg and two for me – which he set down into wooden triangles on the game's wall. I was surprised to see that they were real baseballs, albeit brown and slightly misshapen from a summer's worth of impact with the bottles, the canvas, and the floor. Greg and I didn't need an explanation of how to play the game. The rules were simple – knock over all the milk bottles with a single throw and you were a winner.

Since the bottles weren't nearly as far away as the trippy faces in the other game, I felt pretty confident as I eyed the stool in front of me and threw first, missing everything, my ball sailing high to nail the barn in the painted background with a mighty "thrummpfff."

"Wow, that sucked," I said, trying to play off the embarrassment of my throw.

"Watch and learn," said Greg as he stepped up and made a powerful throw that hit the bottles square on, a metallic "thwack" coming from the initial contact followed by the echo of metal on concrete as the top and bottom right bottles fell to the floor. Still upright, and appearing to defy the laws of physics, a quivering bottom left bottle remained rooted to the stool. Gary astutely stayed off to the side as I quickly launched my second throw, which was better than my first but not as precise as Greg's effort. Somehow it still created an auditory instant replay of Greg's throw as two bottles fell off the stool and clanked around on the floor.

"You want me to set them back up or do you just want to throw at the other stool?" Gary asked Greg.

"Yeah, I'll just throw at that one," said Greg, pointing to the full pyramid of bottles on the far-left stool. Greg made this throw from where he stood at the center of the game, hitting the trio of bottles on an angle. Again, he was dead on and rock solid, leaving a stubborn single bottle shaking on the stool.

"Damn!" exclaimed Greg, "I can't do much better than that."

"Probably not," said Gary with a smile and half a laugh. Then Gary beckoned us over the game's wall with a wave of his upturned right index finger.

"Go ahead – go set up the bottles," he said, with an even bigger grin.

I walked back to my stool, bending over to pick up a bottle with each hand. The one in my right hand was shockingly heavier than the one in my left. I held the bottles up in front of me so I could look into the openings of each one. The bottle in my left hand was hollow. The one in my right hand, which I tilted upward into the light...was filled with concrete!

"Holy fuck – it's fixed!" I said loudly, looking over to Greg at the next stool.

"Say What?"

"This one is hollow," I said, holding out my left hand. "While this one is filled with concrete!" Greg still looked puzzled, then I realized that both of the bottles he was holding were probably filled with concrete.

"Pick up that bottle," I said, pointing with my left bottle to the lone bottle under Greg's stool.

Greg put a bottle on his stool, then picked up the one off the floor with his empty hand.

"Christ, this weighs nothing," he said now turning around to look at Gary, who was smiling from ear-to-ear. "So, the two concrete bottles go on the bottom – does anyone *ever* win?"

"Yeah, it's not impossible," said Gary. "But people don't win very often."

"At a dollar a throw?" I chimed in.

"You get two tries for a dollar. Not bad odds," answered Gary.

"But still in the house's favor?" I continued.

"What did you expect?"

"Are the water guns rigged?" asked Greg.

"No, it's just harder to do. It's pretty much what it seems."

"And this one looks easier...until the bottom bottles weigh ten pounds apiece?" I said, feeling annoyed that something at Playland was "fixed."

"I don't think they're that heavy," said Gary, a little defensive from the innuendo Greg and I were generating, which we only bothered contriving because we really liked Gary.

Other than Greg and Pat, Gary was third on the list of Playland people I knew more than casually. We always talked when we had the chance, and Greg and I had met up with him at the Greene Turtle and the Feed Bag a handful of times throughout the summer. He'd even been over to the condo. And through our many conversations Gary and I had formed a unique bond because we were both desperate to move beyond our current and seemingly fixed places in Playland – me on the karts, Gary on the games – and onto new things. Specifically, running the other rides in the park.

Greg and I reset our stools but had little interest at this point in throwing our arms out trying to knock over the nearly impossible bottles. So we both climbed back over onto the midway and started checking out the prizes lining the walls of the game. They were the usual assortment of cheap stuffed animals from Hong Kong, ranging in size from tiny to trolling. (A "trolling" prize being a super-cute mega-sized animal that some undercover employee might parade around the park to subliminally spread the idea that Playland's games were "winnable.") Although I was viewing these mostly tacky objects through my unsentimental 20-year-old eyes, there was something I'd never seen before hanging on the game's right wall. Miniature stuffed dinosaurs, about the size of a teddy bear, that looked like Dino from *The Flintstones*.

"Hey, those are pretty cool," I said, pointing to the row of long-necked dinosaurs.

"You want one?" asked Gary.

"Sure, is that okay? I mean, I'll throw a couple of bucks into the games' pot if you want."

"Here, give me your backpack – which one do you want?"

"The light blue one with the yellow face."

Gary took my backpack, took a slow and careful look around the park, turning his head to look both directions on the midway, then went over to the wall and stuffed the light blue dinosaur into my bag.

"Just keep it shut tight the rest of the night," said Gary, handing me the backpack as he zipped close its main pocket.

"Sure, sure...thanks!"

"No problem. These animals cost next to nothing. These games make money even when someone wins."

Chapter Twenty-Five

On the Edge

N ot everyone who wanted to ride the go-karts was an idiot, but that was how it felt thanks to my extended and unbroken streak on the ride. It was a default position that Pat had likely reached years ago, yet somehow, he seemed to handle it without the darker overtones that now infected my thinking during a shift. I mean it was a totally unfair assumption on my part, because, in truth, only a small percentage of the people who got on the karts were idiots or troublemakers. But because the potential havoc an idiot could wreak on the karts was greater than on almost any other ride (Ghost Ship excepted), Pat and I always had to be on edge. And we were also on edge for just basic accidents. People who weren't idiots could cause havoc, too. It was this "always on edge" part of the ride that fed my darker emotions.

Yeah, we had the Chase Kart to deal with the idiots. And I'd done my share over the last couple of weeks of running deserving guests into the tires. Of course, in deciding who we were going to run off Pat and I were guilty of selective picking. Neither of us would break the 150-pound mark on a scale, so if our misbehaving rider were, say, 6'2" and built like a linebacker, we'd finger wag and head shake until our fingers and necks got tired. If we sized things up and thought we were "harder" than the offending driver, then in the tires they'd go.

An extra layer of backup for dealing with idiots and assholes was in my back pocket, in the form of a 12"-long pair of heavy-duty slip-joint pliers. They gave off a totally innocent look, like they were just part of the ride, because, of course, someone running the go-karts would need a pair of pliers to fix things. Yet I never dared to touch anything on the karts other than the gas caps. First, it would make Dave very unhappy, something I never wanted to do. And second, if something happened to a kart I "adjusted" – an accident, or somebody got hurt – it would be my fault. I'd be liable, not to mention fired. The innocent aspect of having two prongs of thick metal protruding from my pocket was deliberate on my part. Because, you know, I might have been in the middle of "fixing" something and just happened to have the pliers in my hand when I needed to politely – or not so politely – ask someone to leave the go-kart track. But in reality, the only thing my pliers were meant to adjust was someone's lousy attitude.

That Pat seemed to deal with the on the edge aspect of the karts better than I did...I admired him for that. And I was envious. My rationalization for him being, perhaps, more mature about it all than I was, came down to this – the karts were where Pat wanted to be. This was his ride, and a piece of who he was came from being *the guy* who ran the go-karts. Me, I never wanted to be on the karts in the first place. And during the month of July, they'd turned into a cruel purgatory, completely at odds with the expectations of my now distant early days on the Antique Cars. It was an exile too, as being outside of the park on a ride that required constant focus...it was almost like the inside of the park didn't exist, except for the free food I got from Greg (he was still making a killer butterscotch milkshake). After all this time at Playland, I hardly knew anyone other than Greg, Gary, and Pat, and Pat's high school standing seemed to limit his crossover with the older workers, some of whom I discovered from Greg – who was at least meeting people at the Dairy Queen – were actually school teachers.

I hated to admit it because I liked Pat, but being a go-kart guy wasn't exactly a high-status position in the Playland ride running hierarchy. Well, maybe we weren't looked down on, but there wasn't a line of people beating down the gates for a crack at running the karts. Those who subbed in on Pat's day off seemed like they were just biding time and couldn't wait for the shift to be over (yeah, okay, who could blame them). It was a given on those nights that I'd be giving the instructions and in the lead observation spot all shift long. I also knew I'd be the lead enforcer, as my temporary partners' commitment to the go-kart rules were always more relaxed than mine.

It was all wearing on me. To consider anyone who walked through the go-kart gate to be a potential fuck-up – that was a lot of negative energy to carry around hour after hour and shift after shift. Coming up with ways to synthesize it and burn it off...surfing always helped. But it had gotten to the point where being out on the beach with Greg didn't. On most afternoons one of Ocean City's single-engine banner planes would buzz up and down the coast pulling a long rectangular sign with large red block letters that said "OC's Largest Go-Kart Track – Playland

65th Street." An airborne reminder that I didn't appreciate at this point, but at least it wasn't a personal one, unlike the boy and his friend who cautiously approached Greg and me as we tried to catch some afternoon rays before getting ready for our evening shift at Playland.

"Hey, mister," said the dark-haired and braver of the pair, who were probably no older than twelve. "Don't you run the go-karts at Playland?"

I'd been laying on my stomach facing south, chin propped up on my forearms, listening to WKHI as I watched their start-stop ghost crab-like dart over the mid-afternoon sand to where Greg and I had our towels. Lifting my head, I looked up at the boys, then turned to look at Greg, who was on my right, also stomach down, with his eyes closed tight but also a quivering smile that was, in reality, a suppressed laugh. He was letting me know that I was all on my own.

"Yeah, I do, that's me," I answered, trying to sound enthusiastic.

"Cool!! See I told you," he said, turning to his now impressed slightly shorter friend.

I wasn't sure where things were going from here. They didn't seem in a hurry to wander off, but I really didn't want them hanging around. I'd gladly watch them and keep them out of trouble on the track, but I was not about to sub for mom and dad on the sand at 122nd Street.

"Were you there last night?" I asked, daring to continue the conversation.

"No, we were there on Sunday night. But I think we're coming back tomorrow."

"Good. Well, I'll look for you. Be sure to say 'hi,'" I added, knowing I'd never recognize them if they didn't.

"Okay. You know what? I'm going to run the go-karts when I get older."

"Yeah? Good luck. It'll change your life."

"Okay – bye," he said, looking a little puzzled by my response.

"Bye. See you tomorrow."

The two boys ran off towards the ocean, no doubt to cool their feet off from standing in the miniature piece of Death Valley that surrounded our towels. Greg opened his eyes, picked his head up to see how far the boys had gotten, then looked back at me.

"Well, you're famous, but you're also a miserable fuck, you know that?"

"What? They didn't have a clue," I answered defensively.

"Yeah, so what. They didn't mean anything. They're over with their parents right now saying 'hey, we just met the go-kart guy!'"

Greg was right, but I didn't feel like verbally acknowledging that at the moment. The kids were never really an issue on the karts. They were usually too enamored with driving – the fact that they were actually really driving – to be a problem. Getting on the karts was a mind-blowing privilege for kids who were clearing the height limit for the first time, and they didn't want to throw it away by not following the rules that I mindlessly spat out while standing in front of them.

"I know you've got a lot of shit floating around in your head right now, and we've got Friday to deal with and all, but man, ya' gotta' lighten up. You gotta' get off those karts."

"Yeah, no shit. I've been telling Mark that for weeks."

What Greg said out on the beach had been bouncing around in my head all shift long. He was mostly a cynical bastard, just as I was, but not a contrarian. So, he was giving it to me straight. But to have kids come up to me on the beach...the karts were getting me down enough without that bit of a live-action knife twist. Pat had a good laugh when I'd told him about it. He didn't get why it would bother me, and why being recognized on the beach was like having someone picking at a scab that was never going to heal. Hell, maybe tomorrow the keychain beach picture guy would stop by the towel and try to barter some laps.

So I dug deep on this night and made a conscious effort to be upbeat and remind myself of all the things that made Playland enjoyable. Like being outside in the ocean air, the nightly sunsets that moved both the bay and sky through the yellow and orange sections of a Crayola 64 Box, the smiles and wonder on faces that were experiencing an amusement park for the very first time...the eight tattooed bikers standing at our gate.

Pat and I had seen them pull up earlier in the parking lot. Actually, we heard them first as they rumbled in from Coastal Highway, then picked a distant and deserted piece of the lot to line up their gleaming extended-fork and high-handlebar rides. There'd been no reports of any problems in the park, as, despite our location, we still got "word" of events inside. Like if a rider deposited their dinner in the Rotor, or if the Ghost Ship was on pause for repair. So far, nothing had filtered out to Pat and me about the intimidating group getting ready to enter our ride.

I couldn't tell if they were wearing colors, but their collection of leather and denim vests gave off the impression that they should be. Add in the shoulder length hair, beards that would take me a lifetime to grow, the body-builder arms with a camouflage cover of green-tinged tattoos...I didn't care if it said "Frito Banditos" on their backs, they were some serious dudes. And their appearances had the desired effect because my stomach had flopped and my heart had gone into overdrive, leaving my legs feeling like they were filled with concrete as I moved toward the gate to let them in.

The Hell's Angels come to mind when most people think of motorcycle gangs. For me, they came in third after the Pagans and the Warlocks, two organizations whose "turf" just happened to be the area where I grew up. Not that I ever had direct contact with either entity, but they were part of the local culture. From the rumors of someone's cousin "patching up," to the procession of Pagans and Warlocks that you'd occasionally come across on our local roads, to knowing what bars belonged to what gang. A high school friend of mine even jokingly listed "Pagans' restoration of Marcus Hook" under "Activities" for his senior yearbook profile. Needless to say, it was a joke that didn't make it past the watchful eyes of the year book's faculty advisor.

The bikers ignored me as they passed me by, jangling in an odd metallic harmony as they walked to the karts thanks to the various chains attached to their leather wallets. This matched up with an uneven rhythmic clomp from their street-scuffed work boots, which along with worn-to-the-nub jeans, created their identical waist down uniforms. A shorts and flips flops crowd they were not.

The largest guys had a hell of a time stuffing themselves down into the go-kart seats, yet somehow, they managed. Once they were seated, I tried hard not to stare at their arms, but there were more tattoos concentrated in the kart pit area than I'd seen in my entire lifetime. The elaborate designs went well beyond the pedestrian arrow-hearts and anchors displayed by relatives who'd spent time in the military. There were flying eagles, crosses, crosses with daggers, twisting serpents, skulls, and even a fire-breathing dragon with wings. And the colors, I had no idea that tattoos could be blue or yellow. It was also the first time I'd seen finger tattoos – in person, that is, not on a rock star in *Circus* or *Rolling Stone*. Since the guy was sitting in the back row, I couldn't read what the individual letters said. Not that I wanted to stare too hard.

As luck would have it today, it was my turn to send the karts out. I was still approaching my official sending off position when I looked up at Pat, who was in the rear send-off position behind the karts. Although it wasn't obvious, I could see that Pat was slightly wide-eyed – I'm sure I was too – as he offered a weak smile and a small shrug. Yeah, Pat, I know, I'm on my own.

Looking out over this group I could hear my heart thumping in my ears like the staccato opening notes of Billy Joel's "It's Still Rock and Roll to Me." Wow, I'd missed the various earrings and the bandanas some of the guys were sporting. It was quite the scene to have this group occupying Playland's ground level go-karts with me now lording over them like the Playland jester. It was surreal. And what made it completely Rod Serling surreal (take your pick, *Twilight Zone* or *Night Gallery*) was the fact that most of the guys were *smiling*. Peeking out from their pirate-inspired facial hair were smiles. It would have made one hell of an album cover.

But still, these were some tough, tough guys who could probably melt me with one well-practiced glower. So I tried to say my spiel as evenly as possible, with no hint of the attitude that I offered up to a typical group of kart riders. I also tried to say it as confidently as possible, hoping that I was the only one hearing the slight quiver in my voice. I even improvised to leave off the "lose your ride" part, figuring the last thing I needed to do was give them a dare. With nothing else left to do or say I stepped aside and waved them out, just like I'd done hundreds of other times during the summer. But this was the only time I'd ever felt physically ill after finishing the task. That's because as I watched the back bumper of the final rider disappear around our first left turn, I realized that whatever they wanted to do out there, they were going to do. Pat and I had zero chance of throwing them off, not that either of us would be brave enough – or crazy enough – to confront them about not following the rules. My stupid pair of pliers, and oh, how stupid they seemed at this moment, would give these guys a good laugh. And when the laughing was done, they'd likely plant my "backup" in the back of my head.

Now that they were out on the track...if they wanted to turn our ride into their own personal bumper cars, or, oh fuck, say a demolition derby, then that's what was going to happen. If they decided they wanted to run the karts in the opposite direction, then so be it. If they wanted to make a shortcut through gravel in the middle of the track, the only thing Pat and I would be able to do was to watch whatever mayhem and havoc they created. And for a final totally fucked up thought that put even more fear into my already fear-adrenalized body – would we even be able to get them off the ride, short of calling the cops?

What they did on the track was have one of the most civilized runs that Pat and I had seen all summer. And they had fun. Nobody, not one of them, came close to doing anything wrong. What side-by-side "racing" there was, unfolded almost identically. One of them would move outside and wide on a straightaway, trying to pass the other while having a smile or a half-silly looking "I'm going for it" grin on their face. When the pair of drivers reached the corner, one of them would back off the gas to make sure there was plenty of room for both karts to get through safely. They must have enjoyed the dumfounded looks Pat and I had on our faces. We even gave them a couple of extra laps because things were going so smoothly. I think Pat and I just wanted to fully confirm what we were seeing.

On my signal, Pat started the process of bringing them in, which they did under total control, gently even. They dutifully watched my commands, at least all but one did. But he was immediately admonished by his neighbor – they were side-by-side in the second row – with a "hey dumb shit, stay in your seat." This brought hearty laughs from the other seated drivers, who rose as one when I lifted my arm (in trying to be nonchalant, I used only my left arm for the "raise up" command).

As they got up out of the karts to leave, one of the average sized guys, about my height, but with arms the size of my legs and about three times as much hair on his head and face, walked over to me. A short sleeved blue T-shirt stuck out from the frayed armholes of his denim vest, which had clearly started life as a denim jacket. Multiple tattoos spilled out from both sleeves, a haunting eyeless skull with a bleeding dagger through the top immediately caught my attention. I couldn't see this guy's eyes because of mirror sunglasses, but he reached out his right hand as he moved toward the exit gate.

"Take care, my man," he said with a sly smile, grabbing my hand by the thumb in a surprising soul shake that had me feeling like I'd ridden the Spider and Tilt-A-Whirl consecutively.

"Sure – thanks. You too," was my feeble response.

As I watched him walk away, I noticed that Pat was at my shoulder. I turned my head toward him, letting out an audible sigh as our eyes came together. He was still a bit wide-eyed but looking relieved as he blew out a long deep diaphragm exhale. Then an enormous smile took over his face. Mine too.

"What just happened? I mean, that really did just happen? You saw it too, right?" I asked while turning away from our line so our words would stay private.

"Yeah, I saw it. I've seen it before. They respect the machinery, and the guys working the machinery."

"Me...and you? They respect us? They could have turned this into a demolition derby."

"It works like this – they wouldn't want anybody messing with their machines, so they don't want to be the kind of people to mess with other people's machines."

"Oh..."

"Unless they have a good reason to."

Chapter Twenty-Six

Feeling a Draft

I twisted the key towards me, shutting off the engine and locking the ignition switch on the steering column, feeling my Sunbird's three-pointed red vinyl wheel "clunk" into place as I removed the key from its fitted slot. Pulling off my sunglasses I looked over at Greg, who was staring out the passenger window at the building we were about to enter. The front section of it was a furniture store, but that was not where we were headed.

"Are you ready, man?" I asked.

Greg glanced over with a pained look, a look that I was sure my face was reflecting back at him. Then he turned away for a second take at the white entrance door on the side of the building.

"Fuck!" he shouted, looking back at me. "Fuck – let's get this over with."

The headlines had been building all summer. From a brutally fitting one last month on Friday the 13th to the "read-all-about-it" boldface that jumped off the front of the thick Sunday *Philadelphia Inquirer* that I'd plopped on the dinette table just a few days earlier.

"Draft Sign-Up Given Approval."

It said all we needed to know – but nothing that we really wanted to hear.

The goddamn Middle East. It was forcing those of us of a certain age to pay attention to politics sooner than we cared to. First, there was the Iranian takeover of the American embassy in November, an event that was still front and center in the news because, despite Richard Queen's release two weeks earlier, there were still 52 Americans being held hostage in Tehran. And not long after the embassy takeover the Soviet Union had gotten into the mix, invading Afghanistan, a country that shared a long border with Iran. Even with all this turmoil on the other side of the world I was still shocked to come back from an evening calculus class and hear President Carter use his State of the Union speech to propose restarting the Selective Service. A lot of other people were shocked too, although in dorm room discussions afterward it was concluded that Carter was just saber rattling. There was no way this first step toward an actual draft would really happen. Sure, our thinking carried a certain amount of denial, but we had been old enough to feel America's axis shift when then-President Ford officially eliminated Selective Service registration in 1975. I can personally attest that even 15-year-olds breathed a sigh of relief – not to mention our mothers – as we felt, right down to our bones, that after the strife of the Vietnam years there would never be a draft again. Carter was just blowing a bunch of macho hot air.

But then a registration plan began moving through Congress, receiving House approval in late-April just hours before a hostage rescue attempt by the U.S. Military unraveled into a tragic desert fiasco. When President Carter responded to this failure by vowing to use "every avenue" necessary to free the hostages, it was clear to my friends and me that we were in the crosshairs of a draft revival. Once the Senate gave final approval in June, Greg and I knew it was just a matter of time. The ACLU tried to get in the way, contending that a male-only draft would be unconstitutional, but as of Sunday, the draft sign-up was on for young men born in 1960 and 1961. So here Greg and I were, getting ready to walk into the post office annex on 130th Street and fill out our Selective Service forms.

There had been organized protests around the country, even as Carter tried to assure us that he wasn't in favor of a peacetime draft. That we were all signing up, you know, just in case. Although Greg and I talked about it, neither of us was brave enough to ignore the government's order to give our names to the Selective Service. The "up to five years in jail or a $10,000 fine" was plenty persuasive. We did, however, offer up our own minor protest. Technically, because my birthday was in June, I should have registered on Tuesday. And Greg, with his November birthday, should have come in to register yesterday. In not wanting to waste two trips to 130th Street, and also wanting the moral support of each other, we opted to share the sign-up experience on Friday, which was the designated "make up" day.

We'd come dressed in our Playland work gear even though it was only 3:30 pm, just in case there were any questions as to why somebody with a Pennsylvania or a Delaware driver's license would register for the draft in Maryland. It was a silent walk up to the door, which Greg pulled open from the left, saying, "After you."

Right before I stepped inside it hit me – a light-headed rush, like I'd just finished an extended session pinned to the wall in Playland's Rotor and my body still wanted to spin even though the ride had stopped. This unexpected sensation left stars around the periphery of my vision as I entered the post office, decorating its small rectangular sunlit lobby with a sparkly animated outline. I'd barely gotten my first foot through the door when a woman's voice startled me.

"Do you need a Selective Service form?"

She was a postal employee, easily identified by the "U.S. Mail" eagle sleeve patches on her light blue button-down shirt. Standing just inside the doorway to my left, she was almost directly in front me – but I hadn't seen her at all. Her left hand held a small stack of forms against her chest, while her right hand was poised to give me one. She was well-tanned with grayish blonde hair pulled back in a ponytail, and I took some comfort in her cheerful tone and smile. Maybe this wouldn't be so bad. At least it wasn't the dentist office.

"Are we that obvious?" I asked, trying to pull some humor out of my gallows.

"I've been handing these out all week. I know the 'look.' I'll bet you're not here for stamps."

"We've got almost a full book back in the condo."

"You guys do have your driver's licenses?"

Greg and I both mumbled "hmm-mm" in near unison.

"Good. You can fill these out over on the counter," she said, handing us each a form and pointing to the stomach-high counter that extended along the windows facing out to the Montego Bay Shopping Center. "Then take them up to the clerk at the window when you're done."

Sticking up from holders on the counter were a series of black banker's pens, complete with connecting ball chains that made sure the pens never left the post office. Their services weren't required because Greg and I had come prepared, outfitting ourselves with a couple of stray University of Delaware pens that we'd scavenged from under the seats of the car. In hand, the registration form seemed too small to be official, only being about the size of the top half of a sheet of paper. There were nine lines to fill out, each numbered consecutively and marked clearly with a black box containing a white number. Including, thank goodness, separate lines for both a current and permanent ad-dress. Greg and I had both taken a moment to check out the forms before starting in with our pens. He was standing on my right, and by some coincidence, we looked over at each other at the same time.

"Well, here goes nothing," he said with a smirking smile.

I shook my head in agreement, then looked back down at my form. It was simple enough to fill out: date of birth, sex, full name, current mailing address, permanent residence, current phone number, a signature to witness that your information was true. As I started pushing down hard enough on my pen to start the "J" in June, this was fucking surreal. Looking over to Pappy's where Greg and I celebrated his first night at Playland not so long ago...what were we doing here? Doing something that we never thought we'd have to worry about – filling out draft cards. And just what were we getting ourselves into? I mean, we had to do it, didn't we? It was our duty. But exactly what would our "duty" end up being? An all-expenses-paid tour of Iran or Afghanistan, courtesy of the U.S. Army? These weren't things I ever thought I'd be contemplating during a summer at the beach.

Thanks to my procrastination Greg was finished by the time I got to item number seven (phone number). The post office wasn't all that busy. One other young guy had come in and was now off to Greg's right filling out his own Selective Service form. And there was a tan and professionally dressed woman (beach professional – sleeveless top, granny skirt, and cork-soled sandals) with a handful of manila envelopes at the first of the two clerk windows. Greg walked over to the second window where a tall male clerk with thinning hair and Clark Kent glasses compared Greg's driver's license with the information on the form, then took a quick look at Greg before stamping the form's bottom right corner and handing back the license.

Greg turned around and held up his license.

"I'd rather be using this on a pitcher of Michelob," he said, referring back to our night in Pappy's.

"Good idea, but a little early. We've still got a full shift."

"Yeah, I was only half serious. Or not serious. What was that waitress' name?" said Greg, stepping away to let me hand in my form.

"Ah...Lynda. Right?"

"Yep, that's it."

Before I could respond an unfamiliar and somewhat impatient male voice crashed our conversation.

"Next."

Chapter Twenty-Seven

Expectations

W ell, this summer was certainly turning out different.
That was my overriding thought as I stood at the water's
edge on this almost perfect morning, a morning that I had a
good feeling about before I crawled into my blue sheets the night before.
My anticipation of good things had me out of bed well before the alarm
clock buzzed to life, with my intensifying expectations pushing me out
the back door of the condo, surfboard in hand, just as my watch hit 7:20
am. This enthusiastic awakening was rewarded when I stepped on the
sand and saw only three other surfers out in front of the Caine house at
118th Street. There would soon be more. It was just a matter of how
quickly the lineup would fill in.

Word was going to spread fast now that the sun was up high enough
to start warming the morning air, which sat so still that the ocean shim-
mered like a gigantic green sheet of glass. Surging up from this backlit
horizon-wide reflecting pool were ruler's edge lines of waves, all
stacked up one behind the other like corduroy before they rolled onto
118th Street's low tide receptive sandbar. Once in shallow water, they
turned into translucent head high walls that broke with an almost machine-like cylindrical right-to-left precision. A solid south swell. The
kind of morning that, even as a goofy footer, I dreamed about all through

the struggles of the spring. So why I was still standing on the beach with my board under my arm, feeling something that I never came close to experiencing during the entire previous summer.

Disappointment.

Part of it was Greg. It was finally clear that surfing wasn't his thing. He wasn't going to become a surfer this summer, or probably during any other summer. I took this as a failure on my part, feeling like I'd done something wrong in how I introduced him to the sport. For me, riding a moving wall of ocean while on a six-foot piece of fiberglass was the most amazing thing ever. Even more amazing than strapping on skis and hurtling down a steep snow-covered mountain trail or using a long flexible pole to fly over a 13-foot high crossbar (seems I'd always had a thing for fiberglass-facilitated sports). When I caught my first wave, at this very spot just over a year ago, the rush was overwhelming. The unique buzz, the adrenaline high of a wave, was like nothing else I'd ever felt. And once I felt this buzz, I wanted to share it.

Was there more I could have done to make Greg see just how incredible surfing was?

Something I didn't understand but had to accept was that the sport didn't work for everybody. I'd seen that happen last year with some of the guys from Phillips who came out a few times, then never bothered to get in the water again. And I'd discovered during my limited time in Ocean City that there were a fair number of people who owned surfboards but weren't really surfers. They either couldn't stand up, after years of trying, or were content to sleep in and battle with the surfing beach crowds for a few crumbly leftovers once the sun was high in the sky.

So Greg's decision to permanently undo his leash...maybe the blame didn't totally fall on me. Which didn't mean that I blamed Greg or had any hard feelings because surfing didn't "speak" to him. He gave it a fair shot, he really did, still paddling out until last week. But it was obvious he wasn't having a good time, being stuck in the "almost standing" phase. He could catch the wave, which was an accomplishment itself, but couldn't get to his feet quickly enough. That meant he was either falling off the back of the board or riding toward shore on his stomach – over and over and over. I felt bad that I couldn't offer the right advice to get him past this sticking point. It certainly would have been fun to share this morning with him.

Another thing adding to the disappointment ledger, of course, was Playland. The hours were great, especially compared to last year, but thanks to my extended stay on the go-karts the summer had turned into a six-week-long Monster Mouse ride. A few peaks, a lot of valleys – the Mouse's big first drop being especially appropriate – combined with intermittent whiplash-inducing turns. The days without waves were miserable. I really missed Robin, and my academic inadequacies escaped the cranial crevasses I'd stuffed them in, freely scurrying through my thoughts like roaches along a darkened baseboard.

But the main thrust of my disappointment came in realizing that this summer was going to be "lesser" than the last one. Not bad, necessarily, Greg and I were having a good time. He was, as I'd hoped, a great roommate. And there was still a chance that Mark would move me off the go-karts, although I wasn't sure how much consolation that would be with August just days away. But this feeling of lesser was something I'd been carrying for a while now, even though I'd tried hard to slough it off and ignore it because it carried a complicating emotional layer of me being disappointed with my disappointment. This added disappointment bugged the shit out of me because I knew better. I knew from the day that Greg and I picked up the key from the realtor that expecting a second consecutive "summer of my life" would be a foolish thing to do. So I'd been reminding myself every time I looked at the calendar hanging in my bedroom – last year doesn't matter. Don't compare this year to last. Don't bore Greg with the old days. This was an entirely new summer with new things to do and experience. Just take things as they come and enjoy them.

I was proud of these wonderfully mature thoughts, thinking I'd scoped out and dealt with the potential major pitfall of the summer. But I couldn't pull it off. As the weeks rolled on with Greg not getting anywhere in the water, and me stuck in the go-kart pen in front of Playland...how could I not think of last summer? How could I not have expectations after I'd lived the previous summer's possibilities?

This morning, this glorious morning, hammered my disappointment home hard, like Dr. Van Helsing driving a stake into Dracula's heart. It was now completely and totally official – last summer was not going to be equaled. And it really wasn't even close. All the hopes and expectations that I tried to keep under wraps, that I tried to not even acknowledge having...they now drained out of me with each gentle pulse of frothing whitewater that rolled up over my feet. As always, I squinted and looked hard at the silhouetted surfers in the lineup, desperately hoping that one of them looked familiar. But as usual, none of them did. So I got ready to live out the absolute worst part of my dashed hopes and expectations, doing something that, after last summer, I couldn't imagine myself doing.

Paddling out into a solid late-July south swell...totally alone.

By this time last summer, the service station crews at Phillips had evolved into two distinct taxonomic classifications – surfers and non-surfers. I was on the surfing crew, hand-picked each week by my crew chief Andy, a local surfer who'd been talked into helping me and another "wannabe" surfer one morning in mid-June. At work that night, when word of our "surf lesson" spread throughout both service stations, Andy was obligated to give a command performance the following morning. (Andy being the only one at that point who qualified as a surfer.) After ten guys showed up – and the enthusiasm was so high that many eagerly waited out the morning's acute surfboard shortage for a turn in the water – a precedent had been set and a daily routine established.

It was a routine that I loved. We'd all meet by 8:00 am at a street that Andy picked, based on his local knowledge of the waves and how they might interact with the tides and Ocean City's sandbars, which Andy knew like the back of his hand. Once in the water, we'd surf until the lifeguards came on duty, all the while getting pointers from Andy. Then we'd head to Phillips and load up on the employee breakfast, which was far and away the best employee meal of the day. One of Phillips' most experienced cooks ran the breakfast, a slightly gruff white-clad crew-cutted man who seemed to be straight out of a casting call for a "diner guy." I enjoyed watching him work the enormous flattop grill like a short-order maestro, skillfully frying up French toast, pancakes, and eggs to order, his long spatula subbing for a baton as he internally kept time for each item on the crowded grill.

But my favorite part of breakfast was walking into the crowded employee-only dining room as part of Andy's surf crew. It was big-man-on-campus stuff, as with board shorts and hair still drying we'd take over a six-top to have breakfast and coffee while recounting the morning's surf session.

Then we'd go home for a few hours, or on some days, just an hour, and come back in our uniforms ready for work. Despite the growing demands as the crowds grew both in Ocean City and Phillips' dining rooms, I liked working for Andy and being on the surf crew. He had us hustling all night long making sure each order was filled promptly and properly. Then after the kitchens closed down and we scrubbed every stainless-steel surface spotless, saving the mopping for the last, we'd gather to wind down at Ollie's Pub, a small beer store across 21st Street with two taps (Bud and Busch) and two pinball machines (*Flash* and *Fireball*). It was in Ollie's that Andy would pick the street for the next morning, getting the latest wind updates from the flags flying on top of the Phillips Square Shopping Center.

Through the many mornings in the water together I'd become closest to Jack, John, and Harry. Our differing backgrounds made us an unlikely group, but being beginners who were just stepping into the surfing universe – with guidance from Andy – we had a unique and powerful force uniting us. Thanks to our morning routine the summer was one extended climb upward, both physically and emotionally. Each week our friendship grew stronger, while our surfing improved with each ride. There was also a growing confidence and maturity that came from not only surviving but focusing and doing things right during our ten-hour shifts at Phillips. It all rolled into one massive and incredible wave of adulthood that I took off on at the end of the summer, riding its giant tube of promise into the most significant event of my life.

This wave crested when the four of us walked out of Phillips on a busy Saturday night in August just before the dinner rush. Yeah, it sounds kind of juvenile – my parents thought so – but we had our reasons for leaving the restaurant shorthanded while destroying any chance of ever getting a reference for our months of hard labor. We'd grown tired of waiting on a promised ten cent raise, and days off for a real break from the restaurant were impossible to come by. (The example being when I worked 13 days in a row to get consecutive days off for a trip home to Pennsylvania.) We were also simply burned out from dealing with the organized chaos that seven kitchens and 14 dining rooms generated on a nightly basis. As August counted down we had our eyes on one final thing to consummate our summer of surfing – a surf trip, known in surf lingo as a *surfari*. And we knew exactly where we wanted to go, as Andy had been regaling us with stories of the place for weeks now. Our destination would be Cape Hatteras, North Carolina, the East Coast's "wave magnet." All we needed was time. And since Phillips wouldn't give us the time, we made some for ourselves.

My Sunbird wasn't big enough for the trip, so we ended up putting my surf rack on Jack's parents' vinyl-topped four-door Buick Century, packing its trunk with borrowed tents and blankets before heading south on Route 13 two days later. We had no idea what to expect, but the surf gods delivered glorious Outer Banks' sunshine and the best waves we'd ever seen, including an epic 45-minute session of tube rides for John and me while Harry and Jack were checking out a local surf shop. For three full days we surfed ourselves silly, pushing our sunburned and board-rashed bodies to complete exhaustion. It felt *so* good, and we were *so* stoked. There was no question now, it was official – we were surfers. No one could take this trip away from the Phillips' fantastic surfing foursome.

I floated back to Delaware in September, mounting a photo we'd taken – the four of us lined up with our boards, the Cape Hatteras lighthouse centered between John and Harry – on the bulletin board over my desk. So anytime I looked up from a textbook, that incredible moment in the sun stared back at me. I dreamed about the trips we'd take in the future – Mexico, Hawaii, and why not, maybe Australia. Because as we packed the tents and blankets at the Cape Point Campground, we were already talking about the summer of 1980, making plans to pick up right where we left off.

Little did any of us realize that our fantastic surfing foursome had started to unravel before we made the North Carolina state line. After John was dropped off in Nags Head to hang out with his brother for the final week of the summer...he became a ghost. I'd not heard from him or seen him since. Jack and I did stay in touch, and I was grateful that we'd surfed together earlier this summer. I was also really grateful for his help in getting me into Playland. But as he explained during our surfs, his military career was into a serious phase now, with the summer of 1981 already spoken for. And when he graduated in the spring of 1982, he'd be commissioned as an Army officer. Jack didn't actually say it out loud, yet it hung over our conversation like a cloud of pit area go-kart exhaust – he was never coming back to Ocean City.

As for Harry, we surfed together during the fall, getting some good waves and seemingly having a good time. We even bumped into Andy on a brisk September Saturday morning, saying "hi" but keeping our distance from the group of locals he was surfing with. To keep our surfing going into October Harry generously let me spend weekends with him at his parent's condo on Bayshore Drive. But our relationship got complicated during an ill-advised encore trip to Cape Hatteras just before Halloween. If the first trip had been *The Endless Summer*, the return trip was more *Damnation Alley* – minus the giant cockroaches. There weren't any waves and we got on each other's nerves pretty good, the tension not fully draining out of my car until we said goodbye on Bayshore Drive.

After sparse contact we tried to regroup in January, but through a miscommunication, we'd ended up sharing the condo with Harry's older sister, who made it clear she didn't appreciate us being there. She and a surly friend, as well as a rotating cast of men, closed down the bars and stayed up till all hours fueled by rum and coke and lines of cocaine. It wasn't all Harry's fault, but it was another situation in which I couldn't wait for our time together to end. For all I knew, Harry may have felt the same about me at that point. From there, things had devolved to the point where when Harry showed up at the condo in June – unannounced, and with a couple of guys I didn't like the looks of – I had Greg answer the front door and lie about me being in the water at 118th Street.

That I hadn't run into Andy in almost two months of surfing was really the most surprising thing of all. I used to bump into him regularly in lineups throughout Ocean City before he started up our Phillips summer school. This was a time when I couldn't stand up, so I was always mortified when I saw him, not wanting to reveal the kook-a-fied state of my surfing. Through Doc at Ocean Atlantic I'd learned that this year Andy was glassing boards for the Spyder Surf Shop, which had just opened up in the 45th Street Village Shopping Center. Talking to the Spyder guys, they knew Andy, but all the board work was being done in West Ocean City. So, Andy was never in the shop. And never in the water, as far as I could tell.

As long as Greg was on the path to becoming a surfer, the same path that I'd been on last summer with Jack, John, and Harry, the summer had possibilities. Possibilities that Greg would stand up and be stoked out of his mind, possibilities that he and I would swap great rides and laughs on a morning like this one, possibilities that maybe we'd both quit

Playland before Labor Day and have our own Cape Hatteras pilgrimage where Greg could consecrate his summer in the water. These were all thoughts I'd kept internally, not wanting to make Greg feel like there were any "conditions" for being my roommate, or that I had expectations for him to live up to. I didn't really. That's not what the summer was about. We were doing just fine without the surfing. But as the summer unfolded with me not running into any friendly faces in the water (hell, Harry would do at this point), not finding any surfers at Playland (was I really the only one?), not making any new surfing friends or acquaintances...I'd been leaning on Greg pretty hard, even if he had no idea.

Splashing through the six inches of water covering the tiger-striped nearshore sand...I was lonely. Yeah, the waves were really, really good today, and I'd feel a lot better after a few rides. But I was still going to be alone in the lineup. And that's how it was going to be until Greg and I packed up on Labor Day.

Yep, this summer was certainly turning out different.

Chapter Twenty-Eight

Showdown

Twenty minutes had gone by since the "incident," and Pat and I were still recovering. The tingling sensation that overwhelmed me when Pat mentioned Dave's gun still lingered, and there was an odd queasiness in my stomach and heaviness in my legs as the initial adrenaline surge wore off and my body labored to break down the deluge of norepinephrine that had been released into my synapses. (Hmm...maybe I did learn something in two years of bio.) We continued doing our jobs, pretty much telepathically, as there was hardly any conversation between us. The truth was, I didn't know what to say. Or even what I wanted to say.

Since our disgruntled go-kart riders were nowhere to be seen, it felt like we had a chance to steer the night back onto a normal heading. Maybe they were all talk, I mean, who would really want to hang around here until closing? Comforted by this possibility, I forgave Pat, at least in my head, and was about to walk over to him and start up one of those awkward bygones-be-bygones conversations when...there they were, emerging out of the darkness like phantoms along the fence at the bottom of the track's "L." Except there weren't just the four guys who'd been on the karts. The current tally outside of the fence had somehow doubled to *eight*. And they couldn't have picked a better spot to deliver their message of menace, as our track-facing floodlights left them heavily shadowed, allowing their bodies to ominously disappear and reappear along the fence like they had access to the *Star Trek* Transporter room. In going over my school days' fight record, it wasn't all that extensive, yet I was undefeated (okay, maybe one of them was a draw). Unfortunately, this experience had been limited to one-on-one encounters where your friends and enemies stood around in a circle and screamed for blood. An ebbing and flowing rumble with a group of people was a "joy" I'd not yet experienced. So, having eight males lined up to kick my ass – and these were fit young men, not pre-teen playground boys – I was really, really scared. Not to mention attempting to resurrect my long dormant relationship with God.

It had been my job to send the current group of karts out, so I was still standing up by the pit area when our tormentors reappeared. Pat was down in the middle of the track and really hadn't noticed them until the guy who caused the accident yelled over, "Hey, here we are."

Upon hearing the voice, Pat began backing through the infield to a position directly even with me. Then he hopped across the track and joined me along the access road fence.

"They're back," said Pat.

"Yeah, no shit. And there's eight of them now – double the number that rode the karts," I replied, mentally moving our bygones discussion to the status of "postponed indefinitely."

"We haven't forgotten!" yelled a different voice from outside the fence.

"Fuck!" said Pat tersely.

"You can say that again. Should we tell anybody?"

"No, not yet. Let's just see what they do. I'll talk to Dave on break."

"Okay. Whatever you think."

Pat and I were both standing there trying to look casual and focused, which was absolutely fucking impossible after sneaking a peek at the fence. And fuck, those guys looked like they didn't have a care in the world. A couple of them were milling about in conversation while the guy who caused the accident was leaning on the fence with his fingers wrapped through the chain link. Then it hit me how distracted Pat and I were.

"Umm, I think we need to bring this group in," I said turning to Pat.

"Oh shit, yeah, they've gotten a bunch of extra laps, haven't they?"

We had just finished getting the karts into the pit area when, almost on cue, Calvin showed up for our break. There wasn't a question of who would go first – Pat had to find Dave. Calvin had no idea what was going on, and I needed the situation to stay that way. This meant not only did I send the karts out, but I also casually made my way into the infield to keep Calvin away from the fence. Seemed like my best bet for keeping the situation under wraps was to play dumb and take whatever taunts and abuse came my way.

"Hey, where's the other guy?" came a now familiar voice from the fence. I looked over and shrugged, and for the moment, that was it.

Calvin and I ran two more uneventful groups of karts, which conveniently used up almost the entire 15 minutes of Pat's break. That meant my misdirection play had succeeded...until Calvin's head did a double-take and finally noticed the shadowy human line along the fence.

"What are those guys doing down there?" he asked.

"You'll have to ask Pat," I answered.

"Ask Pat?"

"Yeah, ask Pat."

I exited the conversation by walking over to let the next group of riders through the gate and was grateful to see Pat emerging from the darkness of the back area of the park. With me conveniently at the front of the ride, I pretended to count our line while waiting for Pat to step onto the blacktop.

"Dave is all set. He'll walk us out," whispered Pat as he leaned toward me.

"Okay, guess that's a good thing," I said, whispering back.

"Damn right it is."

"This is still just our party? You didn't let anyone else know?"

"Nope. Because if nothing happens, then nobody knows."

"Dave won't tell?"

"Not a chance. What does he know?" asked Pat while nodding toward Calvin, who was a wall of noise away from our conversation thanks to his position behind the karts.

"That's up to you. Calvin noticed them, and I said to ask you."

"I'll take care of him. Your turn for break, see you in fifteen."

I quickly went out the gate and past the wall with the mascot's face, moving into the dimly lit corridor between Mark's office and the backside of the building that held Playland's games of chance. Before getting to the employee lounge I turned into the park, looking carefully right and then left before scurrying over to the Dairy Queen, hanging off to the right side of the counter while Greg dealt with some customers who were actually going to pay for their food. As they walked away using their tongues and fingers to catch the milky melting runoff from their identical chocolate dip cones, Greg turned his attention to me.

"Man...you don't look right. What's up?" said Greg with a concerned tone.

"Is it that obvious?"

"Well, I've been living with you all summer, so maybe my perception is a little keener, but you look like you've seen a ghost. And not one of those mechanical contraptions clunking around in the Ghost Ship."

"Pat threw a couple of guys off the karts, and they didn't take it too well. They're waiting outside the park for us now."

"What?! Didn't you wave your pliers at them?"

"Hell no. They're in my backpack. I haven't carried those things since the night the bikers were here."

"Oh yeah, I remember that night..."

"Anyway, Pat went off on break to talk to Dave – mechanic Dave – who has a gun. He agreed to walk us out at the end of the night."

"Wait, wait, wait...some guys you threw off the go-karts want to have a fight in the parking lot?"

"I didn't throw them off, Pat did."

"Yeah, that seems a minor detail at this point. They're waiting for you in the parking lot...now?"

"Right now."

"And you're getting an armed escort out of the park."

"Uh-huh. So, if you want to get a ride with Gary or Katie, or get the bus..."

"Are you kidding? I wouldn't miss this for anything. We don't have this type of excitement at Playland every night, you know."

"Easy for you to say."

"Those guys are going to get bored. They'll be long gone by the time we close."

"I hope you're right."

Our "buddies" were still manning their post outside the fence when I returned from break. At least some of them were. The group had been cut in half, down to the four who had actually been on the karts earlier in the evening. They were pretty quiet now, so it was easier for Pat and me to focus on running the ride and find our usual comfortable routine, although with much less "Zen" than on a typical night. We ran four more groups and moved past the ten o'clock hour when I noticed that only two guys were left at the fence. And after two more runs there was no one there at all. Pat sent the next group out, and I caught up with him before heading out onto the infield gravel.

"They're gone, at least from the fence," I said.

"I saw. I really hope they're *gone* gone, and not just hanging out in their cars.

"Me too."

"I still want to walk out with Dave."

"Yeah, me too."

We got notice at 10:45 pm of our official 11:00 pm closing, which meant that Pat and I could shut off the line and maneuver our final runs so the ride closed right at 11:00 pm. We still had to wait for the park to clear before pushing the karts back to the garage area, which was conveniently where Dave would be. The park was dim and quiet by the time Pat, Greg, and I started putting the karts away for the night. Dave watched silently as we came in with the first wave, then with some help from a Monster Mouse guy, we had all the karts put away in two trips.

"You said you didn't see them anymore," asked Dave, who wasn't tipping his hand on the whereabouts of his weapon.

"They weren't hanging along the fence anymore," said Pat.

"You think they're in the parking lot or gone?"

"I don't know."

"Alright then. Let's get out of here."

With the go-kart lights turned off it was a long dark walk down the access road. We were a foursome, Greg, me, Dave, and Pat, crunching over the sandy gravel toward the subdued light of the parking lot, whose towering light poles were just slightly beyond the designation of worthless. Finally, we reached the last corner of the go-kart fence and stepped out, fully exposed, into the parking lot, right at the spot where our jilted and angry riders had been standing not long ago. My hammering heartbeat was all I could hear as we readied for our bayside spaghetti western showdown, Dave, of course, being our tall and unflinching hired gun. The rest of us, the sidekicks as it were, being the scene's lame plot device, our bright yellow "camouflage" Playland shirts symbolizing that we were the good guys.

But then it hit me...what would really happen if they were still out there? Would Dave's gun be enough to make them slink off? Or something I'd not considered before – what if they were armed too? On that thought I swallowed hard and tried to ignore the tightening knot in my stomach and the sweat running down my back, realizing how stupid this would all be, to devolve into an armed duel over a go-kart ride. Shit, what had I gotten myself into? This was fuckin' nuts.

About a dozen cars were left in the lot, and a quick scan of their windshields revealed that they were all completely empty. There were no heads, bodies, or people anywhere to be seen.

"So...they were all talk," said Dave, with a smile and a chuckle.

"I was hoping they were really gone. I couldn't believe those guys would give up that easily," said Pat.

"Well, who'd want to wait out here in the dark for hours? They probably had better things to do," continued Dave.

"Maybe they'll come back?"

"Who cares. You want to wait on them? Just get in your damn car and go home. Ain't nothing easier to do than that."

"I second the motion to go home. You ready Greg?" I said.

"Yep, ready. We didn't need the excitement anyway," said Greg.

"Thanks a lot, Dave, we really appreciate you walking us out," I said, trying to sound as grateful as I felt.

"Yeah Dave, thanks a lot," added Pat.

"No problem, no problem at all. Y'all drive safe. See you tomorrow," said Dave.

"See ya, Dave. Thanks again," I said, pulling out my keys, noticing that my hand was shaking pretty good.

Dave got into his dark Ford F-100 pickup and fired it up, the engine releasing a deep growl that Dave's skilled hands likely added long after the truck left the dealer's showroom. I'd managed to align my car key with the door lock and was finally seated behind the wheel, reaching over with my right hand to open the passenger door for Greg. But as my arm automatically moved back to the steering column to twist on the ignition, I altered this routine by whipping my head around for a careful look into the back seat. I then leaned forward into the curve of the windshield and swiveled my head from right to left, making absolutely sure that we were alone in the parking lot. Greg watched this undeniably paranoid performance and did his best to put me at ease.

"I told you they'd be gone," he said quietly. "They're probably miles away from here now."

Maybe. But wherever they were, I still needed to talk to Mark.

Chapter Twenty-Nine

The Day After

I'd made it over the back railing and "stuck" the landing without incident, feeling a bit shocked that I remained upright despite my eyes being puffy millimeter-wide slits that left me essentially sightless in the overpowering morning sunshine. Neither hat nor sunglasses offered much relief as I directed my unsteady shuffle through the balmy air toward the beach, knowing that I'd probably taken one bong hit too many...ok, several bong hits too many, while hunkered at the dinette table with Greg last night after work. And though I tried mightily, I hadn't succeeded in flushing all of the dissonant life overtones left by my go-kart shift from hell.

But I did sleep like a rock.

Morning blindness and a mouth full of cotton were small prices to pay for my coma-like slumber, as I did not want to wake at 4:00 am replaying not only the previous night's confrontation but also what we should've done or should've said to "fix" the situation. Surely there must have been something...*no, no, no! Just stop!* The answer was simple – I needed to be done with the go-karts.

Stepping off the end of the street and into the uneven area where the roadbed disintegrated into the sand and left jagged flesh-puncturing pebbles of blacktop lurking like land mines just below the surface...yeah, I knew it was going to be flat. There hadn't been any waves since Sunday, but I'd hoped that maybe, just maybe there would be a cosmic karma payback for putting up with the insanity of last night. Perhaps a waist-high mysto swell to rinse it all out of my head and take my weed hangover with it? But nope, that hadn't happened. Not that I was counting on something I had no control over. So, the question now was, what did I have control over? And what could I control so that last night never happened again?

I could talk to Mark. Today. But what control did I really have over his thinking?

Once back in the condo the minutes of the morning ticked by at a snail's pace. The lack of waves, of course, contributed to that, and it seemed like I was trapped forever in the bedroom while waiting for Greg to rouse from his own THC-induced unconsciousness. In trying to be patient, I'd worked my way through almost half of the magazines stacked in the orange Wawa milk crate next to the dresser, with most being dog-eared surf mags that I'd read so many times that I could recite the text almost word for word. And the haunting *Newsweek* with "The Big Bang" headline and an ash-spewing Mt. St. Helens on the cover did little to lift my mood. Finally, I heard Greg rustling out of his sheets and pushed open my bedroom's folding door to walk down the hallway.

"No waves?" asked Greg, who squinted and blinked like a just woken cat as I made my way to the stove.

"Nah, I was hopeful but didn't really expect any. Coffee? Yes?" I said, grabbing the tea kettle and putting it under the faucet in the sink.

"Oh God, please. What time did we – oh, hell, we didn't even put the bong away."

"I'll get it," I said, putting the kettle onto the stove, then pulling the smoke-stained glass stem out of the bong's bulbous bottom before pouring its outhouse-on-fire smelling contents down the drain.

"Do you want to go in early?" asked Greg.

"Well, we've already got the picnic, maybe Mark won't even be there."

"Let me try that again. You need to go in early – and talk to Mark."

"Yeah, you're right. You don't mind getting there ahead of time?"

"Oh, I've got lots of things to do at the DQ. Last night wasn't cool at all. You don't need that type of stupidity."

"Yeah, you're right. I've been twisting on it all morning. Thanks."

I spooned out the instant Maxwell House as the kettle moved to a pre-boil rumble, staring at the brown mound of powder in my cup as if it might have the same telepathic messaging properties as a plate full of mashed potatoes.

The weekday lunchtime traffic was thick, although with the summer being on the cusp of August it shouldn't have been all that surprising. I deliberately steered the Sunbird into the right lane of Coastal Highway at 70th Street, letting one of the city's blunt-nosed white-and-green minibuses run cover for us before turning right at Playland's tall four-posted sign, which sat on the corner of 65th Street just before the entrance to the 64th Street Shopping Center. With the car windows open there was only the sound of flowing air and crunching gravel as I ran the engine up into third gear before coasting across Playland's parking lot to a spot near the go-kart fence, where a handful of cars had settled in like a partially played tic-tac-toe game. Greg and I got out of the car in silence, a silence that continued as we walked up the access road, only broken by a pair of deep-throttling dump trucks maneuvering around in the city maintenance garages to our left. We crossed through the gate and into the park, then under the monorail track before I slowed at Mark's office.

"Good luck – you gotta' do this," Greg said, slowing down to talk, but still continuing on his way toward the employee lounge.

"Thanks, I'll need it," I said, grateful for Greg's encouragement.

Reaching to knock on the door, my heart was pounding just like the day I came for my interview. But this was different. My nerves then had been jangling with excitement. Today, there was a shadow hanging over everything despite the bright midday sun. While I'd been asking Mark for a change, I was prepared now, at least I hoped I was, to demand an exit from the go-karts. What I hadn't figured out yet was this – was I prepared to walk if I didn't like Mark's answer? I mean, I'd walked out of Phillips a year earlier, but that was done without any discussion or confrontation with my supervisor. This year I still felt loyal to Mark despite being stuck on the go-karts for more than a month.

It took a few moments – hell, Greg had time to disappear into the park – but I finally convinced my left hand to knock on Mark's door.

"Come in," said Mark, raising his voice to be heard through the office door.

I pushed the door inward to find Mark sitting at his desk in his air-conditioned cooled office in almost the exact same lighting as the day of my interview. And like that day he was smiling, although today's smile had a flatter and resigned quality to it.

"Hey Earl, I know why you're here. Yeah, I heard about last night. I'm sorry you guys had to deal with that. You should've told us, we'd taken care of them," said Mark in a tone that, as usual, helped me relax.

"Umm...it was decided we shouldn't make a big deal out of it. You know, make something out of nothing."

"Uh-huh. But it might have ended up being a big deal. A really big deal, from what I understand. Sometimes Pat – well, I keep forgetting, he is still a kid. You guys didn't do anything to escalate what happened?"

"No, not a thing. There was an accident. Maybe Pat was a little –"

"But you didn't insult them, or curse them...ask them to step outside?"

"No, nothing. Not even close."

"Then you should have let us know. We need to know. We want to take care of you guys."

Mark was right, and he had gently humbled me into silence. I didn't enjoy not doing the right thing, and wasn't sure what to say, or even what I wanted to say. Then Mark, purposely I was sure, helped me out.

"I know you want off the karts. You've done your job, done a good job. And that's part of the problem. I need you to hang with me for a few more days. You have my word."

"Thanks, Mark. I'm sorry we didn't let somebody know last night."

"That's okay, just remember for next time."

"I'm still out there?" I said, pointing with my left hand toward the go-kart track.

Mark looked up and nodded, "Like I said, give me a couple of days."

"Okay. Thanks."

Stepping outside into the heat while pulling the door shut, I finished taking in Mark's words – and shuddered.

Who in the hell wanted there to be a next time?

I began the short walk to the karts and had almost reached the corner of the games building when I heard the familiar electric engine hum and tire-on-asphalt approach of Moon and Melvin's golf kart. They were coming up from behind me, so I paused to let them zip by and turn left, both acknowledging me with a brief wave as they headed into the main part of the park. Upon reaching the go-kart gate, this was one of the few times I'd beaten Pat to the track. There weren't any karts out yet, and everything was quiet and still, a surreal contrast with the final hours of last night. And surprisingly the tires weren't all that much of a mess, not that I'd noticed what they looked like when we finally turned off the lights. I put my backpack down in its usual place under the far-right end of the picnic bench, which remained in its wobbly see-saw state and probably would for the rest of the summer.

Everything was peaceful and so sedate...did last night really even happen?

The peace and quiet didn't last all that long as another familiar sound filled my ears, and I looked over to see Dave wheeling the first kart of the day into the track. He backed it into place on pit row, then turned to me.

"You okay after last night?" he asked.

"Yeah, glad it turned out to be nothing," I said.

"You still want off, huh? You're ready to be done?"

"All those other rides in there, and I've only run one of them," I said gesturing toward the Ferris wheel. "I need a break."

"You're good with these – no shit."

"Thanks, Dave. I do appreciate it."

"And you can drive the hell out of them, too. Something I've been meaning to ask you. You got any relatives down this way?"

I was momentarily taken aback, as it was an odd question, especially coming so late in the summer. Maybe Dave was just making conversation after the excitement of last night? But whatever his reason to pose the question now, it wasn't a hard one to answer.

"Nope. All of my family is in the Philadelphia area."

Dave didn't say anything right away, pausing for a second like he was thinking hard on what to say. Finally, he offered a small smile.

"Just wondering. I'll go get the other karts."

As Dave strolled out of the gate, an unexpected tingle ran down my spine, and my brain fired up a neurotransmitter storm that completely lifted the fog of last night's kitchen table overindulgence.

I hadn't really lied to Dave – yet I hadn't told him the truth either.

Chapter Thirty

Sky Ride

The employee lounge was at its full evening punch-in bustle as Greg and I entered to take our turn at the time clock. We both weaved around and said "hi" to several semi-familiar exiting Playland faces before reaching the metal time card rack, where I glanced up for a quick look at the night's schedule, my eyes instinctively focusing on "go-karts" before moving rightward to the slot for Tuesday. Hmm...Pat's name was there, but mine wasn't. Where I expected to see "Shores," it said "Ward" instead, that being Perry Ward who occasionally worked with me on the karts when Pat was off. A wave of disorientation scrambled my thoughts. Did I misread the schedule? I pivoted my eyes back to the go-kart line and slid my now shaking left index finger four columns over to Tuesday where the go-kart slot clearly said, Mears and Ward. Okay, deep breath...was I really off the karts, or was it a mistake? Did I have the night off and not know it? No, no, that wasn't right. I was off on Saturday, the first day of the work week. So where had Mark put me? Where would my first night off the karts be?

"Hey, what's up?" asked Greg as he watched my hesitation at the time clock.

I pressed my quivering finger onto the clipboard to make it useful, slowly dragging it down the schedule, slot by slot, by slot...by slot. Finally, there was my name. Paired up with "Price" – that would be Gabe.

I already knew the ride, or at least I was pretty sure of the ride because I'd only ever seen Gabe running one ride. Still, I slid my finger leftward across the paper, finally stopping on the ride column.

"Sky Ride."

Holy shit, I was right. The Sky Ride. I was on the Sky Ride! And off the karts, just as Mark had promised.

"I'm on the Sky Ride! Can you believe it? After seven friggin' weeks," I said looking over to Greg, who was sporting a broad supporting smile.

"High five, man," said Greg, and we raised our arms and slapped together our right palms. "Wow – congratulations. Happy now? I know you're relieved. Man, enjoy it."

"Believe me, I will."

"Woah, what's the matter?" asked Greg as he observed the slight shadow that ran through my eyes.

"I do feel bad about Pat. He's not going to be thrilled."

"But you guys have talked?"

"Yeah, we did. Sort of."

"Nothing more you can do, man. Go have a good time on Sky Ride."

Walking out into the park – actually with Greg because the Sky Ride loading platform was right behind the Dairy Queen – I was more excited than my first night back in June. And I was floating more than walking thanks to the enormous weight that had lifted off my shoulders. Wow...a fresh start. Or more like an "informed" restart. Where I'd been wide-eyed and unsure on that first night, I was now coming off a seven-week stint of running one of the most challenging rides in all of Playland. So for this final phase of summer, I knew exactly what I wanted from working in the park.

And the Sky Ride was going to serve it up on a platter. A full evening on a ride where the ride operator had complete and total control. No more beseeching pre-ride "Green is the gas, red is the brake" spiels. I couldn't imagine the Sky Ride even had a spiel, at least not one that I could remember. It had been years since I'd ridden the thing, but walking up the concrete steps and onto the loading platform it was stunning how familiar everything felt. And they were still here. "They" being the painted sets of footprints that showed each rider where to walk and stand to catch the ride. There were also footprints painted on the other side of the platform to guide riders off and to the exit staircase. Easy non-verbal instructions – I loved this already!

The Sky Ride was another one of Playland's original rides, dating back to the park's opening in 1965 (the same summer Jolly Roger unveiled their nearly identical Skyliner). It was essentially a chair lift for skiing that didn't have a mountain to climb. Instead, it went out over Playland and back, crossing above the miniature golf course, the Scrambler, the Airborne, and then finally over the monorail track and entirely out of the park, lowering down to a short turnaround tower that sat on a concrete island about 20 yards out into the bay. Although it wasn't exactly a thrill ride, there was something both thrilling and unsettling about leaving the boundary of the park and looking down to see your feet dangling over the bay. For some reason that was scarier than having them dangling over the park, even though you'd probably survive a fall into the shallow water, but not one onto Playland's concrete. And the bay turnaround had a knack for offering up a bonus thrill, especially as darkness settled in because the floodlights on the return tower attracted schools of baitfish, which in turn attracted bigger fish...which meant there were often hungry sand sharks gathered in the water below. Their unmistakable streamlined bodies and protruding dorsal fins sending shivers through me long before *Jaws* ever traumatized a single beachgoer. Who needed the Ghost Ship when there were live sharks swimming under the Sky Ride?

Evenly spaced between the Sky Ride's loading platform and bay terminus were three tall support towers that fed the ride's thick cable out and back. Attached to the cable, hanging underneath of it about 15 yards apart, were the cars that people rode in. Consisting of a molded fiberglass bench seat and matching canopy, the Sky Ride cars carried a distinctly dated Space Age quality, and also an exaggerated impression of age thanks to the badly fading colors on the outer shells of the bench seats. After fifteen years of salt air and summer sun, their once vibrant shades of red, orange, and yellow were almost unrecognizable. Some cars appeared to have a hazy waxy buildup that no amount of elbow grease would ever rub off, while others had degraded into splotchy tie-dye patterns, as if they'd taken a bath in paint thinner. Overall the cars just looked unwell, like they had a fungus or some type of disease. But after two months in the park, I trusted that Moon and Melvin had sound reasons for not covering these flaws with a simple coat of spray paint.

Fortunately, there was nothing wrong with the interior of the cars, which still carried their original bright white color. Anytime I looked at an empty Sky Ride car, its smooth white seat contrasting with a tiny ridge of color from the car's exterior, all I could think of was the inside of my family's Coleman cooler chest.

I was leaning against the platform's railing admiring the strength of the ride's seemingly too-thin cable when Gabe began walking up the stairs. From my early days on the Antique Cars I'd learned that Gabe was a permanent fixture on the Sky Ride. It was his ride, there was no doubt about that. An adult in his mid-20s, he was my height but somewhat thicker around the middle, with angled bangs, ear-covering brown hair, and a thick brown mustache – it had probably been years since anyone asked him for ID. He also wore white tennis shorts that seemed a tad too short (this evaluation informed by my summer in "mandatory" tennis shorts at Phillips); had a well-established and continuous flirty dialog with every female in the park; and an overall demeanor that was...shall we say, slightly less masculine than average. Which didn't bother me a bit. He was a fixture in the park. Always a smile, always said "hello" to me, and always seemed to be having a good time working the Sky Ride. And of course, he had a big smile as he came up the steps.

"You look familiar, but I know you're new on this ride." said Gabe extending his hand.

"Earl Shores," I said walking towards him, offering my right hand while pointing to the nearby Antique Cars with my left. "Yeah, I worked over there for about two weeks before getting moved out to the go-karts."

"Go-karts?! How brutal."

"And this is my first night off the karts since June."

"Oh, my God...I'm guessing you wanted off?"

"Oh yeah," I said, shaking my head.

"Well, you're in for a treat tonight. This is about as far from the go-karts as you can get. Hope you're ready for a mellow evening."

Was I ever.

The Sky Ride loading platform sat just about dead center in the park. It was a large waist-high concrete rectangle dominated by three light blue support towers. Maybe ten feet tall, the thick metal towers bisected the platform longways, with a pair at the back anchoring the ride's horizontal drive wheel, while a lone tower with four in-line pulleys sat on its western front edge to feed and receive cable from the taller support towers out in the park. Gabe and I were standing on the loading side of the ride, which faced out to the south midway. On the other side, facing the northern midway, was the exit side of the ride. Other than the three towers, everything was wide open between the two halves of the platform, with the loading area being just a few steps over from the exit area. Gabe moved toward a grey electrical box on the next to last tower and pulled the cover upward, throwing a lever in the box that switched on the power for the ride.

"And now to get the ride up and moving," said Gabe, returning to where I stood while reaching for the oversized green "ON" button that peeked out from a small rectangular grey switch box on the railing. (Just below the green button was an identically-sized red "OFF" button.) At Gabe's push the Sky Ride's engine came to life, filling the air with a vibrant electrical hum that was immediately followed by a rhythmic and steadily speeding "ffht-ffht-ffht-ffht-ffht" as the horizontal drive wheel began rotating overhead, moving the cable and a formerly dormant Sky Ride car past us in the loading area.

"There's another switch on the other railing," said Gabe pointing to an identical switch box straight across from us on the exit side of the platform. "If there's a problem, say something and I can hit the switch. Or hit the switch yourself."

I nodded at Gabe to acknowledge his instruction.

"Otherwise, the ride's pretty simple. The riders follow the footsteps from the stairs to the loading position, the car scoops them up, we make sure the safety bar goes down, and off they go into to sunset. Isn't that an amazing view?" asked Gabe, staring out onto a glowing 180° bay-framed panorama that featured the mini-golf course as a centerpiece, surrounded by a clockwise array of the Bumper Cars, Hurricane, Rotor, Scrambler, Airborne, Monster Mouse, Ghost Ship, and finally the Tilt-A-Whirl, which sat below us just off to the right of the platform.

"Yep, it really is a sight for sore eyes. I haven't seen a sunset in the park for a long time. And never one from a spot like this."

"Oh my God, that's right! You *are* in for a treat. And it just gets better as the sun goes down. I love it up here."

"I can see why."

"You can start the night as the exit guy. When the cars come back, you just pull up the safety bar, tell the riders to follow the footsteps, and make sure they exit off the platform as the car makes its turnaround over to me. Sounds pretty boring, huh?" said Gabe with a sly smile.

"Actually, it sounds absolutely perfect."

Made all the more perfect as the speakers from the nearby Top 40 Club eased into the orchestral opening chords of Christopher Cross' "Sailing." After weeks in the exhaust shrouded maelstrom of the go-karts, these were the calmest Playland waters I'd sailed in for a long time. Gabe got the evening officially underway by pulling a pair of Ray-Ban aviators out of his back pocket and casually slipping them on, a fitting and fashionable preventative measure for an evening that would mostly be spent facing out into a steadily setting sun. Following Gabe's lead, I pulled my similarly styled sunglasses out of my backpack and instantly we were two cool guys running the Sky Ride. And I did feel cool up there like I was center stage in Playland with the sun as my personal natural spotlight.

We had a relaxing start to the night, as most of the early guests walked right by the Sky Ride on their way to other rides. And I was amazed to find that, yes, people did come into the park and play miniature golf. This was easy to see as I had a direct view of the first hole, straight out from my position on the platform. Finally, a trickle of riders began coming our way. And Gabe was the ever-considerate host, having an easy patter and a variety of greetings that made everyone who got on the ride feel a little special.

"C'mon up, c'mon up. How y'all doing tonight? Good, good, now just line your feet up in the footprints there...here comes the car...get ready, get ready...okay, now here comes the bar...off you go!"

He was effortless in directing traffic, sizing up family groups and suggesting how they might want to divide up to get on the ride. (The Sky Ride cars held two adults, an adult and two kids, or three if the passengers were all kids.)

"You want to ride together mom and dad, or ride with the kids? No rush, there's another car coming right behind this one."

And the cars did keep coming, at a leisurely pace that I genuinely welcomed. Gabe set such a positive tone, it was so obvious that he enjoyed every second on the ride. I tried to hold up the vibe on my side and interact with the guests, although I was pretty much relegated to "bar is coming up" and "follow the footprints to the stairs." But the key was, I was willing and wanted to do it because I was enjoying myself in the park again. The change in how I felt from when Greg and I pulled into the parking lot earlier...how was it possible for my thoughts and emotions to shift so dramatically in such a short time? From what would outwardly appear to be a "simple" change?

Like yeah, big deal, I was just running a different ride. But it was *so* much more than that. It was like I'd punched through to some alternate plane of reality, landing back into the "FUN" dimension of Playland. It was fun watching young kids get off and try to match their stride to the adult spaced footprints painted on the platform, just as it was fun watching a parent and child both try to hit the footprints as they headed off the ride. Even adults would sometimes giggle and do some form of "scurry" to the stairs. It seemed to be half the fun of the ride.

But within the fun and relaxed atmosphere I made sure to keep a sharp eye on my side of the platform. In everybody's stretching, hopping, and sometimes running efforts to get off the ride – which I didn't dare scold them for because I'd done the exact same thing years earlier – I had to make sure that no one tripped into the path of the still moving Sky Ride cars. They didn't move all that fast, but the seats were substantial and capable of inflicting a serious knock to any head that got in their way. And I wanted to impress Gabe and be a good partner on the ride. The Sky Ride being "easy" didn't give me an excuse not to pay attention. What I had going for me after all of the time on the karts was that "focused" had pretty much become my default Playland mindset. Ingrained in me now was the fact that *every* ride in the park could be dangerous if the ride operator didn't do their job.

Still, a Sky Ride focus was a less intense and taxing thing than a basic go-kart focus. And I became aware that I was smiling. Naturally, automatically, reflexively, unconsciously, without even being aware that I was doing it. But how could I not be? I was so happy not to have the unceasing sputtering of single-piston engines echoing in my ears. The Top 40 Club playlist was just fine by me, even "Little Jeannie," which was still a park favorite after months of overexposure on KHI. And mixed in with the music were the other sounds of the park. The constant clicking of the Hurricane and Monster Mouse lift chains, the rumbles and squeaks of the Tilt-A-Whirl's clamshell-shaped cars as they spun in circles below me, and the random yet steady "thump" of the Ghost Ship's wooden doors as they were driven open by the "coffin" cars.

"Hey Earl, you doing alright over there?" asked Gabe during a lull on his side.

"Couldn't be better – and how am I doing?"

"You're doing just fine. This is a more relaxing way to spend the evening?"

"Oh yeah, this is...it's unreal. Wish I'd gotten up here much sooner."

"I'll get you on this side of the ride in a bit. I know you can handle it."

"Whatever you want. I'm absolutely fine over here."

A few minutes later Greg emerged from the back door of the Dairy Queen and caught my eye, turning his hands' palms up to pantomime "how's it going." I gave him a thumbs up, and a big smile, both of which he returned before returning to his soft serve obligations.

Gabe sent me on break first, so I made the short walk over to the Dairy Queen where Greg and crew weren't overly busy.

"What do you need?" said Greg, as I stepped up to counter.

"Nothing. Nothing at all. I'm just kind of dazed. It's fun again – the park is fun again."

"Yeah, what's wrong with that?"

"No, nothing...there isn't. But man, all that time out front. I was so..."

I felt a light tap on my right shoulder and turned around to see it was Mark.

"How are you doing? Are you good?" he asked.

"I'm great, I'm having a good time. Thanks. Thanks for the night off," I said, trying to tease out just how "off" the go-karts I was.

"No, you're off the karts for good. That's what you wanted, right?"

"Yeah, it is."

"Don't worry, I've got plans for you," Mark said with an oversized grin.

"Okay. I'd be happy right here for the rest of the summer," I said pointing over to where Gabe was loading up another car.

"Yeah, you could be. We'll see."

"Thanks again, Mark. It's fun tonight."

"Good. Good to hear you say that."

After Mark moved on toward the Hurricane, I did have Greg whip me up a banana milkshake, which I quickly sucked down before walking the five steps back to Sky Ride stairs, excusing myself past three cars worth of people before stepping onto the platform.

"He's back," Gabe yelled to a female employee whose identity was hidden by the support towers.

Gabe then turned back to me. "You can take my place now."

"Okay, sure. Are you sure?" I said, not feeling entirely sure.

"Heck yeah. If you sent those crazy go-karts out, this is a piece of cake."

"I'll do my best."

"Okay, Lindsay, I'm off. I'll be back to relieve you in fifteen."

"Thanks, Gabe. Take your time," answered Lindsay.

I did my best Gabe imitation in filling up the next three cars, asking each set of riders how they were and if they were having a good time in the park. The first two sets of adults seemed to appreciate my efforts, while the early teen pairing in the final car, to them, from the look I got, I was just some doofus ride guy. I'd have to ask Gabe for pointers on that scenario. With the entrance stairs empty, Lindsay moved up to a point on the platform where we could see each other.

"How are you doing? I wasn't sure you even worked here anymore," she said.

"Oh yeah, I still do. You just didn't look hard enough."

"I guess. So what happened?"

"I've been out front on the go-karts since June. Mark just took me off them tonight."

"Oh, were you there the night –"

"Yeah, that was me. I mean, I was mostly a bystander for that 'happening.' I got fried out there. I'd had enough."

"This is better?"

"Oh yeah."

Lindsay let a sort of sneaky smirk take over her face. Not that I knew her all that well, but it wasn't a look I'd seen before, or one that I even anticipated her face could make.

"Did Gabe tell you what happened here a couple of years ago?" she asked, lowering her voice several notches as she stepped across to the support tower in the middle of the platform.

"No, what?" I said

"The night this ride broke down?"

"Broke down? With people?"

"Out over the water and over the park. Oh yeah. The fire department had to come and get everyone down."

"Holy crap, really? That sounds crazy."

"Believe me, it was. Gabe took it hard. This ride is his baby."

"But he didn't do anything wrong?"

"Oh, no, no, no. The cable slipped off one of the pulleys. There was a loud metallic groaning sound, and then the cable just jammed."

"Man, how long did it take to get everyone off?"

"A couple of hours."

"Did the park close down?"

"No, not completely. We shut just down sections of the park as the fire company moved their bucket truck around the rides. They started here at the platform and moved car by car towards the bay."

"The people stuck on the ride must have been totally freaking out."

"They were actually pretty good about it. You should talk to Rick sometime, he was running the Rotor that night," said Lindsay pointing over to the fully lit and rocket-shaped outline of the ride. "The controls are up on the top over the barrel, so he was equal in height to the Sky Ride cars."

"Yeah, I can see...where somebody is standing up at the top of the ride there?"

"Yep. That's where the controls are. Rick spent the entire time talking to two girls who were stuck over the bay."

"Man..."

"Yeah, they had to angle the bucket arm out over the monorail track to get them. They were the last ones off the ride."

"I'm not sure I need to hear any more."

"You've got customers," finished Lindsay, pointing to the stairs on my side. Hopefully, these people hadn't heard too much of the conversation.

It wasn't long before Gabe returned and Lindsay moved on to relieve the young woman running the Tilt-A-Whirl. The last bits of orange had just dropped off the western horizon, leaving our platform illuminated like a concert stage thanks to four corner-mounted floodlights. Riders got sporadic as more of the night passed, but it was still a thrill to put people on the ride and watch their journey over the park, especially when they just seemed to vanish into the darkness once they moved beyond the boundary of the monorail track. Gabe was easy to talk to, as he was just as curious about the go-karts as I was about the Sky Ride.

"We go quiet as it gets later. Mostly kids and families ride the Sky Ride. Teens think they're too cool for it."

"Their loss. Not a bad thing?"

"Nah, it's fine with me. I just listen to the music all night and dig the view."

"Works for me," I said, looking out onto a scene of glowing and spinning rides that fulfilled every ride-running fantasy I'd ever had.

"You did good tonight, it was nice to have someone enthusiastic up here."

"Thanks, Gabe. This was definitely a new start for me. Best night in the park in a long time. I can't even begin –"

"I'm glad. Hope Mark gives us some more shifts together."

"Me too. Me too."

Chapter Thirty-One

Coaster

M ark was certainly keeping his word. Looking at the schedule, just 24 hours removed from my liberating shift on the Sky Ride, my eyes were again doing a double take as I again used my index finger to confirm that I was actually seeing what I was seeing. Moving down from the "Wednesday" at the top of the clipboard I found my name paired with "Dylan." And we were both in a slot directly across from one of my favorite words.

"Coaster."

The Hurricane might not have been in the center of the park, but it was Playland's centerpiece and most iconic ride. It had been that way since the gates first opened in 1965 when the newly built wooden coaster gave the park a defining feature unlike anything at Trimper's or Jolly Roger. And that still held true in 1980. There was nothing else like the Hurricane in Ocean City or on the entire Eastern Shore, with the next nearest wooden coasters being hours away in Hershey (PA) or Wildwood (NJ). So, the ride was still something special. And despite its compact size, at least in coaster terms, it was the largest ride in Playland and the largest ride in all of Ocean City, being a landmark that was visible from miles away on Coastal Highway, especially when the sun went down, and the ride's illuminated outline spilled into the 65th Street night sky. The Monster Mouse might have been the most thrilling ride in the park – its first drop was bigger than the Hurricane's – but it lacked the throaty rumble of a multi-car coaster train hurtling over a wood-framed track. Which to me was one of the most thrilling sounds in the entire world.

"Alright!" I said softly and reflexively to myself in the nearly empty employee lounge. Greg was off, so I'd have to share my excitement with him later, but just having a second consecutive shift inside the park, as opposed to an exasperating evening out front with the go-karts, that was a thrill all by itself. Then to top it off with the coaster...it was like a perfect drop into the biggest and best wave of the summer, carrying just enough buzz to have me excited yet still in control, with a full grasp of how significant this opportunity was. Because during those hopeless weeks inhaling go-kart exhaust a night like this seemed a pipe dream. But right now, turning onto the southern midway to take in the coaster's lift hill rising skyward against a shimmering backdrop of bay, fantasy had become a reality. My reality and I floated toward the immense wooden structure like I was locked in the eye of a tubing wave, totally focused and oblivious to all else around me.

"If you're walking into the park that must be a good thing?" asked Gabe, startling me with his question as he leaned against the red railing of the Sky Ride platform.

"Uh, yeah, yeah...it is. I've got the coaster tonight," I sputtered out in reply.

"Nice! Pretty sure you're working with Travis. Yeah, you'll have a good time there."

"Thanks. Yeah, I'm looking forward to it," I said, exchanging a wave as I continued my walk to the back corner of the park.

Although I'd been up on the coaster when Greg worked it, I'd felt like an interloper and had done my best to stay out of the way. Tonight, as I passed under the red-lettered "Exit Only" sign and stepped onto the orange boards of the long upsloping Exit ramp, things were different. I belonged here, I was going to be part of the ride. And looking up at the crisscrossing framework of sturdy yellow boards while sliding my hand along the waist-high orange railing on my right, I could see that the ride was a stunning piece of carpentry. Its original color had been the standard "roller coaster white," but then somewhere along the way that had been changed to yellow, with the accent color on the ramps, railings, and walkways now a Crayola red-orange.

Making my way up onto the enormous loading platform, which was probably the length of the go-kart track's backstretch, all was quiet, with the coaster train empty and awaiting riders as the flags lining the upper level of the ride pointed northward while flapping lightly in the breeze. The loading area was not only the biggest in all of Playland, it also sat at least eight feet off the ground and offered a stunning overlook of the west end of the park. But my eyes weren't drawn to the view, at least just yet. They were pulled down the platform to the lift hill, which angled high up into the wispy blue of the sky like a magic two-railed escalator. Due to the compact layout of the coaster the loading platform and lift hill were right next to each other, a cozy setup that left the coaster train usually needing a push to make it onto the lift chain. The coaster train itself consisted of three connected silver waist-high cars, each having three seats apiece with slanted backward rectangular openings that allowed the riders to get in and out of the padded red bench seats inside. Keeping the riders safe during their journey around the track was a backward "D"-shaped metal restraint bar that hinged down and locked over each seat.

I was admiring the purposeful design of the thick silver running boards on the sides of the coaster train, a feature that would prevent a rider's foot from sliding between the train and the platform, when Travis came up the Exit ramp. Thanks to Greg's early nights on the coaster I knew Travis well enough to say "hello" any time our paths crossed during a shift. There were a bunch of us in the park who, due to our indeterminate teen-to-twenties age, late summer tans, and park-required uniforms, all kind of looked alike. Travis was one of these people. He and I shared the same slim build, the same "average" slightly under six-foot height, and were probably the same age, give or take six to nine months.

His distinguishing features were dark curly mid-ear hair and a slightly darker shade of tan than I'd cultivated through my countless hours in the surf and on the go-karts. Somehow, I pictured him with a hat, but he wasn't wearing one tonight, so he'd started up the ramp squinting into the evening sun, his face scrunched into an awkward half sneer that had me a little worried. But his face relaxed into a smile by the time he reached me.

"Oh, you're Greg's roommate!" he said enthusiastically, which was a relief.

"Yeah, I am. Earl," I said, extending a right hand.

"It's funny...we've sort of known each other, but not known each other," he said with a laugh and a firm grasp of my hand. "Travis – welcome aboard!"

"Thanks, it's good to be here," I said, sounding like a slightly stoned rock star who couldn't remember what city he was in. Christ, was that the best I could come up with?

"Come on over," said Travis, waving me along as he stepped on the connector between the second and third coaster cars and hopped down onto the narrow platform on the other side of the tracks. I followed, climbing through and down onto the orange painted wood planking, which sloped slightly downward toward the lift hill. Travis continued walking to the base of the lift hill with me following along like a new puppy.

"This ride isn't all that hard to run, just a bit tricky. And the tricky part is this," said Travis, grabbing the orange chest-high wooden brake lever, a refashioned two-by-six that sat upright like a blade, its top having been shaved into a thinner handle section that could easily be grabbed and controlled. At the moment the brake was angled almost 45° toward the lift hill, which I presumed was the "on" position. Travis then went over to a gray electrical box, opened it, and flicked an L-shaped switch upward.

"The power is on now. There are 'on' and 'off' buttons for the lift chain," Travis continued, pointing to a smaller gray electrical box on the wooden railing near the brake. "The chain is always on as long as the ride is up and running. That way, if the brakeman misses the train...well, the riders just get another turn."

I nodded and watched as Travis pushed the green button to turn on the chain, starting up the familiar lubricated rattle created by the beefy playing card-sized brownish links as they moved up the hill. Also activated was the chain's pungent grease gun aroma, a smell that was familiar to anyone who'd ever ridden up a lift hill.

"Okay, let's take it for a test run," said Travis, pushing the brake lever forward to release the coaster train. Slowly it drifted past us toward the hill, the front car going slightly upward, almost catching the chain, but then leisurely rolling backward to settle just a little short. "Damn, I thought the humidity was down today. Oh, well, it's a pushing night. Go on over to the other side, I'll take this side."

"Back between the cars?" I asked, wanting to make sure I didn't do anything wrong.

"Yeah, don't step on the track if you don't have to. You'll have slippery shoes from the grease."

I stepped between the second and third cars and back onto the loading platform, then moved to the rear of the coaster train, grabbing the back of the last seat with both hands.

"Okay, it won't take much, and watch it when the cars catch. This thing's going to jolt away from us," said Travis.

"Okay. Ready when you are."

"One...two...three!"

With one good push, the cars caught the chain and started clanking methodically up the hill. It didn't take long for them to reach the top and release into the first turn, rumbling through a banked horseshoe-shaped left while giving our phantom riders a breathtaking view of the bay and the Route 90 bridge. Those riders got a quick glimpse of the ocean and Ocean City's beachfront skyline before heading into the Hurricane's main drop, a hill that almost reached ground level while angling back through the center of the ride to help form the layout's figure eight shape. Watching the empty cars accelerate down the hill was a rush because I could feel the entire structure vibrating under my feet as our imaginary riders thundered past and climbed into a banked horseshoe right turn at the other end of the ride. This pointed the cars back into the middle of the ride for a short dip and a camel hump, which bridged over the main drop and completed the "X" in the center of the figure eight. The coaster train "whooshed" by into the lower level of the ride, taking on a banked horseshoe left that wormed through an opening in the framework supporting the lift hill. From here the cars shot out into the open on a short back straightaway, negotiating a small hump before tunneling leftward back into the ride's sea of lumber.

I'd stayed on the passenger platform for the run and now observed Travis as he gauged the coaster train's movements through this final 180°. Just as there wasn't much distance between the loading area and the lift hill, there wasn't a whole lot of footage between the last turn and the loading area, Travis' definition of "tricky" now plain to see. He'd taken on a coiled posture, his right foot parallel to the track and nearly even with the base of the brake, his left foot pointing at the track and anchored flat on the wood planking. Both arms were fully extended, and his hands were spaced about a foot apart with a tight grip on the brake lever. The entire loading platform shook as the speeding coaster snaked toward us through a forest of yellow, and when the distinctive tri-head-light design on the front car appeared in the wood-framed opening at the head of the straightaway, Travis uncoiled, pulling the brake lever with his arms while leaning his body backward to get more leverage. A subdued scraping and slight squeal came from under the cars as they hit the brake plates and skidded a full 15-yards, coming to a dramatic halt just a few feet up from where I was standing. It all happened so fast that I wasn't sure exactly what had happened, other than the coaster had come to a stop. I looked over with a big smile at a now relaxed Travis.

"Ah, it wasn't bad for the first pull. I can do better," said Travis.

"Looked good to me. The rides are always more impressive when you work them."

"Yeah, that's true. I know this thing looks small, but it really is a fun coaster. We run the cars around twice because it is such a short ride. Don't want people to feel cheated."

"Who feels cheated on a wooden coaster?"

"Oh, you'd be surprised. Here, let me show you the lap bars," said Travis, waving me to walk with him up to where the coaster came to a halt. "Step through again."

I did as Travis said and ended up standing next to him near the front of the first car.

"You see anything out of the ordinary on this side of the cars?" he asked. It took me a second, then my eyes focused in on a tall, elongated triangle of thin metal pointing downward on the back corner of each car.

"Those things on the end," I said, pointing at the first car.

"Yep," said Travis, walking over to the train and pulling up on the triangle. "This releases the lap bars. Just pull up. They're spring loaded and retract right back down. Go ahead, do the other two cars."

I walked past Travis and pulled up on the oddly hinging triangles, hearing a set of almost simultaneous metallic clicks under and in the car. For curiosity, I pulled up the lap bar of the last seat in the train.

"Leave it up. If it falls back down it will lock again," Travis said hurriedly, making sure I didn't let the bar down. "Of course, you could just release it again. But when we're working, we don't need any extra complications in the routine."

"And just what is the routine?"

"You let them on, check the bars, and I'll send them out."

"And when the ride ends?"

"If you can undo the bars it makes my life easier. Then let them off, and get the next group on."

"I should be on this platform when the coaster goes out?"

"Not necessarily. It's easier pushing from the other side, and probably a little safer. See what works for you, it's not like we'll have a giant line."

"Okay, sounds good. Thanks, Travis. Let me know if you want something done differently."

"Don't worry, I will. Oh, and the bars on the third seat in the second car, and the second seat in the third car – they don't lock. So just play dumb when you check them."

"Uh...whatever you say. It's safe that way?"

"Yeah, this coaster's not rough enough to throw anybody out of a car. We do have a height limit so don't forget to check that. And they can be three feet tall and ride with a parent."

"Okay, will do."

With the lesson over I climbed back through the cars and onto the loading platform. It was subdivided by a second railing which ran parallel to the ride's main railing and allowed riders to be up on the platform as they waited for their turn on the coaster. This second railing had the "In" and "Exit" openings that I would tend to while letting people on and off, with chains across both openings keeping order until I took them down. In finally taking a moment...the view from the platform stopped me in my tracks. Although I wasn't in the center of the park like last night, the coaster platform was higher off the ground with wide open sight lines. Like last night, the miniature golf course was directly in front of me, being surrounded by the towering Rotor, the Scrambler, then the Paratrooper and the Monster Mouse, which both had the reflective motion of the bay as a blank canvas behind them. Straight across at eye level was the ominous skeleton face of the Ghost Ship, whose ghoulish gaze cast down on the Tilt-A-Whirl and the Hot Rods.

Then, looking beyond the perimeter fence and out into the openness of the bay...there was sparkling blue water stretching northward for as far as I could see, blending into narrow strips of mostly pristine and sandy land on the western horizon. Along the water's eastern edge were the numerous meandering back bays of Ocean City, dominated by green waist-high marsh grass and empty mazes of man-made canals that still awaited the arrival of a construction company's bulldozer. Closer towards Coastal Highway there were clusters of light-colored low-rise buildings along the southbound lanes, then the busy accumulation of multi-story buildings sitting oceanside, all of which appeared identical until I located the 9400 Building, where Ocean City's Condo Row just beyond was doing its best imitation of Miami Beach under the flattering yellowish hue of early evening light. As the multiple high-rises on the north end of the Gold Coast skyline blended into a jagged blur, the sophisticated guitar-piano interplay of Boz Scagg's "JoJo" came over the PA system.

Yep, it was time to go to work.

This was all that I had dreamed of during those humid back bedroom nights on Dorchester Street when my heavy eyes fought off fatigue while listening to the sounds of Trimper's Wild Mouse echo through the southern streets of Ocean City. Not that Gabe could have done anything more last night to welcome me back into the Playland fold, and not that the Sky Ride wasn't fun to work on, but the coaster was...well, it was a unique piece of Ocean City. A true landmark. And to be standing on its elevated platform getting people on and off the ride, this was the big time, the "major leagues" of ride running.

This wasn't work. This, whatever it was, was thoroughly enjoyable. Opening the chain to let people on, counting the riders, helping people get in the cars, checking the lap bars, letting Travis know we were all clear, then pushing the train toward the lift chain, watching the cars click up the lift hill...it was a thrill to do it. Every single time. And the sound! There was something exhilarating in just hearing the coaster out on the track, then having the cars swoop down the first drop and rumble past the loading area before ascending up into the banked turn just above where I stood. Not only watching and hearing the ride, but I also could feel it, the intense downward pressure on the structure as the coaster moved around the layout, reacting and moving to every force that was put upon it, reverberating under my feet like it was a living and breathing thing. After a while, I could tell where the coaster was without even looking at it. That's how precisely the ride's framework reacted to the motion of the cars.

Something else new I was getting in tune with were people's screams. There wasn't a whole of lot screaming, at least screams of excitement, on the go-karts or the Sky Ride (a ride where screaming probably meant that something terrible was happening). Every run on the coaster had a screamer or two, or three or four. Usually, it was female in origin, but not always, with the first hill being the lead scream generator. And the first hill, of course, produced the loudest screams, with both the intensity and frequency lessening as the ride went on. So just like vibrations, it wasn't long before I could guess where the coaster was on the layout based on the screams I was or wasn't hearing.

But the absolute best thing about the ride were the smiles on people's faces when Travis finally brought the coaster to a stop. Without fail, people were smiling and laughing when they got off the ride. There was just something magical about a wooden coaster, even one as small as ours, that made people happy.

Travis was incredibly skillful with the brake, slowing the coaster down just enough as it came through to start a second lap, catching the train for a brief second then letting the cars go without giving a hint of whiplash to riders. I had no desire to touch the brake lever, being totally happy just to be part of the "show" under the bright and strategically placed floodlights that did indeed illuminate the loading platform like it was an enormous outdoor stage. This was so much fun. Waiting for Travis to bring the coaster to a complete stop, pulling up the lap bar releases, following the riders as they got out of their seats and ushering them across the loading platform and off the ride, turning to let the next group in – my feet were barely touching the ground. In my younger days when I imagined being a ride operator, yeah, this was it.

It absolutely was.

Chapter Thirty-Two

The Original Playland

M arty's Playland was a fixture of just about every visit I'd ever made to Ocean City. In fact, Playland was such an essential part of my Ocean City experience that "disappointment" was the overriding recollection I had from off-season visits when the arcade was closed. Located on the boardwalk at the south corner of Worcester Street, it was Ocean City's original "Playland," beating my current employer to the name by at least two decades. It was also one of the resort's main boardwalk arcades, the other being Sportland, a neighbor and competitor located on the north corner of Worcester Street. Playland had always been my family's arcade of choice. The reason for this was never explained, but I presumed it was because we had a longstanding relationship with Mr. Gaffin, who ran the place and never failed to stop for a conversation whenever he saw my family. (And Marlene would always make a fuss whenever she was at the change counter.) So, spanning from my earliest stroller moments through my teen years – and hell, I'd even snuck down there a couple of times earlier this summer – Playland was a unique portal that linked my Ocean City past seamlessly to my present.

That's because, like Trimper's and the inlet beach, the white building with the tilting neon capital letters spelling out "PLAYLAND" had become part of me long before I had any conscious awareness of Ocean City. My amusement riding history started there, on the array of coin-operated kiddie rides that were seductively positioned along the edge of the boardwalk every morning. Where your local supermarket or discount store might have a single coin-op horse or boat in their front entrance, Playland's ride offerings almost reached double digits, making the arcade a coin-op wonderland. There were three different rocket rides, a tugboat, a speedboat, a galloping horse, a see-saw, an antique car, a mini-Ferris wheel, and a full sit-down drivemobile, all of which were interspersed among brightly colored soda machines, those instant photo booths with a pull-across curtain, and a glass-walled fortune telling machine with a mechanical gypsy woman inside. (I kept my distance from this thing, just as I did the mechanical laughing lady in the funhouse.)

The proof of my amusement riding career starting at Playland came in the form of some not quite-in-focus photos that my parents had of me, just over a year old, sporting a white bucket hat and a dumb look on my face, chained into the red seat of the miniature coin-op "Musical Ferris Wheel." This oversized tombstone-shaped contraption had a spinning circular interior section with a dancing clown figure painted on it. Once a coin was inserted the clown began turning slowly in a clockwise direction, moving the seat up and around the circular section as a speaker on the side of the machine played a garbled calliope version of "Wooden Soldiers on Parade."

My parents had other equally blurry photos that proved that I'd been plopped into the Western saddle of a frozen in mid-gallop horse named Sandy who rocked back and forth after being fed a dime. When I finally had enough awareness to make my own choice about these rides, I gravitated to the more exciting items on Playland's front line, like the fully detailed yet kid-sized Traffic Police motorcycle, and also the drivemobile, a 1950s vintage driving simulator with a full-sized steering wheel. The object of the drivemobile was to navigate a slot car-sized metal vehicle over a miniature rotating streetscape, turning the wheel to keep the car on the curving and undulating "road" in the glass-enclosed display that served as your windshield. For realism, the seat pivoted as you turned the wheel, with the machine offering a final verdict on your driving ability, ranging from "creeper," all the way up to "wizard."

After finishing with the coin-op rides it was on to the extended row of Skee-Ball machines inside, their sleek alleys and net-covered scoring areas taking up an entire wall of Playland's interior. There was nothing like standing at the end of the long upward sloping alley, dropping in a dime and pulling back on the thin metal handle by the coin slot, hearing the loud mechanical "frzzzeeet" and "clunk" that released nine wooden balls into the long open slot on the right side of the game. Then the rumble of the ball rolling up the green alley, finally going silent as it lifted into the air and landed, hopefully, in one of the small circular target holes with a "40" or "50" marking on it. (The machines would "ding" whenever a 50 score was rolled.) And all scoring throws were accompanied by the whirring "th-th-th-th-tink" of the game's tin score plates adding up your point total.

Sitting right across from the Skee-Ball machines were a gleaming row of Shuffle Bowl games, something that I really wasn't into, maybe because I still wasn't tall enough to get good leverage on the waist-high adult-sized alleys. Yet I still liked sliding the heavy silver metal puck down the sand lubricated surface and hearing the swift "kaarrunk" as the white plastic pins folded upward just before the puck thudded into the bumper at the end of the game and rebounded back to where you were standing. Something that I was into, in a big way, was the scaled-down bowling alleys that sat just a few steps beyond the Skee-Ball machines. Unlike Shuffle Bowl, where the dimensions of the games were designed for adults, these bowling machines were perfectly sized for an eight-year-old, being knee high off the ground (for me) and even having ball returns that sat at waist level. On the ball returns were baseball-sized rubber balls that you rolled down a short wooden alley toward a set of miniature plastic pins. The ball didn't hit the pins, it rolled underneath of them activating wire-like relay switches that made the pins fold back up into the game. Instructions printed on the alley helped you aim the ball, with red arrows and red lines forming "Strike Zones" on both sides of the head pin. A glowing glass backboard on top of the pinsetter kept score automatically, its number dials turning over with each throw as an unseen bell dinged with every spare and strike.

When my bowling was done, I'd move on to the mechanical cranes in the back of Playland. The prizes inside these games might have been cheap junk, but there was something wondrous about getting lost in the "forest" of tall and handsome dark wood cabinets, their large panes of rectangular glass all aligned together at the same height, giving the illusion that you were surrounded by an almost endless set of machines. And there was something about being able to crank the shiny silver lattice crane arm to just the right position and watch the machine's three-pointed claw drop dramatically downward to grab your "chosen" item as well as a few pieces of the colorful gravel from the bottom of the game. And then the anticipation as the claw retracted upward and the crane started its journey back to its original position over the drop hole...would the machine hold onto your prize or let it slip back into the game? The suspense, especially if you had a lucky "double prize pickup" going, was just about all an eight-year-old could handle. *C'mon, c'mon, hurry up, hurry up, drop it in the slot already!* Finally, the crane would pull back into a nearly complete upright position, and the claw would open, dropping your prize with a "clink" into the outward hinging metal drawer in the front of the game. Success! As junky as these items were, they would still travel home with you as prized catches from your Ocean City vacation.

Probably the coolest thing about Playland was that from a very early age I was allowed to wander around inside unaccompanied. An adult I was related to was always nearby, but I pretty much had the run of the place until my allowance ran out. Often, I'd find my adult keeper sitting with other adults on the padded stools in front of the *Pokerino* machines. Initially, this was an utterly mystifying game where grownups rolled small rubber balls down a slanted and glass-topped wooden alley toward a massive array of holes at the back of the game. Each hole represented a card value – there were 9s, 10s, Jacks, Queens, Kings, and Aces (six of each). When a ball landed in a hole, the card and the suit of the card lit up in white on the game's pale green glass backboard. The goal of the game was to roll a winning poker hand with the five balls the machine gave you on each play. Two pairs or three-of-a-kind were the minimum needed for a *Pokerino* "win," then you could get fancy and go for a full house, a straight, or a flush.

My perception of this being an "old person's" game lasted until I understood poker and finally sat down and dropped a few coins into a *Pokerino* machine, quickly discovering that it had the most generous ticket payout – tickets that could be turned in for the prizes displayed on Playland's walls and ceiling – of any game in the arcade. Turned out the grownups were actually pretty smart.

Another cool thing about Playland that I discovered over time was that you didn't really outgrow the place. As I got too big for the coin-op rides and started viewing Skee-Ball and the claw machines as baby stuff, I worked my way into the more "mature" games scattered around the arcade. I still didn't quite get pinball, but I was familiar with the pinball section of Playland because that was where the pitch-and-bat baseball games were located. These games looked like a pinball machine, at least from the outside, but they didn't have flippers and bumpers. Instead, they had a baseball diamond laid out under their glass top, with a retractable slot that pitched a metal ball to a bat inside the game. A button (or buttons) on top of the left side of the game controlled the pitcher, while a bat-shaped handle on top of the right side of the game made the bat swing. Two players could play the game – one to pitch and one to bat – or you could play it yourself, which was a perfect option for an only child like myself. The fate of a "hit" was determined by where the ball went within the game, hitting one of the target panels along the back edge of the outfield ("Single," "Double," "Triple," or "Out"), or elevating on a narrow metal ramp to land in the upper deck "Home Run" area. My favorite part of these games was the eye-level glass-enclosed miniature baseball stadium diorama in the back of the game. It sat underneath the backlit scoreboard with a complete 3-D infield of players, including a pitcher, batter, catcher, an umpire, and players that popped up and ran the bases.

That was pretty high tech for the mid-1960s, but I had no idea how much the arcade gaming world was going to change over the next few years – and how lucky I was to be just the right age to enjoy these changes as they happened.

Playland always had new games on display. Some years, especially with baseball games, it was just a different configuration on the field or a different way to get a home run. The basic parts of the game, the scoreboard, and the stadium diorama stayed the same. But the hint of new and different arcade "things" showed up one year in the late 1960s right smack in the middle of Playland's boardwalk front line. There had been shoot-em games out there in the past (both Western and military types), but there had never been anything like the giant naval battle game called *Periscope*. It was one of the biggest games in all of Playland, being as tall as a phone booth and almost twice as wide. On its front was a life-sized submarine periscope that overlooked a glass-enclosed 3-D ocean diorama complete with white-capped waves and naval ships on its surface. At the back of the game a variety of naval ships sailed continuously across the ocean's "horizon," with a player needing to sight one of these moving ships in the periscope and push the launch button to send a torpedo – which had underwater sounds and a lighted trail that you could follow across the ocean's molded plastic surface – toward the doomed ship. A direct hit made the ship disappear from the horizon with a flash and loud echoing "ka-boom!" I wasn't really all that good at the game, but I loved looking into the periscope and firing the torpedo. Another notable thing about the game was that it cost a quarter. Most games in Playland at this point could still be played for ten cents.

Also showing up around this time was a game called *Speedway*, which had an authentic three-point racing steering wheel, an accelerator pedal, and a backlit display screen with a race car that you drove around a perpetual track filled with other race cars. This was all new arcade technology, as was the revving engine sound that matched up with the position of the accelerator pedal. And you could even have an accident – no one who ever put a quarter into a *Speedway* game will ever forget the trashcan lid sounding "crash" and the vibrating "thacka-thacka-thacka" of the steering wheel as you waited for your car to get back in the race. Then it wasn't long before the insistent clacking of Air Hockey overtook all the arcades in Ocean City, and the popularity wave that *Pong* rode in on...I'd never seen anything like it. Even with the games being everywhere it was still hard to find an empty one to play.

But even as more *Pong*-like electronic games started showing up in Playland, a funny thing happened – I'd begun dabbling with pinball machines. *Fireball's* colorful and comic book-inspired artwork caught my eye, so much so that I couldn't resist playing the thing. And after a few turns...there was something about its spinning rubberized center disc and multiple ball play that intrigued me. I didn't have the usual "well, that was pretty dumb" reaction that my previous tries at pinball had generated. Somehow, this time it made sense. Listening to the sounds and actually "feeling" the machine, the ball being launched and dropping into play for a dramatic and almost too fast to see "ding-ding-ding-ding-ding" back and forth between the bumpers, the "clunk" of the flippers as I started to understand how they worked, not panicking when the ball got near them, catching the ball in the heel of the flipper instead of whacking it right back into play, relaxing and aiming for targets, saving "lost" balls by tipping them from one flipper to the other...and finally, experiencing the rush of a ball that seemed to stay in play forever, making the game ding continuously with each turn of the score dial...it was intoxicating. And really, really fun. I finally got pinball – and pinball had me.

From that point on, I'd played a lot of pinball. "A lot" being defined as so much pinball that I got to know what brand of game I liked to play. Bally and Williams were my preferred machines, as I'd try out any game they made, even searching in the back of Playland and Sportland for machines from the 1950s and 1960s as a previously unexpressed geek gene compelled me to have a "hand's on" understanding of pinball history. Playland also had a number of Gottlieb pinball machines, all of which had colorful and creative backglass images that made you want to stop and play the game. But no matter how much I tried, I found the Gottlieb machines extremely challenging. Their interiors were sparser with fewer bumpers and targets, and the overall play was slower, at least these were the impressions I always came away with. The patience needed to play a Gottlieb machine well...I just didn't have it. But they were still good practice for my favorite Bally and Williams' machines.

Pinball got a significant shot in the arm when the movie *Tommy* came out in 1975, thanks to a dramatic pinball showdown scene where Tommy (played by The Who singer Roger Daltry) defeated the larger than life Pinball Wizard (who happened to be played by the equally larger than life Elton John). Elton and his band had also re-recorded "Pinball Wizard" for the *Tommy* soundtrack, and the song became a radio staple during this time. Bally even came out with a *Pinball Wizard* game that had Daltry and co-star Ann-Margret on the front, following that up with a *Capt. Fantastic* machine that featured Elton John's Pinball Wizard persona on the scoreboard. All this publicity made the pinball sections of Ocean City arcades more crowded, at least for a little while. But for most people, the *Tommy* influence faded quickly.

Not that it ever mattered for me. Last summer I'd played *Flash* and *Fireball* after almost every shift at Phillips, making it the most prolific pinball period of my life. That meant I'd come into this summer looking for new challenges, and found one during my boardwalk outings in early June. Tucked in the back corner of Playland was a *Surf Champ* pinball machine. *Surf Champ* was a Gottlieb model with a glowing comic book-like surfing scene on its backglass, an image that I was entirely taken in by, even though the male surfers were outfitted in Speedo-type swim-suits. It felt "right" during the handful of games that I played on it, or so I thought. While I was pretty sure that the previous summer had readied me for almost any type of pinball challenge, I knew there was a distinct possibility that the surfing theme had me overlooking the usual Gottlieb pitfalls. To settle the matter, I wanted one more serious session with the game, something I'd have to squeeze in around work and the August crowds before Greg and I packed up the condo on Labor Day weekend.

And if I didn't get a clear answer about my pinball skills from *Surf Champ*, then, maybe it was finally time to drop a coin in the mechanical fortune teller.

Chapter Thirty-Three

Airborne

Experience the thrill of a parachute jump on the ever popular AIRBORNE RIDE.

This was a ride I'd been waiting for. It might not have been the most exciting thing in Playland, but for me, it was one of *the* rides I remembered from my earliest visits to the park in the mid-1960s. Maybe that was because at that time it sat on the edge of Kiddie Land, right next to the Antique Cars, in fact, leaving me transfixed as I suffered through my youngness and lack of height while making the rounds on the buzzing and honking umbrellas rides, the whip, and the kiddie coaster. But watching this ride rise up effortlessly to spin against the darkened Ocean City night sky, its cathedral dome-shaped center-piece pointing upward and lit in bright yellow, the "parachutes" above the swinging chairs all outlined in rings of white light, the smiling faces of the riders as they flew so high in the air...it was an image that was burned into my brain. I'd never seen anything quite like it. Well, maybe that wasn't totally true, I had seen something similar on the pier. But this ride, the Playland version, ran so smoothly and so elegantly that even my very young eyes knew that this was a better version of what was on the pier. Instantly it was one of my favorite rides, even if I couldn't ride it yet. And this ride, a ride that had once captured my imagination, I was going to be at the controls of it tonight.

That ride was the Airborne.

The Airborne was another Playland original that dated back to 1965. It was a more sophisticated version of the Paratrooper, a ride that had been featured on the pier during the 1960s and early 1970s. The pier's Paratrooper was a "fixed" model, meaning that its spinning wheel was already elevated off the ground and mounted on top of a sturdy metal support tower to its preset running angle. This configuration made the ride load like a Ferris wheel, with only a single car being able to sit in the loading area when the ride was stopped. So passengers had to wait until everybody else got off or on before their turn on the ride even started. A large throaty gasoline engine powered the Paratrooper, doing serious work to bring the ride up to speed, including a "medium" speed stage when the free-swinging umbrella cars swayed violently back and forth as they moved up to the apex of the ride and back down to the loading area. This jerking phase could be unsettling, especially your first time on the ride. But eventually the wheel got up to speed, and the centrifugal forces evened out, pushing the cars into a smooth sailing outward angle that made the ride a blast.

Witnessing the Airborne for the first time, I couldn't believe what I was seeing. It started off on the ground, that is the wheel of the ride was down and parallel to the ground with all of the hanging parachute cars accessible from an elevated platform that encircled the ride. This platform allowed Airborne riders to load on and off all at once, a significant advantage over the Paratrooper as no time and effort was wasted moving the wheel around to load or unload an individual car. The next design advantage the Airborne had was that it got up to speed while still on the ground, making the cars go from stopped and vertical to moving and freely swinging in a transition that was so smooth that it was hard to notice the ride's increasing speed. Not to mention that this was all accomplished with a discreetly humming electrical motor that moved the ride with ease. Then came the final movement, when with just a little more electrical humming a pair of hydraulic lifts pushed the Airborne's long metal support arm upward, dramatically elevating the counterclockwise spinning wheel into the air at a 45° angle as the cars maintained their outward pointing angles. I swore that at the top of the ride the cars swung up beyond vertical, something that I'd never seen on a Paratrooper. Then after a few minutes, the ride lowered back down just as smoothly as it had moved upward. And once in the down position, it would gradually slow until the cars all came to a gentle stop. From the very first time I saw the Airborne, I thought its choreographed sequence of movements was magical. And all these years later, even in the age of looping roller coasters, I still loved watching the ride (and riding it, too). It was a mechanical marvel. So much of what it did...well, it just all made sense.

My opinion of the Airborne being a great ride was undoubtedly colored by nostalgia. And it probably was an antiquated notion to have in 1980, as evidenced by the Airborne's current location in Playland – stuffed behind the Scrambler up against the western edge of the perimeter fence. Or maybe that was the only place the ride would fit when the park was reconfigured sometime in the early 1970s. (The Hot Rods, with an expanded track that ran behind the Ghost Ship, now occupied the Airborne's original location.) Overlooking the bay, it really was a beautiful location, giving the riders nothing but sky to look at as they spun upward over the main hill of the Monster Mouse.

After seeing my assignment on the clipboard, I'd thoroughly enjoyed my walk to the ride, saying "hi" to Gabe as I helped Greg open up the front of the Dairy Queen, then getting a "bummer, you'll have a good time" from Travis after stopping to let him know that I wasn't helping him run the coaster tonight. Finally, I felt like I was part of the park. And it felt so good to shed the social limbo of the go-karts. Late *was* better than never, especially considering that for most of the summer "late" seemed beyond the realm of possibilities.

Grabbing the Airborne's waist-high chain link "IN" gate, I exchanged waves with the tanned and pony-tailed blond over at the Scrambler, who I knew by sight but not by name, and then walked up onto a small elevated area that was attached to the ride's circular loading platform. This auxiliary platform was where the Airborne's control booth sat. (Yes, my own personal control booth!) It looked like an oversized phone booth, about the same height but with slightly more square footage inside. A side entrance with no door faced out to the park, with the bottom third of the booth being wood-paneled and painted white. Decorating these outward-facing white walls were large diamond-like geometric designs, done in red and seeming to illustrate speed or movement, or something. The upper parts of the booth were painted brown and blue, framing a plexiglass front window that looked out onto the ride, a partial side window that looked out to the bay, and a sliding screen back window that made sure the ride operator didn't suffocate.

Inside, a narrow wooden counter sat just below the front window. There was a cutout at the counter's midpoint, and protruding up through this opening was a gray metal control panel. About the size of a shoe box, the control panel was mounted on a metal post that came up from the floor, and attached to both sides of the post were thin, counter-high metal handles, the left one having catch points and a release mechanism. But the coolest thing in the booth didn't have anything to do with the ride controls. Sitting against the back wall was a gray metal stool. This would be the first ride I'd ever run where sitting was an accepted part of the job.

I put my backpack down next to the doorway, purposely on the outside as I didn't want to be presumptuous about taking over the booth before anybody showed me how things worked. Then I stepped out onto the ride's loading platform, noticing that its surface was actually a handsome deck made from stained and parallel wooden planks. In addition, the platform's circular shape was created by dozens of straight segments with angled edges, and these segments were pieced together around the ride like sectional furniture. On the inside edge of each segment there was decorative metal fencing, purposely placed to keep curious or careless riders from wandering into the circular opening that the support arm moved in and out of during the ride. It was a unique setup, unlike any other ride in the park.

I couldn't help myself from wandering around the platform, counting the cars as they hung motionless over the planking, their latticework metal parachutes high enough off the ground so I didn't have to duck when I walked under them. I was up to four in my count when, without thinking, I looked up and out over the bay.

It was a clear view all the way across to the other side, a full 180° early evening vista of Assawoman Bay. A few small fishing boats were still bobbing in the evening sunshine, partially backlit on the water that sparkled like it was overlaid with diamonds. And to the north, where the green of the western shoreline turned into the jagged blue openings of distant coves and creeks, a speeding Sunfish moved swiftly southward on the power of its rainbow-striped sail. Damn, it was beautiful

here. And peaceful too, at least with the park still mostly quiet and waiting on our opening song. Sure, the Rotor was just a few steps away on
my left, and the Monster Mouse was only a few strides around the platform to my right, but for the moment, neither of them was in my view.
What a place to spend the night, a fantastic spot even if I wasn't working.
And that I was getting an entire shift here...holy hell, had I died and gone
to heaven?

The skidding sound on the nearby pavement made it clear that I
hadn't. Looking over – and I knew who it was when the skidding started
– Moon and Melvin were parked in front of my ride. Their matching
smiles told me that they were already having a good night.

"Moving up in the world I see," said Melvin, who was at the wheel of
the cart tonight. "This is one of the best locations in the park. The view,
the breeze, and it's a nice ride."

"Good to hear. Yeah, it is really nice here," I said, stepping down off
the platform and moving toward where they had come to a stop just
beyond my fence. A pair of fishing rods extended off the bed of their
cart, and Moon was pointing to a plastic five-gallon paint bucket that sat
upright behind their seats. As I stepped over the Airborne's perimeter
fence, the white bucket rocked back and forth with an echoing "thump"
and a "splish-splash." I flinched, taking a quick step backward, and the
park's fixit duo got the laughs that they came for.

"Ah, they don't bite," said Moon with more laughter.

"Never know, they just might, especially if you were out in the bay
with'em," said Melvin, turning to look back over his seat into the bucket.
It tipped back and forth on its edges again, and moving closer I saw a
gray tail, a gray dorsal fin, and then another tail flipped over and
splashed into view. A pair of small sand sharks were in the bucket.

"Dinner?" I asked with a grin and a smart-ass upward inflection of
the word's final syllable.

"Dinner, he said," repeated Melvin looking over at Moon. As usual,
they were having a good time.

"These really ain't that good for eating," added Melvin.

"Yeah, they're nothing but cartilage at that size. Wouldn't even be
worth peeling the skin off. Could be bait for something bigger?" I said,
letting them know I knew a little something about fishing. Melvin turned
to Moon with a growing grin on his face.

"I told you this boy could probably fish, didn't I?"

Moon nodded and looked up at me while putting a Winston into his mouth – which he didn't light. There wasn't anything puzzling about that, but why in the hell had they been speculating about my fishing prowess?

"I need to ask you something," said Melvin, and I quickly sensed that my puzzlement wasn't going to last all that long.

"Your last name is Shores, right?"

"Yes. It is."

"You got any family down this way?"

Ah, that question again. Dave had caught me totally by surprise when he asked, and my reflexive "no" was completely honest. In my head, and in my everyday thinking, I had no relatives in this area. None were talked about, none were ever visited. And no one from down this way ever visited us. What I said to Dave – that all of my relatives were in the Philadelphia area – was true. But after Dave walked off and I took a moment to roll his question around in my head...yeah, I actually did have family down here. Supposedly.

Awkward was the only way to describe the current pause in the conversation. Doubly awkward because I never expected any interaction with Moon and Melvin to delve into serious territory. Sensitive territory, too. And I needed to come up with an answer. My "lie" to Dave had been an accident. What came out of my mouth I believed to be totally true. This, on the other hand, would be a deliberate lie. Maybe not a big deal, maybe just a little "white lie," one that would, for the immediate moment, make my life easier. But I wasn't a very good liar, and I wasn't going to feel very good about the rest of the shift, regardless of the scenic setting and the chance to run one of my favorite rides. I didn't have my sunglasses on, so maybe Melvin could see the battle going on behind my eyes. I wasn't sure where the conversation was heading, but throwing a lie into it felt wrong. I couldn't do it.

"I never met him, but my grandfather was originally from down here," I said, feeling a flush and sweat on my back.

"His name's Leland, right?" said Melvin.

"Yeah, it is."

"Weellll, what'a you know? We know Leland. He's out near Pittsville right now," said Melvin, as Moon nodded in agreement. "He drove trucks, big ones, and fixed'em too. But he's retired now. He also did some race car driving."

These facts were vaguely familiar. I couldn't swear who in the family had passed them on, as my grandfather, at least this one on my father's side was rarely ever mentioned, let alone talked about. That's why my initial answer to Dave had been so automatic. As far as my family was concerned, he just didn't exist.

"A helluva' driver. I seen him race a couple of times when I was a kid, at what was it...it was either the Loves or the Volunteer Speedway. Used to be up near Rehoboth."

"Yeah, I'd heard something like that about him."

"But you never met him?"

"Nope. Never even seen a photo."

Melvin went quiet, turning away from me as his chin dropped and the smile he'd maintained until this point drained from his face. Since Moon and Melvin weren't ones to leave space in a conversation, or to seemingly contemplate too hard on what they were going to say, the current silence between us was surprising. And agonizing. Finally, Melvin turned back with a thoughtful look I'd not seen before.

"That's too bad," he said, the playful tone gone from his voice. "Oh, well, you have a good night with this thing. Runs like a Swiss watch."

"Thanks, I will," I said, barely getting the words all out before Melvin hit the gas. Although I'd gotten used to being speechless whenever Moon and Melvin drove away, this was a whole different level of bewilderment. Complete and total shock was the only way to describe it.

With Moon and Melvin off and showing the "catch of the day" to the guys over at the Ghost Ship I was relieved to see Lindsay walking up to my gate. She had no idea how welcomed her presence was. Or how hard I was trying not to outwardly look like two guys with a bucket full of sharks in their golf cart had just told me the whereabouts of my long-lost grandfather.

Thanks to my comfort level with Lindsay it was easy to re-center and focus on her instructions for running the Airborne. The controls were relatively simple. In addition to the matching pair of waist-high levers, there were three large buttons on the control panel. Button No. 1 lit up yellow when pushed and got the ride going. Then once the wheel was up to speed, I pulled the right handle toward me, activating the hydraulics to lift the support arm into the air. When the arm reached its preset 45° angle, I pushed button No. 2, which lit up green and maintained the ride's speed while it was in the upright position. After I thought my riders had been on long enough, I pushed button No. 3 (it lit up white), and moved the right handle away from me, bringing the wheel back to the ground. My final step once the wheel was down was to push the left handle forward – it was the brake – and bring the ride to a complete stop. Then I set the brake and unloaded the ride.

I only needed a single turn at the controls before I felt comfortable with the ride. The other duties that Lindsay assigned were checking each car's restraint bar lock – yes, even the empty ones, because a loose bar would flap around during the ride – and see that the riders were distributed somewhat evenly around the ride. The balance didn't have to be perfect, but it wasn't a good idea to have four consecutive cars full of riders on one part of the wheel while leaving all the other cars empty. And the ride did have a height limit, although a less stringent one than the go-karts.

Once Lindsay said goodbye I was able to finish my counting. Twelve cars were hanging below the ride's wheel, each a sort of a rounded off version of a Ferris wheel car, minus the footrest. Tubular white metal formed the framework of each car, with sheet metal panels between the framing filling in to create an exposed exterior "skin" that was painted beige, red, or blue. (This coloring went for the entire car, with different colored cars alternating around the wheel.) The interior consisted of a padded bench seat, and additional padding all around the curved and enclosed backrest, with the color of the padding matching the car's exterior shade. A hand-width metal restraint bar hinged across the opening of the cars, designed to keep passengers inside and latch on the outside so the ride operator could walk around the platform and quickly check all the bars and locks before starting up the ride. Connecting the cars to the wheel was a thick fishing hook-shaped metal post that snaked down from the parachutes to the back of each bench seat, terminating in a large bolt that secured the post to the car's framework. At the top of the post, where the ride connected into the wheel with a heavy-duty swinging hinge, there was a rear mounted automobile shock absorber to even out the forces exerted on the cars. It was the most elaborate set-up I'd seen on a ride so far.

With the roulette wheel spin of thoughts from Moon and Melvin's visit finally subsiding, I heard the introductory cymbal crash and the ascending chord pattern of "Misunderstanding" ring out from the PA system. Finally, we were open. The song had been getting a lot of play over the last month, and I did like it, initially at least. But I'd kind of had my fill of the song at this point, having owned the *Duke* album since it came out in March. Although there were there certainly worse songs to start the night with.

Presumably, people were drifting into the park now. Being all the way at the back by the bay I figured it would take a bit for guests to work their way back here. Let's face it, nobody was making a bee-line for the Airborne. The Coaster and the Rotor, maybe, but people would get to my gate when they were ready. And to get ready, I'd walked over and propped my gate open as sort of a "welcome" sign, then retreated back to the opening of the control booth.

"Come on in, it's open," I said to a pair of lightly-sunburned early-teen girls who hesitated when they got near the gate. "Go ahead and pick out a car. It might be a few minutes, I want to see if we can get a few more riders."

They didn't say anything, just smiled as they walked to a red car on the bayside of the ride, opening the restraint bar and hopping up into the seat. A father and pre-teen son came in next, getting the same "pick your seat" spiel that I'd given to the girls. Then quickly I had four sun-burned and early-teen boys, all apparently friends, and probably looking for a possible evening "pick-up" of the two girls already on the ride. And right behind them came a mother, daughter, son trio, the girl likely an early teen, the boy likely on the cusp of junior high.

"Can three go in a car?" the mom asked as they began climbing the four steps up to the loading platform. That wasn't something Lindsay had given me instructions about, but after a quick look over to the cars, it was pretty clear that three would be a comfortable fit.

"Sure can, easy," I replied, trying to sound as welcoming as I could. As the family began loading themselves into a car on the Monster Mouse side of the ride, I walked down to the gate and closed it, then headed back up onto the platform to check everyone's restraint bars. Walking up the stairs next to the control booth I could see that the riders had done a nice job of distributing themselves around the ride so I wouldn't have to ask anyone to move. The descending sun was directly in my eyes as I walked clockwise around the platform checking the locks, which entailed slowing down to grab and rattle the restraint bar to see if it stayed shut. As I got to the car with young teen girls, I noticed that they were both wearing flip-flops, which I could envision flying into the bay or over onto the Monster Mouse track. Here was another scenario for which Lindsay hadn't offered any instructions, but I'd been in the park long enough to improvise an answer.

"You might want to sit on them, or keep your toes curled during the ride," I said pointing to their feet.

"Oh, these?" said the braces-wearing brunette on the left side, holding up her feet while flapping her blue-soled flip-flops at the same time. "They won't come off."

"Okay, just giving a heads up," I said, noticing that both girls now had their toes curled tightly against the footbed of their flip-flops.

I moved on, finishing up the restraint bar check on all 12 cars, and was just about to duck into the control booth when I paused for a second and yelled out to the riders "Is everybody ready? Alright, here we go."

Sitting down behind the controls, I put on my sunglasses and I undid the brake lever, pushing button No. 1 which lit up to let me know the night and the ride were underway. As I watched the riders speed by, almost all with smiles and squinting into the golden glow bathing the ride...yeah, there was no question that this was my favorite night in the park. Working with Gabe had been great, I wouldn't forget my first night off the karts. And running the coaster with Travis had fulfilled many of my ride-running fantasies. But tonight, I was in complete control of a ride that was pretty special to me. All those years ago I did wonder how much fun it would be to run this ride. So I couldn't help but smile as I pulled the hydraulics lever and watched the Airborne rise into the air.

It was still a beautiful site – and an equally beautiful feeling.

Chapter Thirty-Four

The Spider

I'd tried to take in all I could from Aaron during my first two nights on the Spider. Just as Pat was the go-kart guy, Aaron was the Spider guy, or Spider-man if you wanted to be silly about it (a nickname that he didn't care for one bit). The shifts had been a blast with me doing most of the heavy work of loading and unloading the fluorescent green cars. Aaron had given me some time on the controls, and I ran the ride myself while he was on break last night. But I still wasn't sure I was completely ready for tonight's assignment – running the Spider all by myself on Aaron's night off.

Having Mark pencil my name into the Spider slot was flattering. I did feel like a park "veteran" at this point, with a hell of a lot more ride running experience than I had just a few weeks ago. And I'd been hoping for a chance on the Spider if for no other reason than I knew that Jack had run it during his summer in the park, including on a brutally hot day when he and his partner left some interesting hieroglyphics on the back of the ride's control box.

Playland's Spider was one of the first rides that guests saw upon entering the park, sitting between the north and south midways within a circular waist-high chain-link "pen" just past the Ferris wheel. It was an updated version of the Octopus, a ride that both Trimper's and the pier had in their amusement lineups throughout the 1960s. The Octopus was notable for several reasons, the first being that it looked like no other ride. Extending out from its center, or "head," were eight long red arms, each with a pair of white ladybug shaped cars on the end that could spin a full 360°. These arms not only moved up and down, but they also circled completely around the ride, creating a wavy forward motion to go with the independent spinning of the individual cars. Which brings up the other notable attribute of the Octopus – it was basically a motion sickness generator, like something NASA would have created to test astronauts before sending them into space. Although the ride had never taken me fully out, it had done in my dad, my mom, my aunt, and several childhood friends. Let's just say I wasn't disappointed when the Octopus eventually vanished from Trimper's and the pier. Our Spider did everything an Octopus did, including test your tolerance for motion, except with six arms instead of eight. (Yeah, the company making the ride seemed to have missed an Entomology lesson or two.) And the arms, instead of being straight, were curved to look insect- or spider-like. A pair of cars still sat on the end of each arm, giving me a total of 12 to look after on my upcoming solo shift.

The Spider was actually Playland's newest ride, a $90,000 addition that arrived in the summer of 1978 to be the park's featured attraction. (Ocean City's first Spider had shown up at Jolly Roger a few years earlier.) Of course, as something new, people couldn't help themselves from trying out the ride despite its fairly obvious nausea-inducing properties...which led to a fateful day in July of 1978.

In Jack's telling, it was a sweltering sunny afternoon, a day where shimmering waves of heat rose from Playland's midways to make the park feel like a pizza oven. The gates had opened early for a weekday corporate picnic, and a smoldering haze of Kingsford charcoal and pit-barbequed chicken hung in the air in a less than mouth-watering way. People were moving slowly in the stifling heat, sweat-stained and guzzling Solo cups of lemonade to deal with the oppressive conditions. Jack and his partner were only a few runs in when they had a rider decorate the interior of a car with an intestinal "abstract" of chewed chicken pieces, briefly closing the ride while Playland's cleanup boys came on the scene to disinfect and hose out the car. Then not long after the ride was up and running – oops – they had another rider paint the white interior of a car with his stomach contents. Once again, the ride was shut down to let the cleanup boys come out and perform their industrial disinfectant magic, expertly using their spray bottles to remove every spec of vomit out of the offending car.

During this unexpected opportunity to get out of the sun, Jack and his partner retreated to the employee lounge where they were "inspired" as only 18-year-olds working at an amusement park can be inspired. They decided to keep score of the riders who got sick, with the idea of also gently creating the conditions that would add to their tally. Just an extra minute or so of twisting and turning for every group that got on the ride. An added benefit of this strategy was producing riders who weren't physically ill, yet shaken-and-stirred enough to not bother getting on the Spider again.

By the late afternoon the cleanup boys had visited the Spider seven times, an unofficial Playland record that still stood as far as I knew. And there was no line, as word of the Spider's toll had spread quickly through the picnic goers. Hearing Jack's unassuming southern Delaware delivery recount this slightly twisted and somewhat incredulous tale made it seem all the more surreal...and hilarious. But Jack swore that this day really did happen, and the proof was in the marks etched into the Spider's control box.

So the first thing I did on my very first Spider shift was to look for these marks, realizing that it was possible that they may have been painted over since Jack worked on the ride. The control box wasn't hard to find, looking like a turned-on-end metal briefcase just inside the entrance on the north side of the ride. Welded to an oval metal pole it sat maybe 18" off the ground, making the top edge of the box about waist high. It was a heavy-duty setup, which it had to be, because the Spider's control levers were mounted on a metal plate on top of the box. After letting myself into the ride, I moved around to the back of the control box, kneeled down, and sure enough, scratched crudely into the paint was "7/19/78." Then etched right below were four vertical lines with a diagonal slash, and two lonely vertical lines that seemed to be waiting for company that would never arrive. Jack was no bullshitter, so I'd expected nothing less. And the next time we talked, I'd be sure to tell him that his "Etchings of 65th Street" were still intact.

I couldn't recall the last time I'd ridden a Spider, although there was a faded memory of bouncing up and down with Jolly Roger scenery spinning before my eyes. Jolly Roger still had their version of the ride, which was pretty much identical to ours except it had red cars instead of green ones. I liked Playland's better, there was something more diabolical about our fluorescent green, especially when matched against the white interiors of the cars. (The white being a functional part of the ride's design, keeping the car interiors bearable to sit on during 90° days.) As with all the other rides I worked on in Playland, the Spider was much more impressive from a ride running perspective than from a rider's perspective. To look at it, sitting on a white circular concrete slab that had been specially poured to create a level surface strong enough to hold the ride's elongated girder-like legs and the weight of its massive centerpiece – which seemed to be overflowing with manhole cover-sized gears and drive chains the width of motorcycle tires – the thing was a beast. And this was not even taking into consideration the long, curving muscular arms that did, in fact, look tarantula-like, at least in a 1950s horror movie sort of way. It was, without a doubt, the most mechanically impressive ride I'd worked on all summer. And this was before Aaron even turned the damned thing on.

While the Airborne's smooth and measured movements were like a gymnast swinging on a horizontal bar or a diver gracefully twisting and turning before knifing into the water with hardly a splash, the Spider was something totally different. All raw power and brute force, like a barrel-chested 300-pound weight lifter clean and jerking a 500-pound bar over his head. That's how I felt the first time I stood next to Aaron as he moved the Spider controls into the full "go" position. Watching the cars go from ground level to 20 feet in the air in the blink of an eye was spectacular. This ride was serious – and intimidating. A little later during my first shift, a parent leaned over the perimeter fence and caught my attention, asking "How's the ride?" I took a quick peek at the Spider as it bobbed and revolved in its yellow and green nighttime glory, then turned back to the man and rendered my evaluation.

"I wouldn't ride it," I said while still trying to sound like a polite and cheerful Playland employee.

"Thanks, I wouldn't either. But my kids will," he said with a laugh.

Aaron broke me in slowly on my first shift, having me load and unload the cars as he kept tabs on the "advanced" parts of the Spider – the line, how many cars were filled, how the cars were balanced, and actually running the ride. The loading part was more challenging than it looked, as the first thing I had to do once Aaron maneuvered one of the Spider arms into the loading area was pick which car I was working on – always the left one first according to Aaron – and physically spin it around so its front end was facing me. Then I could grab the thin ball-handled black lever that stuck out of the front of the car and pull it forward, releasing the front half of the car, which dropped down to let the passengers out. And this dropping of the front end was not just something that you stood back and let happen. You had to catch it and control it, bringing it down as gently as you could after grabbing onto a different black handle that ran across the top of the car.

A split open Spider car was a pretty ingenious thing because a rectangular cutout on the top, which looked like a wide white racing stripe when the ride was running, became an opening for riders to get in and out of the car. And the riders got help from two steps that were built into the nose of each car and only accessible when the front section was dropped down for loading. Another clever Spider component was a pair of tubular restraint bars that folded snugly up against the riders when the front section was pushed back up and locked into place. This permanently mounted pairing, which popped up like an oversized set of paper clips when the car was opened, gave the riders something to hold onto and kept them from sliding around on the car's slippery bench seat.

With the Spider being one of Playland's busier rides the first night was more of a blur than any other first night I'd had, including the go-karts. We were steady from the moment the park opened with things going something like this: Aaron brought one of the arms down into the loading area; I went over to orient and open up the pair of cars while Aaron checked heights and sent two cars worth of riders over to me (usually it was two people per car but, three could squeeze in for a snug fit); I loaded the riders on the car, asked them if they were "All set," then closed up the front end, hearing and feeling the solid "ker-thunk" as the car locked back together; I tugged on the front of the car for good measure to make extra sure the lock was fully engaged; repeat the exact same procedure for the second car; then with both cars locked and ready to go I stepped away from ride, giving Aaron a thumbs-up signal to bring the next set of cars down into the loading area.

Because Aaron needed to balance the ride, the next set of cars we filled may or may not have been on an adjacent arm. What got loaded next depended on our line. For example, if there were eight people in line, we loaded two cars on one arm (two people per car), and then Aaron moved that arm all the way around the ride up to the 12 o'clock position. The final four passengers then got loaded into the two cars on the opposite arm, which now sat in the loading area at the 6 o'clock position. So you needed to watch the line and calculate your next move, really paying attention to all that was going on, both on and off the ride. At least to run the ride properly, which Aaron took great pride in doing.

This was good for me, as I got to see exactly what it took to run the Spider. The night started to slow and come into focus as the loading process became routine, and I started doing my own calculations with the line to see if they matched Aaron's. I was extra focused and did a lot of listening early on because I wasn't sure Aaron and I were "clicking" on a personal level. We were getting along fine, but like Pat had done when I first showed up on the karts, Aaron seemed to be holding me at a distance while he sized me up – not that I took it personally. I sensed it from the moment I introduced myself and tried to "break the ice" by telling Aaron about the marks on the control box, which prompted a half-hearted smile, a brief look, and a forced "huh" that made it clear he wasn't overly impressed with my Spider history lesson. When he added that he didn't know or remember Jack, I understood that it was a night to put my head down, work hard, and do as I was told.

Through surfing and running the go-karts I was in top shape by this point in the summer, but my upper body was starting to feel all the repetitive spinning, pushing, and pulling I was doing with the molded fiberglass cars. They weren't overly heavy, it wasn't like you needed to be a bodybuilder to do the job. Yet doing the motions over and over and over...I wasn't used to it. Of course, when Aaron asked how I was doing, I had a single word reply.

"Fine."

Aaron returned from his break with a warmer vibe, as it seemed like he'd decided that I was worthy of being on the Spider. Not that he directly voiced a change in his judgment of me, but I did receive this invitation.

"After you finish there I'll show you how the controls work."

"Sure, great," I said waiting for a final set of passengers to load onto the ride. After pushing up and locking the front end of their car I went over and stood next to Aaron behind the control box.

Sitting side-by-side on a plate on top of the control box were two black metal levers, each looking the like the right half of a motorcycle handlebar. They were designed to hinge and pivot over two curved strips of sturdy upward protruding metal teeth, these teeth allowing the ride operator to "set" the levers into place when manipulating the motion of the Spider's arms.

Two levers...how hard could this be? Aaron was about to show me.

"The ride has a clutch, which you need to activate before moving either lever," said Aaron, hinging the right lever up from where it had been sitting in the most forward metal tooth on its curved strip. Then, with an underhand grip he began pulling the lever carefully back toward his body, making the Spider arms slowly move counterclockwise, picking up speed the further Aaron pulled the lever over the teeth.

"You've got to feel the thing and feather it along, you just can't yank it," said Aaron, in fact giving the lever a short yank, which made something in the spinning center framework of the ride groan unhappily. "See, it didn't like that a bit."

I nodded, wide-eyed and trying to take in all that I could see and hear as Aaron continued to pull the lever toward his body, guiding it over the semi-circle of teeth until finally, he gave the lever an extra little tug and lowered it down so that it locked into place behind the strip's bottom tooth.

"The speed is set now – we'll just wait a few seconds and let it come up a little more," said Aaron, which I interpreted to mean the ride was going to keep picking up speed and rotate faster.

"Now this lever," said Aaron hinging up the left one, which I noticed had more of an upward angle, allowing it to pass over the nearby right lever. As Aaron feathered this lever toward his body, the Spider began to change its axis point, meaning the "down" position of the cars was slowly migrating out of the loading zone and moving around the ride.

"Again, we've got the clutch to deal with, and look at the offset post – the thing in the center with the lit-up ball – that's what this lever is controlling."

High up in the center of the ride, moving gradually in a clockwise direction, was the Spider's offset post. Looking like an oversized pencil sharpener handle, it was mounted to the top of the ride and covered with a glowing globe of yellow and white light bulbs. And in looking closely I could see that the ride's arms, in addition to being anchored to the base of the ride, were also connected to the offset post just below the glowing globe. So as the Spider's arms moved counterclockwise around the base, the offset post moved in the opposite direction, its long metal support rods pulling the ride up and down as the distance between the arms and the offset post lengthened and shortened with each rotation. It was this unique movement that made both the Spider and Octopus the rides that they were, and put the "motion" into your sickness.

"Here, you can get this one going and secure the lever into place," said Aaron, moving a step to his right to let me take a position directly behind the controls, all the while keeping the lever tilted upward and in place until I got situated.

"Okay, take the handle – don't let it drop."

"Got it," I said, grabbing the lever with both hands, an underhand grip with my right, an overhand with my left.

"Now bring it slowly toward you...do you feel it catching?"

"Yeah, I think so," I said, feeling some resistance in the handle as the offset post continued to rotate slowly clockwise, moving the "down" side of the ride to almost directly opposite the loading area.

"Good, now go ahead and pull it all the way toward you."

The night sped up again, as did my heart rate, and my palms went clammy against the forged metal of the lever. There was a slight groaning from the clutch and more resistance as I pulled, then I hit the sweet spot and the cars high in the air to our left came swooping down towards the control box with such a sudden and forceful directional change that I almost took a reflexive step backward. And no sooner were the cars at eye level directly in front of us, then they were flung instantly 20' into the air above, the numerous lights of yellow and green on each arm seeming to leave trails in the night as they passed by.

"Some feeling, huh? Pulling the left-hand lever?" asked Aaron.

"Yeah, it's wild. The —"

"Power?"

"Yeah, I'm not sure I've experienced anything like it before."

"You haven't. And there's nothing else in the park that comes close."

Aaron was right about that. I'd had fun on every ride I'd worked on since the go-karts, but the Spider was different, not only in how it ran, but how it needed to be run. So being on my own with it for an entire shift...I was nervous. My feel for the clutch was still a work in progress, and I couldn't bring the cars down into the loading area like Aaron could with one seemingly nonchalant lever flip. This was his second full summer on the Spider, and I'd been behind the controls for probably a half an hour total. The comparison really wasn't fair. But I wanted to look like I knew what I was doing. Spending the night trying not to embarrass myself, that wouldn't be any fun at all. What I needed to do was take my time and relax. It wasn't a big deal if I had to gradually bring the arms into the loading area, as hell, without Aaron around to "show off" most guests wouldn't even know that I'd only been running the Spider for two nights. Just be sure to check everyone's height, make sure the cars were locked, and the ride was balanced. This night is what I wanted right? One of those I'd dreamed about for so many years?

Ah, maybe.

In checking out the ride before the park opened I was able to get some practice in, rotating each of the arms through the loading area to open and close all 12 cars. And I even got a full test run in without a hint of complaint from the clutch. So I was feeling pretty confident by the time the synth-heavy opening to Kim Carnes' "More Love" cascaded out of the doors of the nearby Top 40 Club. We were open – and I was ready.

I only had three arms full on my first run, a leisurely start that I was grateful for. The clutch again stayed quiet, and it was still a thrill to pull the Spider's left lever and watch the cars bounce and swoop through the air, the full ones spinning more than the empty ones thanks to the weight of the riders. It was an uneventful three minutes, and when the time was up, I eased the offset post around to get the cars down in the loading area, then pulled up the right lever and pushed it forward to bring the ride to a stop. Wow, I did it. Not that it was easy, but if I trusted myself and had a light touch on the levers, this night would be okay. Now for the next challenge – loading and reloading the ride. I was well practiced at getting people off and showing them the exit, that went off like clockwork, but now, going back to the "IN" gate for the next set of riders, this was a new part of the routine. Heights were all good, loading and checking the cars, okay back to the controls. Check the line, feather the right lever to bring the next arm into place, and repeat the process all over again. And again. And again. And again.

Before long, my line was long enough to make things easy. Well, maybe not exactly easy, but the decision making was out of my hands as every run was going to be a full load. That meant I needed to keep serious track of which riders were the first and the last ones on, not the easiest task with 24 different faces spread around the ride. Although I wasn't overly worried, sure that any "forgotten" car would let me know they needed to get off before enduring back-to-back sessions on the Spider.

As darkness settled over the park, and it was coming earlier now than it had back in June, I was in control. Sort of in a groove, sort of comfortable, and in a place where I was confident and really starting to enjoy the night. It had taken all the focus I could...well, focus, to reach such a point. Including making sure that each group of riders got just about three minutes on the now fully illuminated ride, whose constantly moving green and yellow lights created a glowing circular island in the middle of Playland. Three minutes might not sound like much, but Aaron warned me that leaving the ride going any longer could be a problem. A four-minute run, he said, put the riders in the "danger zone," without needing to elaborate about the exact danger the riders were being exposed to. I'd been diligent with my timing, checking my watch as soon as the offset lever was locked into place, and then stopping the ride's up and down motion right around the three-minute mark, having gotten a good feel for three minutes during the previous two shifts. Things had gone smoothly despite having full loads, with nobody even being disqualified by the height limit.

And time had flown by quickly. It was already 8:30 pm and almost time for my break – I couldn't wait to tell Greg how well things had gone, especially after bringing this current group down almost perfectly into the loading area. Man, that was a good one. I felt like I belonged on the ride, like I'd been working it all summer. Then, as the arms came to a complete stop, I was startled by a series of taps on my right shoulder.

A chill shuddered through me despite the humidity of the night, and I turned to find myself face-to-face with a man, apparently a father, with an unsmiling and a concerned look on his face. He didn't say anything, leaning over the railing while reaching his outstretched right arm around me to point up at the ride, guiding my eyes to the car up at the apex of the ride, a position that was as high off the ground and as far away from the loading area as any car could get. I didn't understand what I supposed to see because the car was facing away from us and bathed in the ghostly green of the Spider's fluorescent lights. I squinted into the night sky as the car gently rocked to a stop, then turned back to the man, my eyebrows raised, feeling the moment extend out like an uncomfortable eternity as my nervous system ratcheted up into a gear I hadn't used since walking out with Dave for the parking lot showdown.

"He's sick," the man said calmly, but directly.

"Oh, okay, right. I'll get'em down," I said, feeling relieved that it wasn't something worse – but also bad that I felt relieved about somebody being sick. I held up my left index finger up indicating that I needed a moment, then ran over to the pair of cars that I'd just proudly placed in the loading area.

"There's someone sick on the top of the ride, I need to get them off first," I said, turning away before they had a chance to respond, making a sprint back to control box where I grabbed the right lever and moved the arm with the sick rider down into the loading area. In the slowly rotating car on the left was a pre-teen trio of boys, all so stricken looking that I couldn't tell which one had gotten sick. Then, realizing that if the sick one had hurled well before the three-minute mark as the ride was still bobbing and weaving through the air...the thought made me a little queasy. Arriving at the car I took a breath and grabbed the ball-handled release lever, dropping the front section down, and out wafted a foul and sour smelling cloud – like a Dairy Queen trash can at the end of a hot day – that made me gasp and take a deep sideways inhale that I planned to hold in for as long as I could.

The yellow t-shirt of the dark-haired boy sitting in the center of the car was stained and wet down the front, and he kept his hand over his mouth as he stood up and jumped out onto the ground, his friends contorting their bodies sideways while staring off into some alternate dimension beyond the fetid confines of the car. I couldn't tell how much collateral damage they'd taken, and to be honest, I was trying not to even look. But I couldn't help notice that the stricken boy's black low-top Converse were wet and glistening, the white rubber toe caps covered with small pale pieces of what looked like chopped clams. I fought off a dry heave as he jogged toward the darkness of the exit, then turned back to the car to help the other boys out, focusing only on their pale faces because I really didn't want to know the volume of vomit still sloshing around in the car. The other boys exited without saying a word, hurrying over to the exit gate with me following close behind. Just beyond the fence the boy in yellow was being consoled by the man who tapped me on the shoulder, and as the other boys went out to join them, the man turned toward me.

"He'll be alright, thanks for getting him off."

"Sure, sure. You're welcome – I'm sorry. I can get somebody, there are paper towels over in bathrooms," I said, pointing the Men's Room entrance next to the Top 40 Club.

"Thanks. We'll be okay," said the man, before they all walked off gingerly toward the benches in front of the Antique Cars.

Returning back to the still open car...there was something dripping out of the bottom of it. I turned my head away and grabbed the car's front handle, hoping not to feel something wet on my fingers as I closed up the car. Luckily, I didn't, although I didn't linger around the dark spot on the concrete, moving immediately over to unload the other car, apologizing for the delay in getting them off. Obviously, I didn't load anybody onto the ride, and once back at the controls I made an announcement to my line.

"After I get everybody off I need to clean up the ride, so it's going to be shut down for a while. Sorry."

"How long?" came the question from a heavily shadowed face along the ride's fence.

"Shouldn't be long. Maybe twenty minutes or so. Sorry."

I finished unloading the ride, then brought the vomit-marinated car down into the loading area, again telling some just arriving line stragglers that the ride was closed for now. It didn't seem right to leave the things unattended, so I stood outside my gate scanning the park for Calvin, Lindsay, or someone official, when I spotted Jason walking toward me carrying the broom and long-handled dustpan he used to sweep up the trash in the park. Being one of our cleanup boys, he was just the person I needed to see. And I was happy to see him, too. He was a nice kid, very tan, very blonde, and was way too polite with subadults like me.

"I need your help," I said as he got closer.

"You got a sick one?"

"Yeah, the car on the left."

"Let me take a look," said Jason as he opened the gate to go inside the ride. We both walked over to the car, and I again took a deep breath before grabbing the ball-handled lever to drop down the front section. I couldn't believe it when Jason stepped right up into the car, then turned around with his smile still totally intact.

"Looks like chili to me," he said, giving me more information than I needed, my brain diving in to stifle the dry heave that my body wanted to perform. I fought for a long second to keep my composure, and my stomach contents where it belonged.

"I'll go get the hose," said Jason, unwittingly diverting my attention from the wave of nausea that mercifully didn't break.

"What do you need me to do," I finally asked after a hard swallow.

"Nothing at all. I'll take care of it."

"So, I'm down until you're finished?"

"Yep."

"And you don't need me hanging around?"

"Nope. I'll find you when I'm done. Enjoy your time off."

"Sure, thanks," I said, thinking the cleanup set up was too good to be true. Especially if you did it seven times during a single shift.

Chapter Thirty-Five

Big Wheel

"Whatcha' got tonight?"

That was the running joke now with me, Greg and Gary. Checking the schedule had turned into a pleasant mystery, as I'd become Playland's "fill-in" guy. If there was a short-term vacancy on a ride, I'd fill it, with seemingly no rhyme or reason to where I ended up each night. Not that I was complaining. As long as I never saw "go-karts" penciled in next to my name – and my go-kart days were now a far-off distant memory even though I'd only been off them for a couple of weeks – I was happy. Tickled even, the summer was definitely finishing on a high note. It turned out that all I needed was a change of scenery.

Mark had been leaving my slots blank during the week, presumably filling them in during the day whenever something unexpected came up. So, most nights were a surprise, which I didn't mind at all.

"It says 'Ferris wheel.'"

"Wow, that's a new one," said Greg.

"Wasn't really on my list, but I'll take it."

"Man, you'll run them all by the end of the month."

"We'll see. There are some that I don't need to run if you know what I mean."

"Yeah, I know. There are some I wouldn't want to do either. I'm not that far away from you tonight, so I'll come check on you later."

"Thanks. Talk to you in a bit."

The only downside of being the fill-in guy, and it was a minor complaint that I'd only ever voice to Greg, was the social part. In bouncing all over the park I wasn't developing a "got-your-back" partnership with anyone like the guys on the Mouse and the Ghost Ship had, or like I'd had with Pat, the one thing I did miss about the karts. Everybody was always super nice, but it was a given that I was just passing through. I was really hoping to stick on the Spider. Those three glorious and tantalizing nights on the ride were the high points of the summer. I wouldn't trade them for anything.

The Ferris wheel might not have been on my "must run" list, but it still fit my ride requirements at this point. People got on, and after I closed the restraint bar, they were just passengers along for the ride. The on and off, the stops and starts, were all under my control. The Ferris wheel fit this to a "T." And how hard could it be to run the thing, anyway?

The ride was located just inside the main entrance directly behind the Lord of the Lot, purposely centered between the north and south midways to be the first thing you'd see upon entering the park. This might sound like a prime location, but in actuality, it was kind of a weird spot. That's because it was easy to walk right by the Ferris wheel, even as an employee, without noticing the thing. Yeah, you'd think it would be hard not to notice something rising up behind the jester, yet the location was isolated, at least in terms of Playland's rides. Nearby but not in Kiddie Land, and several football fields removed from the "thrill" section by the bay, the Ferris wheel sat all by itself at the front entrance. Almost an afterthought, as people entering the park didn't usually get their bearings until they'd walked past the ride. It took commitment to ride Playland's Ferris wheel because you weren't going to accidentally stroll by it once you were in the park.

I split off from Greg on the southern midway walking past the Spider and the games of chance before making a left at the short metal fence that encircled the base of the ride, noticing for the first time this summer the "IN" and "OUT" gates that formed a small "Y" at its entrance. No one was around as I entered the ride, but I knew that somebody would soon be along to show me how things worked. That had been the routine since I'd gotten off the karts, which were now just off to my right. Standing under the Ferris wheel, looking over to the go-kart entrance, yeah, I had some serious pangs of guilt about abandoning Pat.

We did still talk, but I think he took it personally that I wanted off the karts. I think he tried to understand that I'd reached a breaking point, but I'm not sure he really did understand.

On the other hand, as harsh as it sounded, I didn't really care. I was so much happier now – coming to the park was fun again. Most nights I had something entirely new to figure out, and I was getting a crack at running the *real* rides, or at least some of the rides I'd always dreamed of running. It was exactly what I signed up for, and all that I hoped it would be when I first slipped a Playland shirt over my head in Mark's office.

As my go-kart guilt drifted off on the night's pleasant northeasterly breeze, I discovered that straight ahead was a camera viewfinder perspective of the parking lot, framed by the back of the Playland sign and a pair of parallel monorail supports. But it was an obstructed view as ten-yards dead ahead was one of the towering light poles that were spaced like illuminated vertebrae down the spine of the park. And just beyond that pole was a trio of support posts that snaked up to the heels of the Playland jester. I'd never noticed that he had extra help to keep him in place on the sign. I'd also never noticed how much of the view from the Ferris wheel consisted of the jester's red-striped backside.

In looking at the ride, it was a deceptively large structure. I mean, it had to be to do what it did, moving people up and around an enormous steel circle. Yet I was still taken aback by its size. Getting on and off quickly as a rider didn't give you a sense for how substantial the ride was. No doubt my experience around the park the last couple weeks helped me put the size in perspective. Gazing up at the wheel's bewildering silver web of angular metal and crisscrossing cables...I was totally in awe.

The ride was taller than the nearby light pole, and heck, it was even taller than the hat of the jester. There were one, two, four, six, eight...twelve cars on the wheel, alternating in a four-color pattern of red, green, yellow and blue. Within the wheel, a ring of long slender beams had been adorned with white fluorescent lights that would be visible all along Coastal Highway when I switched them on later this evening. And within this ring a series of diagonally-mounted metal support pieces angled themselves into a six-pointed star, its spinning yellow fluorescent outline soon to cast a celestial glow over the front of the park. Holding all of this up was a pair of tall erector set-like lattice girders that cradled each side of the wheel's sturdy center hub. These girders were assisted in their task by a matching pair of extended lateral support arms that angled down to form a right triangle with the ground.

Speaking of the ground, I'd never noticed before that our Ferris wheel was actually mounted on the ground, not on a moveable trailer like a carnival Ferris wheel. I wasn't sure whether Moon, Melvin, and Dave took it down in the winter, but things didn't look like they could be easily dismantled. Especially since the wheel was pretty much wired to the ground thanks to a slim and unending cable that ran around the entire circumference of the wheel before exiting down to a series of large pulleys that were somehow connected by thick black industrial belts to a trash can-sized electric motor behind the ride. Again, I'd just never paid enough attention to see that a cable turned the wheel. It was such a Rube Goldberg looking setup – was this really enough to make the wheel go?

I was trying to figure out how the darn thing worked when Ed, one of the relief guys who had worked at the park for a number of years, walked up to the ride. Ed and I were well acquainted because he'd often filled in on the karts when Pat took his break. Neatly trimmed hair, always a clean and proper Playland uniform, Ed was a straight shooter type. I'd guessed that he was beyond student age, but I'd never had doubts or any qualms about running the karts with him. Like Pat and I, he did it by the book. And hopefully, I'd earned his respect during our brief intervals together. He sure had mine.

"Wow, a night off the go-karts. Aren't you lucky?" said Ed coming through the front gate.

"Actually, I haven't been there in a while. I felt like I'd done my time," I said.

"How'd Pat take it?"

"We still talk...obviously not as much as we used too."

"Yeah, I'll bet. You haven't run this thing before, right?"

"No, I've been bouncing around all over the park the last couple of weeks."

"Enjoying it?

I nodded quickly in the affirmative, with a big smile.

"This one is a little different. It takes more finesse than some of the other rides," continued Ed, walking back toward the motor and flipping open a large grey metal electric box that held the power switch for the ride. Ed clicked on the switch and the engine hummed, but neither the pulleys nor the wheel moved. "It's an Eli 12-car wheel. Not the park's original Ferris wheel, but it's been here a long time."

The wheel's brand meant nothing to me, although it was a thrill to run the same rides that I'd been on in Playland as a kid. A yellow car sat motionless in the loading area. Ed moved toward it while waving me over with his hand, stopping next to a short metal knee-high ramp that led up to the car. The ramp had a hinged section that extended under the car's footrest, and coming off the right side of the ramp was what looked like a silver brake pedal. Ed went over and grabbed the side of the car with his right hand.

"Okay, this is important...watch this," he said gently rocking the car back and forth on its mount. "When you take people on or off the ride, you've got to step on the pedal."

As Ed stepped on the pedal the metal "under" section of the ramp, which had three parallel rubber strips on it, rose up to meet the footrest and hold the car in place.

"You step down on the pedal and make sure you stay on it until the passengers get on or off. Trust me, you don't want them spilling forward onto the ground – or the footrest to swing up toward your head."

I took a hard look at the pedal.

"Go ahead, step on it. Get the feel," encouraged Ed.

I did as I was told, stepping down to feel a gentle "thunk" as the stabilizer section met the footrest. Ed had put his left foot against the edge of the footrest to illustrate how the car was set in place.

"See? It doesn't rock now. Go ahead and open the restraint bar."

The thin metal restraint bar – I'd always thought Ferris wheel restraint bars were on the flimsy side – had a spring-loaded black plastic nob coming out of the right side of the car. I pulled out the nob with my right hand, allowing the bar to swing slightly up and leftward to let my imaginary passengers on.

"Now hook it back," said Ed, which I did by swinging the bar back into place, seeing the lock catch as the black nob moved slightly and clicked.

"Always give the bar a jiggle," said Ed, continuing his tutorial. I shook the bar and it stayed locked in place. "And watch out for that thing. People like to 'help' and shut the bar themselves – just make sure your body isn't in the way. Okay, now let's step away and release the car," which I did by stepping off the pedal. Ed then turned toward the waist-high silver lever that was next to the ramp.

"Now the fun part. Making the wheel go," said Ed, putting his hand on the lever. The top was tapered into a handle, and coming off the handle was a smaller squeezable lever that looked like the handlebar clutch of a motorcycle. In following the longer lever to the ground, I could see it was mounted to the supporting framework of the ride, being anchored to a protractor-shaped piece of metal that had sharp pointed teeth protruding from its upper edge. At the moment it was pointing away from the ride at a 45° angle.

"You have to squeeze this to unlock the position," said Ed pointing at the hand lever. "The engine has a clutch. You engage the clutch as you push the tall lever forward, making the cable and the wheel move."

Ed took the squeezable lever and handle together in his right hand with a firm grasp, and not the gorilla-type grab that I imagined the crude-looking contraption might require. Then he moved the tall control lever steadily toward the ride with some slight metallic grunting and squeaking as the clutch went to work and engaged the pulleys with the cable. Slowly the ride started to turn, with the car we just worked on rising backward as the wheel began moving in a counter-clockwise direction.

"I'm gonna' catch it at the top, so we can pretend like we're loading another set of passengers. You need to balance the wheel and load the cars opposite each other," said Ed as he slowed the wheel to a stop with our yellow car directly overhead and a blue car in the loading area. I watched him effortlessly move the lever to the forward "off" position, letting go of the squeezable locking mechanism before giving the handle a slight tug to make sure it was secured in the teeth of the protractor piece.

"Okay, step on the pedal," said Ed and I dutifully followed his command. "Undo the bar with your right hand, and swing it open with your left...good, good, now steady the car with your right hand as the people get on...okay, now they're on so close the bar, use your left hand...jiggle, jiggle...good, good, now release the pedal. Done!"

I stepped back from the car completely discombobulated. Not from the physical part of the task, but from the focus of piecing the loading process together. I needed a checklist. Nothing about this felt natural. And I hadn't even run the wheel yet.

"See? Piece of cake," said Ed. "Now let's take it for a spin. Grab a handful of handle – make sure you squeeze the lever to unlock it."

Squeezing the lever felt natural enough, then I started gently pushing the handle forward. Nothing was happening at first. The wheel wasn't moving and I wasn't feeling anything engaging. Then I could sense some tugging on the handle, kind of like having a giant fish on a line, and the wheel started to move. I pushed it harder trying to get it beyond the 90° mark when the cable and wheel groaned and squawked, jerking a bit in unison with the tug I felt in the handle.

"Easy, easy, easy...you've got to coax this baby to get it going. You can't go from zero to fifty in one Incredible Hulk shove. Just hold the thing in place for a moment and let the cable catch."

I did as Ed instructed, watching the wheel pick up speed as the pulleys cranked harder, bringing the cable off the wheel at an increasing rate.

"Okay, keep moving to full speed. Doesn't have to be slow, but just feel it as the handle moves," said Ed.

"I'm trying. The tension you mean?"

"Yeah, that's one way to describe it."

The handle reached a position where it was pointing toward the ride at a 45° angle. It couldn't go any further, so I let go of the squeezable lever and the handle stayed in place.

"Check it, make sure it's set good. You don't want it to come loose."

Again, I followed Ed's directions and gave the handle a shake.

"Seems good."

We both stood back and watched the wheel pick up speed, which was a little startling as a stiff man-made breeze started coming off of it like it was some kind of giant Hollywood soundstage fan.

"I had no idea these things went this fast. It doesn't seem like it when you're on the ride," I said, fighting with myself not to move back from the speeding wheel.

"Yeah, this thing will go. Give it a few more turns and you can slow it down and unload it."

After a couple of more turns, I grabbed the handle, squeezing the hand lever at the same time to unlock its position.

"Just feel things start to slow down, take your time. There's no rush," said Ed, as I began pulling the handle toward me to slow down the wheel. It had stopped giving off a breeze, but it still wasn't something you'd want to get in the way of. The inertia of the thing, at least when standing right next to it, was unsettling.

"Okay, looking good. See this blue one that just went by?" said Ed pointing to a blue car that was now moving up and away from the loading area. "Try to stop on that one. When it reaches the 12 o'clock position, get on the handle good."

It wasn't the hottest of nights, but I was sweating like it was mid-afternoon. None of the other rides I'd worked on had been this much of a challenge, although the Spider wasn't exactly easy. When the blue car got to the top I brought the handle toward me, my clumsy efforts generating a piercing squeal from somewhere in the cable path, along with a metallic groaning that let me know things weren't quite right. Ed didn't say anything, so I feathered the handle back a bit, eliminating the squealing while still managing to slow the wheel. I fixated on the blue car as it continued to drift downward, gauging its position and speed with the angle of the control lever as my eyes and hands joined as one to keep things under control. When the red car in front of my blue one moved through the loading area, I pulled the handle firmly toward me, bringing the wheel to a halt – my car hanging a good four feet above the loading area.

"That's not bad, you're better off being a little short," said Ed encouragingly. "You can glide it in from here. When you go past, the people have to go up and over again."

With a little more feathering of the handle I got the car into the loading area and aligned it with the hinged section of the ramp. My back was wet from sweat and my heart was racing like I'd been chased by a set wave. I looked at Ed, took a deep breath, and tried to reassemble in my head the sequence of things I needed to do to get my invisible passengers off.

Step on the pedal with my right foot then stabilize the car (check); pull the black knob of the restraint bar lock with my right hand (check); swing the bar up and out of the way with my left hand (check); put my right hand on the footrest so the car doesn't move as the passengers leave (check); invite the next set of passengers onto the ride while still holding the car and still standing on the pedal (check); close the restraint bar without getting whacked by it (check); jiggle the bar (check); step off the pedal (check); and grab the handle to start the ride (check). Somehow, I'd strung all the steps together – this time.

"That was good, see? You'll get the hang of it. Be patient with the handle and take your time. And remember to balance as you load people on. Twelve and six, nine and three, etc."

"You don't want to hang out for a bit and make sure I don't kill someone?" I asked half seriously, feeling seriously uneasy about the rest of the night. Something about the ride felt...kind of wrong.

"Ah, you'll be fine. You've been working here for what, two months now, right? And it's a Tuesday. You probably won't be that busy."

"I hope not."

"Feel free to keep practicing until someone shows up," said Ed, leaving through the "OUT" gate at the front of the ride.

"Thanks – not sure that will help."

A quick snare-plus-tom-tom four beat came over the PA system, followed by an immediate see-sawing fiddle line. Shit. Were we really opening the gates to "The Devil Went Down to Georgia?"

Crabs and Beer

It was unusual for Greg and me to be heading south on Coastal Highway just before midnight, at least at this point in the summer. Our post-work outings, as I knew they would, had diminished as Ocean City night spots became inundated with vacationers. Even the Feed Bag had lost its charm, as our last shooter-Monday excursion found us standing around the crowded bar while waiting for a table. We threw in the towel before getting seated, settling for a Billy's Sub Shop stop for a late-night snack of cheesesteaks. Not that any place in Ocean City knew how to make an authentic Philly cheesesteak. But Billy's could come close if you specified, very precisely, that no, you really didn't want lettuce, tomato, or raw onions. And for God's sake, no mayo on the damned thing. That abominable combination of condiments was sacrilege in the hoagie shops where I grew up (and no, no mayo on hoagies, either).

We passed the Gold Coast Mall where a small group of cars was clustered around the doors of the still open A&P. This contrasted with the southern end of the mall, where the vehicles of people partying in The Family Fish House filled nearly half the lot. Greg and I had been there once – which was enough.

"Glad we're not going there," said Greg looking out the passenger window.

"Yeah, it really wasn't my scene," I answered, enjoying the sparse traffic in front of the mall.

"Me neither. Looks like they even have a line tonight."

"Plus, a cover at the door – there's just no way."

"Nope. Way too many people. Much rather do what we're doing."

"Without a doubt."

Traffic thinned even more after we cleared the 94th Street Plaza, continuing past the parked-out nightspots lining Coastal Highway. The Hobbit at 82nd Street; B.J.'s at 75th Street; the older crowd hangout of The Jackspot at 73rd Street; then ear-splitting disco-dance worlds of the Hurricane at 71st Street and Crystal City at 68th Street; and the Natty Boh rock n' roll sweatbox that was the Back of the Rack at 66th Street.

Finally, it was time to turn – back into the Playland parking lot for the second time in less than seven hours.

There were probably 20 cars in the spaces next to the go-kart track, even though the interior of the park was in total darkness except for a scattering of security floodlights. Fortunately, the light towers in the parking lot were still on, covering Greg and me with an eerie haze that made it feel like we were part of someone's grainy home movie.

"Feels weird being here now, doesn't it?" said Greg standing up out of the car.

"Yeah, not only being here now, but not being in uniform," I said, looking across the roof of the car at Greg.

"And you don't even have a hat."

"You're right. I'm almost naked."

"Well, then let's get inside!"

Greg and I had hustled home for quick showers and were now walking up the access road cleaned up and refreshed. The circular indent of my hat was gone from my hair, and I was decked out in my "out for the evening" surf wear ensemble No. 2 – sky blue Lightning Bolt polo shirt, tan OP shorts, and, of course, Rainbow flip-flops. We hadn't seen any movement inside the park by the time we stepped through the open gate, although, I had to admit, my attention had been diverted to the skeletal outline of the Ferris wheel, which looked so peaceful and innocuous against a backdrop of night sky. Far removed from the 15-round sparring session we'd had together during the night. The ride had been a surprising shift-long challenge.

Greg and I continued our walk, using the employee corridor to reach the southern midway, where we were greeted by Mick Jagger's cooing falsetto as it wove a path through the bass and electric piano interplay of "Emotional Rescue." The song was coming out of the open doors of the Top 40 Club, mixing in with the sounds of cheerful voices, laughter, and the "bang-bang" of purposeful hammer blows. And as we moved closer to the lighted doorway a very familiar aroma filled our nostrils.

It was Old Bay – welcome to the Playland Crabs and Beer after-party.

The party was an official park event that management held once a month. Greg and I missed the June outing, having to wait until July to get our first taste of this generous Playland tradition. There was something about its simplicity, the Maryland-ness of it, perhaps, that made the gesture of appreciation feel genuine. It was an incredibly thoughtful thing to do, to offer your employees a supervised and safe place to socialize and unwind after work. Something that was in a totally different universe from the employee house parties I'd attended last summer, which always seemed to end with the police at the front door. This month's after-party was probably the most appreciated of all since it gave us the chance to avoid the sunburned throngs packing all those night spots we'd just passed on Coastal Highway. A civilized and comfortable night out in our own private space – chez "Club Playland" – was just what the doctor ordered.

We stepped through the doorway and into the soft glow of the laundromat-sized interior, which had a DJ booth in the back corner, and rows of picnic tables taking up most of the floor space. Playland employees filled out about half of the tables, arranging themselves among the rolls of white paper towels that pointed upward at random intervals. Some of my co-workers already had piles of spice-coated crabs sitting on the brown paper that covered the tabletops. Others seemed content with conversation, likely debating whether they were up for ritualistic crustacean dismantling at this time of night. I wasn't sure that I was. They certainly were good-looking crabs. "Larges" for sure, and although I couldn't tell until I handled one, I was betting that they were on the heavy side. Delicious, but a ton of work to get at the meat inside.

In looking around, I was having a flashback to last month, because once again I was on my heels over the number of "unfamiliar" faces in the room. Our Playland uniforms had come to define us during the summer (and in my case, I'm sure my Montego Bay Hardware hat was also part of the package). Now, with the majority of people in the Top 40 Club out of uniform...I was having trouble recognizing my Playland colleagues. Especially the women, who for safety reasons, often worked the rides with hair that was pinned up or in a ponytail. With their hair now down and their boxy Playland shirts replaced with flattering and form-fitting summer tops, many looked completely different from how they did just hours earlier. I never realized we had so many "wow's" working at Playland. And I'd never say it out loud, but I hoped that by removing my hat and putting on my carefully coordinated surfer clothes I'd had a similar metamorphosis. Not that I was going to go walk over and ask someone for an opinion.

"Do you want to get a beer first?" I asked Greg, not getting an immediate answer. Greg was scanning the room for Katie, who worked the counter at the Dairy Queen. Their relationship had recently moved beyond the friendship stage, and they were trying to maximize their time together as the weeks of the summer wound down. While Greg looked for Katie, I scanned for Pat, half hoping not to see him. Tonight would be an opportunity for us to have the "sit down" conversation about the go-karts that we'd still not had. Then Greg found Katie, and I didn't find Pat. So, we were both happy.

"Yeah, let's grab one," said Greg, as he and I moved toward three large Coleman cooler chests that were on the floor along the wall on our right. I leaned over and flipped open the first chest, finding only cans of Coke, Sprite, and Tab peeking out from the thick bed of ice in the bottom. After letting the lid fall back into place, I opened the second cooler and looked up at Greg.

"Budweiser or National Premium?" I said.

"Does it matter?" said Greg, with a bit of impatience in his tone.

"If we're having crabs it should be a Maryland beer?"

"Yeah, I guess you're right."

I fished two dripping cans out of the cooler and stood up, giving the can in my right hand to Greg. We then walked over to sit down with Katie, who was in conversation with a tanned and attractive blonde woman beside her that I couldn't quite place. They didn't have any crabs yet, but they both had beers. Greg and I took seats directly across from them.

"You made it!" Greg said to Katie, who smiled sweetly back. She was the definition of "natural beauty," with penetrating blue eyes, sun-bleached hair, and model-worthy cheekbones. And there wasn't a dab of makeup on her smooth face.

"We beat you guys!" Katie said with a laugh.

"It was my fault, I had to get rid of my hat hair," I interjected, trying to absolve Greg of whatever he might need absolving of. Then I looked over at the friend, who I still couldn't place. Maybe it was the mascara and the orange-tinged lip gloss?

"Is this your roommate?" I continued.

Katie and her friend both started laughing, the friend going slightly red in the face.

"Oh, sorry. You work here, don't you?" I said, trying to recover from my clumsy attempt at being "social."

"The Scrambler, the Tilt-A-Whirl," she said with a growing smile.

"Oh...I know who you are! Now let's flip it around. Do you know who I am? What do I work on?"

She looked over for help from Katie, who didn't offer any. Then they both started laughing again, the friend blushing once more under her tan. Finally, she looked across the table and shrugged.

"We've been neighbors recently. I was on the Airborne last Friday and did some shifts with Travis on the coaster. I was up front with the Ferris wheel tonight."

"Yes! Now I recognize you!" she said, pointing at me with an extended index finger. "You look really different without the hat. I'm Karen."

"And you look really different with your hair down. Nice to meet you, Karen. I'm Earl. I'm also Greg's roommate," I said, nodding at Greg as I reached my right hand across the table.

"How was the Ferris wheel? You have run it before?" asked Karen, with what seemed like genuine interest.

"No, no I haven't. It wasn't easy. There's a lot going on, especially trying to work the clutch and getting the cars to stop where you want them," I said, shifting my gaze from Greg to Katie, and then back to Karen.

"That's what I've heard," said Karen.

"And the wheel moves faster than you realize."

"But it went okay?" said Karen, continuing her curiosity.

"Nothing serious, thank goodness. Let's just say, it was an awkward night. The clutch did a lot of groaning, and there were extra trips around the wheel for a lot of riders.

"Glad you survived – and that nobody got hurt."

"Well, not exactly 'nobody.' Here, feel that," I said to Greg, having him put his hand on the back of my head.

"Holy shit!" he gasped back, his eyes narrowing in concern.

"Nice, huh?" I said flippantly.

"What happened?" asked Karen.

"The restraint bar. It has to be open, obviously, to load riders on. And once they're seated, they want to reflexively pull the bar shut. The problem is, the ride operator's head is sometimes in the way."

"Oh, man," said Greg, pulling his hand away from the bulge on the back of my cranium.

"Are you okay?" said Katie, with her own look of concern.

"I'm fine. A couple of bumps on the head will make you figure things out real quick."

"So, you're all set when you run it again?" said Karen, tilting her head and holding my eye.

"I'd really rather not," I said, finally picking up my beer for a healthy swig.

Greg and I did make our way to the table against the back wall with the trio of silver crab pots. Then together with Katie and Karen we cracked open and picked our way through a dozen crabs, with the "flowers" of white backfin meat – a Phillips' old-timer had taught me the technique – being spicy and succulent. We'd also cracked our way through a couple of more beers, and were in a thoroughly relaxed state of mind. A stream of Playland colleagues who were friends with Katie and Karen stopped by, and I'd even felt comfortable enough to make the rounds at other tables, sitting down with Travis and Gabe to meet their circle of friends.

And on top of it all, I had an extra buzz that wasn't alcohol related thanks to some random entreaties I'd gotten about my identity. The inquirers were female, all saying that they were surprised they hadn't noticed me in the park before. (There was a butterfly lurking under my hat!) Not that I was looking for a rendezvous of any type. I was happily "taken." But I didn't mind the attention.

By 1:45 am, I was ready to call it a night and walked over to Mark, who'd been overseeing the evening.

"This is a such a cool thing to do, Mark. There's something...I don't know, I feel like you guys genuinely appreciate us. I mean, I know you do, but this is special."

"Thanks! I appreciate you saying that."

"And I'd say it even without the free beer. The crabs, on the other hand..."

"How'd you like the Ferris wheel?"

"Ah, it was a challenge."

"Yeah, it is. Don't worry, though, you're just a backup there. I needed someone else to have experience with the ride. You never know."

"No, that's fine. You know, there's something I've been wondering since my first day in the park. Why does the Top 40 Club look like a barn?"

"That's a good question," said Mark with a deep laugh. "A couple of years ago this was the Fiesta Mexicana puppet theater."

"The what?"

"Yeah, that was most people's reaction. We paid a group from Texas to come in and put it on. It only lasted a year. So we just left the space as it was and called it the Top 40 Club. The speakers and wiring are left over from the puppets."

"Huh. That's not as interesting as I'd hoped it would be."

"Well, the truth is like that sometimes."

"Yeah, it is. Anyway, I'm heading out. Thanks again. See you tomorrow – I mean later today."

"Be safe getting home."

"Always."

I left Mark to let Greg and Katie know that I was leaving. Greg would get a ride home from Katie, if he came home at all.

"I hear you're ready for that trek to Busch Gardens?" I said to Katie, referring to something Greg and I were putting together for the final week of August. A double-date day trip to Williamsburg for Katie, Greg, Robin, and me.

"Yep, I sure am," answered Katie, who was leaning against Greg, holding his hand.

"We're going to tame the Loch Ness Monster! It's supposed to be the tallest and fastest roller coaster in the world."

"I might have to think about that," said Greg. "The riding the Monster part. I'm set for the trip."

"We need something like that here in Playland."

"That ride is huge. It's got two loops, it would take up the whole park."

"No, I mean just something that loops. Travis was just saying that the park needs something like the Lightning Loops ride at Great Adventure."

"What's that?"

"You go forward through the loop, and then the ride reverses and you go backward through the loop, ending up where you started. I rode it last year."

"Just sounds like an excuse to go upside down. Where would we put it?"

"Travis was speculating that we could rip out the Sky Ride and the mini golf. Put it right in the middle of the park."

"You realize the Dairy Queen would go, too?"

"Oh yeah —"

"Sounds like you need some sleep."

"I was just coming over to say goodnight."

"Okay. Goodnight. Don't wait up."

"Not a chance. Goodnight Katie. See you guys later."

Chapter Thirty-Seven

Hot Rods

After my shifts on the Sky Ride, Hurricane, Airborne, Spider, and the Ferris wheel, this wasn't fun at all. It was a weird ride, in a weird place, arguably the most dated looking thing in the entire park. Noisy, smelly, it was never on my "must run" list, and probably placed in the Top 5 of Playland rides that I had absolutely no interest in running at all. And this was before I spent most of the summer stuck on the go-karts, which happened to be this particular ride's direct offspring. Not helping things were my Playland ride running partners, who seemed unimpressed with the massive amount of experience I had with cars that were much more dangerous and difficult to deal with than this friggin' glorified kiddie ride. So, I just kept my mouth shut and stuck to my task as the "catcher" on the Hot Rods.

The Hot Rods were Playland's original go-karts, or at least the park's original driveable gas-powered cars. They ran on a single-lane oval track in front of the coaster when Playland first opened, but moved in the ensuing years to a larger location next to the Ghost Ship, in a spot that had once been occupied by the Airborne and the Broadway Trip (a walk-through funhouse that I'd never had the chance to experience). In this updated location the cars were still confined to a single lane of track, but it was a much longer layout that snaked through multiple twisting turns in the shadow of the monorail station before embarking on a long straightaway that ran behind the Ghost Ship and fed into a dogleg section on the other side of the building. From here the cars went back behind the Ghost Ship (on a parallel inside lane), emerging into a pair of turns that returned them to the loading area. My job, as a car came in, was to hop on the narrow driver side running board, grab the steering wheel to take control, and put my foot on the oversized exterior brake pedal to bring the car to a safe stop.

Basically, I was the whiplash preventer. There to make sure that nobody exiting from a car got blasted from behind by an out of control driver – a scenario that Pat and I battled on a daily basis with the go-

karts. There were many a night when we would have killed for the opportunity to hop on the side of our karts and personally guide them to
the pit area.

Which should have offered me some consolation for being back in
the world of combustion engine rides, but not enough. The Hot Rod cars
were rumbling jalopies that didn't go all that much faster than the Antique Cars, being powered by puttering and prehistoric lawn mower
engines that burned more oil than a Marcus Hook refinery. They also
put out a caustic funk that could be best described as "First Day in Freshman Chem Lab," with one car seeming to emit more noxious fumes than
an entire squad of go-karts. Maybe it was because the cars sat in a long
idling row before they were sent onto the track, meaning that there
were always exhaust fumes spewing into the loading area. (At least with
the go-karts Pat and I could send them all out at once and spread the
exhaust around.)

The bottom line here seemed to be, everything was just old, including the fiberglass car body shells that gave the Hot Rods their identity.
They'd been designed to look like miniature 1960s Corvettes, which
wasn't necessarily a bad thing, but years of sun, heat, and exhaust had
taken a toll, leaving the lighter colored cars looking like they had a
bumper-to-bumper case of mange. Not that the cars weren't kept up.
Like the Sky Ride cars, it was just their natural state of being after seasons and seasons of use. And unfortunately, adding the dingy and dated
elements all together, there was no way around it – the ride was kind of
sad.

Yet I understood why the Hot Rods were still part of the park. They
offered a gas-powered driving experience for the kids who weren't tall
enough for the go-karts. I wasn't sure exactly what the Hot Rod height
limit was, just that it was definitely not as strict as the go-karts. If a kid
was as tall as the wood cutout of Dennis The Menace standing at the
entrance, they could drive a Hot Rod all by themselves. If they weren't
tall enough, but with a parent or sibling who did meet the height limit,
they could still go along for the ride because the Hot Rods had a left-
side steering wheel just like a real car, and also a bench seat with room
for passengers. Depending on how a family wanted to break it down
(three was a squeeze, but possible if the passengers were kids), they
could all go out for a drive in a situation that was much more controlled
than the "let's race!" vibe of the go-karts.

Part of the control, in addition to a yellow-shirted Playland worker bringing the cars to a stop, was in the track itself. Its single lane of asphalt was bordered on both sides by a shin-high wooden guardrail, which conveniently kept the cars on the road and moving forward. Unless a car completely conked out during a ride, there was no way for a driver to get stuck on the track. And the cars were sent out one at a time with plenty of space in between so that even if someone was a not-so-great driver who bumped along the guard rails for the entire circuit, the car behind it wouldn't catch up. That only happened when people played games with the gas pedal.

There were three of us running the ride, with Jacob, who I got the feeling was *the* Hot Rod guy, putting people in the cars and sending them out. Ty was the middle guy who kept the cars moving through the loading area, and gave me a hand if two cars did happen to return close together. And I was at the back, bringing the cars in for a soft landing. There was plenty of room for all of us along the loading area, which consisted of a shallow 15-yard long concrete channel that looked a lot like an actual race track pit area. Matching up seamlessly with the channel were the track's guardrails, allowing the ever-vibrating Hot Rods to migrate through the loading area like they were on an invisible conveyor belt. On the other side of the channel was a sidewalk-like concrete platform with two extended lanes of cattle chute fencing to manage the ride's lines. From what I'd seen during the summer, this setup – being the most extensive line layout in all of Playland – was overkill, at least in 1980. But it was a testament to how popular the Hot Rods had been in Playland's past.

At my back, within spitting distance, was the two-story cinderblock east wall of the Ghost Ship, something that added an odd and claustrophobic element to the night, because every other ride I'd run had been wide open with no buildings or walls encroaching on their space. Having an oversized orange rectangle block my view of the bay was...different. But on the positive side, it created the only shade in the park I'd ever experienced, with the wall casting a long shadow over the track that had the evening air feeling comfortable long before the sun disappeared over the horizon. An additional and not so endearing feature of the wall was that it doubled as an echo chamber, adding a jackhammer quality to the engine noise bouncing off its oversized masonry surface. Still, for one night, and hopefully this was a one-night stint, I could deal with it.

It was kind of mindless, at least what I was doing. I'd just finished delivering a car without incident into the loading area, allowing the thin metal bumper that encircled the car to gently click against the bumper of the car in front, when a father with a young girl at the back of our line caught my eye and called me over.

"Ty? Ty? Can you watch my spot for a second?" I said, in a voice loud enough to be heard over the idling Hot Rods. Ty nodded, and I went over to the railing where the father and daughter stood.

"Yessir!" I greeted them, with my best Playland helper voice.

"He said she wasn't tall enough to get on the ride," said the man, pointing to where Jacob stood at the front of the Hot Rod line.

"I can measure her again if you want," I said, not sure what etiquette I might be breaching if Jacob and I came to different conclusions. Hopping over the railing and onto the midway, I walked with them down to our smiling cutout of Dennis The Menace. Approaching Dennis, it was already apparent that she was too short, but I asked her to stand against the cutout anyway.

"Go ahead, put your back up against Dennis," I said, anchoring my left hand above her head as a measuring guide. With the base of my palm against Dennis and my fingers outstretched and flat, there was at least an inch of Dennis' painted yellow "hair" visible above my knuckles.

"I'm sorry – you're close, but just not tall enough," I said to the girl, who seemed to take the bad news in stride. But dad was a different story. "I'm sorry, sir, she's not tall enough to drive the cars."

"That's just not right. It's not fair, she can drive those things," he spit back with some force. "We paid good money to come in here…"

"I'm sorry, sir. She can't go on by herself."

"That's just crazy. Outrageous, it really is."

Now he was just wasting my time and venting on me because I was there and still listening. I didn't appreciate being this asshole's chew toy and could feel my temper kick into low gear. I needed to pull the plug on this conversation before I said something that I'd regret.

"I'm sorry, sir. There's nothing more I can do here. You'll have to talk to the manager."

"Well, I believe I will. What's his name?"

"Mark Davis. His office is in the front of the park."

"And your name?"

"Earl Shores."

"We'll see about this..."

Oh my, God – what a *dick!* I never got that much shit on the go-karts, and we had some severely disappointed kids over there. Christ, my first night on these lame-ass Hot Rods and I get myself in trouble over an eight-year-old girl. Fuck. What was wrong with people?

I hopped back over the perimeter fence and went to my post at the back the Hot Rods, but before I settled in...

"Hey! Hey, you!!" said a raspy male voice whose volume was set on "yell." Fuck – now what? It couldn't be the same guy, could it? And where the hell was Ty? In turning around...no, this was a different guy, but it was easy to see that he was even more unhappy than the last guy. And in my quick assessment of his dingy yellow tank top and fur-covered neck and shoulders, the fun here was just beginning.

"Did you see what just happened?" he shouted at me as I walked toward him at the fence. I didn't appreciate being jumped, even if it was only verbally, and my anger rocketed as I looked down onto his stubbled face.

"No sir, I didn't. I was down there measuring somebody for the ride," I said, pointing with my left hand down to the entrance.

"Someone rammed into the back of my son's car just as he was trying to get out."

"I'm sorry, sir, I'm sorry that happened. But I wasn't here, and I didn't see it," I said, trying to keep a measured tone while knowing that Ty had left me out to dry.

"You young people just stand around with your hands up your ass, not paying attention to anything – somebody could get seriously hurt, and you guys don't care."

Oh, this dude was going for the throat, wasn't he? And it was working, too, especially after I'd just sent dickhead No. 1 off to the office with my name. My pulse thundered in my ears, as a state of pissed-off-ed-ness I'd not experienced this summer came over me. Still, I tried.

"Sir, I'm really, really sorry that happened. Believe me, we do care."

"Bullshit, you guys stand around..."

Rage. That was all I felt. Flat out, unadulterated rage. And it was wrapped in the frustration and poison from all those weeks on the go-karts. I wasn't going to let this guy stand in the park and insult me and curse me over an honest mistake. My employee decorum was about to go, and in all likelihood, so was my job.

"Then you go talk to my manager!" I shouted at him, jabbing my left index finger towards his chest for emphasis.

"Well, well...I will!" he shouted back, surprised that I'd broken "character." And I wasn't finished, at least with more words that would surely finish off my night and my summer employment.

"Yeah, you tell'em that Earl Shores sent you. You got that? S-H-O-R-E-S. Shores!"

He looked back at me, stunned I guess, with an "I never" kind of look stuck on his face. I was stunned too, but still...fuck you, fuck your kid, and the fuck the first guy too. At least that's what I hoped my eyes were saying. The guy didn't say anything more and walked off with his son, who'd been late to the conversation but witnessed the "best" parts. I guess I'd won the verbal battle, but the war was lost. I'd been unprofessional, rude, and made a scene. And I was embarrassed now. How did I let those two idiots get the best of me? All summer long I'd been a "pro" on the go-karts and held it in, but now...I'd just lost it. Completely. And what I'd lost – there was no way I wanted to stay around to deal with all the shit I'd just stirred up. On the fucking Hot Rods! Probably the shittiest ride in the entire park. Fuck, what did I just do?

Like a cornered animal my "fight or flight" response was on overdrive, and since I'd just had the fight, it was time for flight. So I hurried back through the line of cars and grabbed my backpack, flinging it over my shoulder while turning around to get the hell out of the park. I'd just started to step through cars when Calvin cut me off. Calvin? What the hell...did he relieve Ty?

"Earl, Earl, Earl – what are you doing?!!" said Calvin.

"I quit. I'm done. I'm not taking shit from these people anymore. I've had a summer's worth. I'm tired," I said, looking off to the parking lot, wishing I could magically transport myself to the driver's seat of my Sunbird. It was a surprise to feel Calvin grab me, put his hands on my shoulders, and maneuver me around so that we were eye-to-eye.

"No, no, no!! It's okay. Trust me. I was here, I saw it. Even with the little girl – I walked right by you. I'll talk to Mark. It's okay. Calm down and take a breath. It will be okay."

I wanted to leave, and even tried to take a step, but Calvin had a firm grip on me. I didn't answer him, unable to slow down all the thoughts and emotions that spun like a whirlpool in my head. Calvin wouldn't let go, determined to get an answer.

"Trust me, okay? Trust me," he said firmly, now being just inches from my face.

In a moment of clarity – I think the drain gurgled as my whirlpool spun dry – I knew I didn't want things to end like this.

"Okay," I said, nodding at Calvin.

"Good, good. Now go do the kind of job you always do," said Calvin, letting go of me and breaking into a smile. "It's going to be okay."

I again took up my place as the catcher, feeling weak and a little wobbly, likely from the stress, but probably just as likely from the exhaust fumes. And who in the hell was bringing the cars in while Calvin talked me down? Were we in a lull? Those moments were lost time – I had absolutely no awareness of what had gone on around me. Jacob was still up at the front, still doing his job as if nothing had happened. Or maybe stuff like this happened every night, and it was just part of the Hot Rod "show?" I was dying to go on break. Calvin should have relieved me once Ty returned, but he asked me to be patient, disappearing for what seemed like an eternity while he was presumably off apprising Mark about my "difficulties" with the ride. When Calvin returned to put me on break, I felt like I'd gotten a reprieve from the warden.

Things were still a blur as I took my first few strides away from Hot Rods, but I hadn't gotten very far when I noticed Mark coming my way. Oh well, I was going to have to face up to all this sooner or later. This was just a little sooner than I wanted, and my stomach quickly reverted to the sour state it had been in for much of the night. At least Mark didn't look all that upset.

"So, we go two months and I never hear anything, then you get two complaints in fifteen minutes. Guess you were up too late last night, huh?" he said, almost teasingly I thought.

"I am so sorry, Mark. I lost it with the second guy. I mean, he was right, sort of. But I had been doing my job. That's what pissed me off."

"Don't worry about it. Calvin filled me in. Plus, I got a sense of what you were dealing with when I talked with them. I don't think you could have pleased either one. They were looking for something to be upset about."

"And then I joined in. I am sorry, Mark."

"No more tonight, then. Three strikes and you're out."

"No more, I promise. But speaking of being out...I'm not going to finish the summer. My last day is going to be a week from Saturday. The 23rd."

I held my breath as I said this, half figuring that if Mark wanted me out tonight, then so be it. Mark's expression didn't change, and he tilted his head slightly while stroking his chin with his right hand.

"You're sure? You'll lose your bonus you know?"

"I know, I know. I just really need some time off before I go back to school," I said, feeling good about being upfront with Mark. This was the absolute truth. I wanted some vacation time, and time to reflect. Things were going to be different at Delaware this semester, with little margin for error.

"So that's like a week and a half from now?"

"Yeah – about. I'll give you two weeks' notice if you want. I just need some time."

"No, that's fine. I appreciate you letting me know."

"And can I ask one final favor?"

"Probably," said Mark with half a laugh.

"Please don't make me run these things again. I'll gladly do the Antique Cars. Just not them," I pleaded, pointing back at the Hot Rods.

"No more problems tonight."

"Deal. I promise."

Chapter Thirty-Eight

Rotor

If the park had a throne, this would be it.

That was all I could think as I looked out on a twilight panorama of Playland from my crow's nest perch on the Rotor. I'd actually had to climb a fully vertical fire escape ladder to get up to this sort of mini metal lifeguard stand, a climb that elevated me to the highest ride-running location in the park, and actually in all of Ocean City. I mean, I was looking down on the monorail as it moved along to my left, spying through its transparent, dome-like covering on the unsuspecting passengers during their clockwise tour of the park. (And they thought they had a great view of the sunset!) Directing my gaze to the front gate...not only was I even in height with the jester, the ocean was visible off on the horizon, its deep blue not far from the color of the sky as we neared the point in the evening when the park lights would need to come on.

Perhaps the ultimate testament to just how unique this location was came from a story my ride running partner Rick Machado told me earlier in the evening. He'd been running the Rotor the night the Sky Ride broke down and found himself being the closest person in Playland to the lone occupied car stuck out over the bay. And what Rick did, was strike up a conversation with the pair of teen girls in that car, keeping them distracted and calm during the almost three hours it took for the Ocean City Firefighters to work their way, car by hanging car, to the back of the park where the girls were stranded. Finally, after Rick learned that, among other things, the girls went to Albert Einstein High School just outside of D.C., and that their parents had a place near the Gateway Hotel, the firemen maneuvered their bucket truck up to the perimeter fence between the Rotor and the Airborne and plucked the girls out of the Ocean City night sky.

"Rotor" was actually the formal name for the ride. I'd known it while growing up and riding the one at Trimper's as the "Hell Hole." In fact, I knew what a Hell Hole was long before I ever saw one in person, that's how common the ride's colorful nickname was. And without a doubt, Hell Hole was a good description for a two-story tall, industrial carpet-lined drum that spun fast enough to pin riders against its walls with centrifugal force. But that was just the beginning, because once the riders were "secured" to the walls, the floor dropped out, settling about a yard-stick-length below the riders' now dangling feet. Screams and gasps always echoed out of the drum when the floor started to move, as there the riders were, suspended with no straps, bars, or supports, just stuck to the walls like bugs splattered on a windshield. After a few minutes in G-force hell, the floor came back up, and the drum slowed to a stop, finally giving the riders a chance to peel themselves off the walls while dealing with their still-spinning vestibular fluid. "Seeing stars" was a common Rotor side effect, not to mention an unsteadiness that made it a challenge to walk out of the ride.

Time was just about up for the group I had spinning now, and looking down on them from my control "throne" above, I admired their determination. And their youth, too. That's because although I'd put countless strips of Trimper's blue tickets into the Rotor through the years, my Hell Hole days were over. Not that I couldn't *take* the ride anymore – I still could handle its just-shy-of-nausea experience. It was that I didn't see the point of putting up with the G-force abuse the ride dished out. In all honesty, the ride wasn't that fun. It was all about that moment when the floor fell away, and you found yourself stuck to the walls, seemingly defying the laws of gravity. But once you did that a handful of times – trying to turn yourself sideways or maybe upside down during the ride – the novelty was gone. For me, anyway. (Although Rick claimed that he and some of the other Playland guys could actually stand up on the walls and "surf" the Rotor, giving a bizarre twist to the term "getting barreled.") For serious thrills, I'd take the Zipper over the Rotor any day.

Surprisingly, running the Rotor wasn't all that hard. Off to my right, mounted on a white waist-high steel post, was a thin wand-like lever that controlled the ride. Pushing the foot-long silver shaft forward got the drum spinning while pulling it back slowed the ride and engaged the brake. And when the ride was up to speed and everyone was pinned to the walls, there was a broomstick-like handle that I pushed forward to drop the floor. Pulling the handle toward me brought the floor back up to the riders, and the handle could be manipulated to lower the floor swiftly, slowly, or somewhere in between, depending on how I felt. The most intimidating part of running the ride was the microphone just off to my right, which I was supposed to use to ask the riders if they wanted to go faster. It was intimidating because Rick was a master at working the "crowd" in the drum, having all the polish and poise of an improv comedian. Effortlessly he engaged the riders, knowing just the right time to say something that made everyone scream in unison. I was trying but felt that every word I uttered into the microphone was contrived and unconvincing. And the harder I tried, the lamer I sounded. But I still was having a great time running the ride.

Rick had advised that three to four minutes was enough of a Rotor session for most riders, so I flipped my right wrist over to see my watch needing just 15 more ticks to reach the three-minute mark for the current group. This had me looking over the right-side railing down to Rick, who was working the loading deck below. Once I caught his eye I pointed at my watch to pantomime a question of "time" that I'd otherwise have to shout over a two-layered torrent of noise that combined the hum of our hard-working motor with the speed-generated whir of the drum into something that could be best described as an invisible swarm of seagull-sized bees. Rick shook his head "yes," and I pulled the handle to raise the floor quickly up to the riders. After the floor locked back into place with an echoing "boom," I pulled the silver wand toward me and felt the brake slow the ride, watching closely in the drum to make sure no one had passed out, and also that no one was in front of the exit door that Rick would need to open inward. As the drum slowed to a stop, my oversized bees returned to their invisible hive. The tricky part of stopping the ride was that I had to align the doors of the drum with the doors in the metal outer shell of the ride. This time I got them set just about perfect, making Rick's job easy as he let the riders exit out of the drum.

Of course, now that I was on short time and the summer was almost over, I'd bumped into Rick. He was in his fifth season at Playland, and one of the coolest people I'd met, which was saying something, considering how many genuinely nice people there were in the park. He'd handed me the Rotor controls for a significant chunk of the night, saying that he'd watched people go around in circles enough for a lifetime. It was surprising to discover that, despite Rick's half-decade of Playland experience, we were the same age. This was possible because he'd begun working at the park when he was just 15, starting as a cleanup boy, then moving to the mini-golf, and later on to just about everything else, eventually becoming a Rotor and Monster Mouse specialist, the two rides he'd been rotating between this summer. He was even trusted to work after hours, helping with repairs and firing up Playland's barbecue pits on the days the picnics came in.

Funny and unassuming while showing me the ins and outs of the ride, he morphed into quite the character once the park opened, sliding on his mirror shades and rolling up the sleeves of his Playland shirt to show off his biceps. But this was just the start of the performance that Rick put on as I climbed up and down the ladder to watch and learn during the early part of the night. "Do you want to go faster?" Rick would ask as the riders spun below us. He then pretended not the hear the loudly yelled "Yeah!" that came back up out of the drum. "Do you want to go faster?" Rick would ask again, leading to an even louder "Yeah!!" This time Rick would oblige, speeding up the ride and dropping the floor out so quickly that the collective scream of the riders was heard throughout the entire park. And then Rick playfully taunted the riders with "Now you know what a fly on flypaper feels like!" I also learned about "wall wedgies," as on one of the runs several riders slid below the yellow line painted on the inside of the drum. For the ride operator this line represented the "up" position of the floor, and any body parts hanging below it could be pinched when the floor returned to its start position. Rick fixed the situation by slowing the drum enough to let the riders gently slide down the walls to the floor, their clothes wanting to stay fixed in place as their flesh and bones succumbed to gravity. It was funny to open the drum door and see everyone tugging at the bottom of their shorts.

"Hey Earl," Rick yelled up before he let the next group of riders into the drum. "Go ahead and turn the rest of the lights on."

"Sure, Rick. Thanks," I said.

There was already a series of support-post mounted floodlights shining down into the drum, which would've been pretty uninviting without this bit of illumination because we were well past the point of daylight reaching into the ride. One of the funny things about the Rotor was that it was easy to overlook, at least during the daytime. There was something about its location, tucked back by the bay in the shadow of the coaster hill, and also something about its upright stature – instead of spreading out over the ground like the Scrambler or the Airborne – that helped it almost hide in plain sight. Yet when its lights were turned on, man, it was like somebody crossed a rocket ship with a wedding cake and decorated it with a box of sparklers.

All I could see was the glow when I flicked the breaker for the lights, but I knew that both of our angled metal walkways were now lit by overhanging pole-mounted "stars" that would continue twinkling for the rest of the night. And that high up on the front of the ride's embossed gold outer shell, "ROTOR" was spelled out in luminous three-foot-tall letters. But, oh, the lights I could see from my control perch...radiating over me, the drum, and the observation platform was a large two-tiered flashing ring of white, seeming to endow the ride with an enormous flickering crown. Then curving upward off the top of the crown was a series of thin, light-covered metal beams, all converging together into a smaller illuminated crown high up over the drum, giving the ride a glittering circus tent-like peak of lights. Looking up to the night sky through this canopy of flashing artificial stars, then panning down...wispy strips of orange still off on the horizon to my left, the slowly undulating surface of the bay reflecting soft-focused mirror images of the coaster, Rotor, and Airborne, the lift hill clicking at my back as the Sky Ride cars floated by at eye level, the bobbing and weaving luminous arms of the Spider playing peek-a-boo with the Dairy Queen sign, the forward-spinning fluorescent star of the Ferris wheel seeming to want to spin right out onto Coastal Highway, our jester looming up from the shadows to truly look like a giant...this was beyond all the ride running dreams I'd ever had. Every one of them. And the Rotor wasn't even something I'd thought about when the summer started. Again, it took a while to even *see* that we had one. But here I was, in a moment uncolored by any preconceived expectations about what such a moment might be like, floating over the park at what seemed a higher altitude than my already elevated post on the ride.

The night moved by like a tape recorder on fast-forward, with Rick being a big part of that. He'd made me feel welcome right away, not displaying a hint of skepticism about whether I was "worthy" of the ride. We were simply two Playland veterans with a job to do on the Rotor. This implicit trust was flattering because I knew that after five seasons in the park, Rick had seen it all. Whatever ride running wisdom he wanted to share, I was happy to soak it in like a sponge. Because I really wanted Rick's night to be as easy as he was making mine.

"Here they come again," said Rick, watching a group of five boys scurry up the "ON" ramp for their fifth consecutive spin in the Rotor.

"Take it easy, take it easy, we weren't leaving without you," said Rick with a laugh as the boys reached the chain he was guarding. In my estimation, they were likely 6th graders or just into junior high, all still in the "gangly" stage with hormones dripping into their thoughts but not yet filling out the formless arms and legs that protruded from their T-shirts and shorts. And I would have bet my paycheck that their sun exposure in Ocean City had been identical, yet their varying complexions had yielded varying results in how their bodies reacted to an overdose of UV rays, ranging from bitchin' surfer brown to ready-to-peel red. It was obvious that they were playing a game amongst themselves, one of those utterly juvenile male contests – think hornless adolescent goats butting heads in a farmyard– to see who would back down first. Who would crack and be the first to say "no more," or who would stay stupidly silent, maintaining his male "code of honor" right up until the moment his stomach contents reached the back of his throat.

They really weren't harming anyone with their, shall I say, exuberance, other than being slightly annoying when they charged up and down the Rotor's walkways, sounding like soldiers on a parade ground as their feet "whomp-whomp-whomp-whomped" over the thick metal plates.

After Rick loaded them and a handful of other riders into the drum, I kneeled down under my safety railing to quietly ask a question.

"Should I help them out?" I said.

Rick chuckled, knowing exactly what I was thinking, his face moving into a corners-of-eye smile that I was pretty sure meant "yes."

"That's up to you," he said, being verbally noncommittal.

"Then you don't have a problem – it wouldn't be...wrong?"

"It's probably going to happen sooner or later. If you just want to get on with it..."

"Okay," I said, standing back up to start the ride.

It didn't take long to get the ride up and humming, with me making a quick glance at my watch before dropping the floor. Looking down at the shadowed faces spinning round and round, the five boys had aligned themselves together, and just like the previous four spins, were trying to outdo each other by getting into different silly positions on the wall. All in all, they were still just bugs on a windshield, yet bugs that kept up a constant stream of chatter and laughter as the revolutions mounted. I was checking the other riders, too, as I'd noticed that they had family watching from the observation area. In my channeling of Jack and his Spider running partner, I was having second thoughts about making this an extended session. Not for the boys, I was fine with keeping them on, because they'd been trying to test themselves since they first stepped foot in the ride. If they wanted a test, I was more than happy to accommodate them. But my other riders – it really wasn't fair to potentially ruin their night. They were innocent bystanders just trying to have a good time in Playland. So as my watch neared the four-minute mark, I grabbed the handle with my right hand to raise the floor...but didn't pull it toward me.

Overtime had begun...10 seconds...20 seconds, I looked down at Rick, who was looking up at me as he paced the platform...30 seconds, the drum had gone silent...40 seconds, all was still silent and my guilt was building...50 seconds, I felt like a complete shit and pulled the handle toward me, finally shutting down the ride near the 75 second mark.

Watching the drum slow, listening to my bees fly back to their hive, I was a little disappointed that my plan had failed. And relieved at the same time. This had been an enjoyable night. Why did I want to spoil it by letting my dark side take over? Well, at least that run was finished. So what if the boys came back for round six? Just let them spin. They'll go away eventually. I looked down briefly to my right where Rick was emptying out the riders, then turned around to watch the coaster click by at eye-level on the lift hill.

"Hey, Earl?" called Rick, from inside the drum.

"Yeah? What is it?" I said, turning back to see Rick standing in the middle of the blue metal floor pointing down to a large puddle. It was, indeed, vomit.

"On the way out. Someone didn't make it."

"One of the boys?"

"Yep."

"Darn," I said, smiling down at Rick.

"Yep. Oh, darn. I'll go find somebody. Time to get out the Zep!"

I hated to admit it, but I didn't feel bad. Not in the least.

Chapter Thirty-Nine

Rain

"**M**an, this really sucks."

Travis was at my side on the loading platform as he rendered this succinct and accurate evaluation of the evening, both of us huddled under damp hats and sweatshirts to counter the chilly rain that bounced off the orange planks under our feet. Stretched out before us was the fully lit park, enveloped in a misting drizzle that had the rides eerily empty and the employees shivering and annoyed. Travis and I usually had a good time when we worked together on the coaster, but not tonight. Not that we weren't getting along, we just didn't want to be here. That's because we'd spent most of the day not expecting to be here, thanks to a frontal system that had camped over Ocean City, blotting out the sun with dense gray clouds while flooding the beaches and Coastal Highway with rain.

"I can't believe we even opened...we really shouldn't be here. I mean you and me," Travis said, raising his arm to point at the coaster train. "This thing does not like the rain."

I had no doubt Travis was right about the coaster, as he knew the ride almost as well as Moon and Melvin did. And he was such an easy-going guy that his unease about the night was not something I took lightly. If he was on edge, then I was too, even though there was little I could offer besides mindless chatter to help the situation.

This night was still young, but the depth of darkness that had descended over the park made it feel like late-October instead of late-August, with the usual orange-toned sunset shades on the western horizon being replaced by an unyielding curtain of black. The only things visible across the bay were the occasional downward flashbulb flares of lightning, which unfortunately weren't close enough to chase us off the ride. At least not yet.

"Whoa! Did you see that bolt over there? It went all the way down to the ground." I said, trying to fill the silence.

"Yeah, hopefully it will come our way. Man, I just can't believe it," said Travis, again pointing over to the parked coaster. "You saw already. That thing is a bear in the rain,"

"That was a healthy push it needed to get on the chain."

"You should've felt how it slid through the brake. I didn't think it was going to stop."

"I thought you did that on purpose."

"The hell I did. Man...at least if we were working the Airborne or the miniature golf we'd have a booth to sit in."

"The Ghost Ship guys have cover, too," I said looking across through the floodlit drops to the porch like outcropping that covered the ride's loading area.

"Yeah, but they've got all that electrical stuff going on inside. Think I'd rather be out in the rain."

That was definitely something I hadn't considered.

We paced the platform aimlessly for a few more minutes, the rain seeming to let up even though we could still see flashes of lightning far off on the mainland to our left. I was still looking westward when Calvin started up our "Exit" ramp.

"Come on Calvin, shut us down. This is a total washout," said Travis.

"Wouldn't count on it. Remember, the park's only open for another week and a half, so we've got to make every night count," said Calvin, who'd just arrived at the chained opening on our inner railing.

"But you know this ride doesn't like the rain," said Travis, continuing to plead his case.

"Seems to be letting up, it should be able to dry out. Here, I brought you guys some towels for the seats."

I stepped forward and took the thick white wad of folded towels that Calvin was offering and stuffed them under my arm. In looking down and making a rough count, it seemed like there were at least half a dozen.

"Also, word is that a ride inspector might be in the park tonight," continued Calvin. "So, don't let anybody sit in the seats where the bars don't lock."

"Tonight? Hell, the giveaway will be that he'll be the only one on the ride," said Travis, finally easing up with a smile and a laugh.

"Give it time. People will show now that the rain has stopped."

"We'll see. I'd bet you if I had any money."

Calvin was right. Once the rain let up, people seemed eager to get out and find something to do after spending the day cooped up in their condos and hotel rooms. And Playland, with its lights fully ablaze, was visible from all up and down Coastal Highway. Maybe we weren't the original destination, but someone could be on the road at 45th Street or 90th Street and see that the park was open. So why take a chance on driving all the way to the boardwalk, Trimper's, or Jolly Roger, when heck, you could just pull into an obviously up and running Playland? This "lights on at all cost" strategy paid off as more and more people came through the front gates. Not that we were overly busy, but we'd gone through all the towels and had them scattered around the loading platform like family beach towels on a hotel balcony railing. A simple fact of the evening was that anybody who came into the park had to reconcile themselves with having a wet bottom, no matter what we ride operators did.

Traffic on the ride was steady, albeit light, with Travis and me even sending out a couple of runs with just a pair of guests in the coaster train, which was running at warp-speed and engaged in an ornery ongoing battle with the brake and the lift hill. The chain and coaster train had actually frozen a few runs earlier, seeming to ponder for a moment whether they wanted to keep working on this miserable night (I know I didn't) before jolting back to life and dragging our half dozen riders the rest of the way up the hill. Since the incident was at least 20 minutes in the distant past, I'd let it slide out of my worries until the cars I'd just pushed onto the chain stopped dead – two-thirds of the way up the hill, easily 50 feet off the ground.

Oh my God. What I was I seeing? It couldn't be, this couldn't really be happening, could it? How could the cars just go dead in the middle of the hill...on a night a ride inspector was in the park?

Thanks to the anti-rollback mechanism – the clicking heard on every coaster hill – the cars weren't in any danger of rolling backward. At least, that's what I assumed. But my nervous system kicked into high gear when I looked over at Travis, seeing his open-mouthed astonishment as he stared up at the crippled coaster train.

"Oh, shit-shit-shit," he mumbled to no one in particular, pivoting away from the brake lever to switch the ride's main power off and then back on, apparently hoping for some sort of reset in the circuitry. He then began working the green "On" button like a hurried man in an elevator, frantically flicking his thumb as if he needed 30 presses to get to the 30th floor. The coaster didn't budge an inch. The chain was still dead.

Travis repeated the process as my gaze shifted anxiously between the coaster and the shadowed corner where Travis was trying to revive the ride. And our natives were getting restless.

"Hey! Hey man, what's up down there?" came a loud male voice from a car I couldn't identify.

"Give us a moment, we're working on it," Travis yelled back, without looking up to the hill.

We're working on it?

While it was nice to be included, I had nothing to do with the coaster being stuck, or unstuck. And despite a third reset try, Travis still couldn't bring the chain back to life. He abandoned his resuscitation efforts and stood up, looking me dead in the eye.

"Fuck. We'll have to go up and get them," Travis spat out in what could best be described as a violent whisper.

"Uh, okay, sure. How?" I asked with really not much on my mind other than my fear of heights. So, I'd always wanted to work on a roller coaster...

"You go up on the right walkway, I'll go up on the left. I'll release the restraint bars, and you walk them down and off the ride. All the way off – make sure they go down the ramp. Then come back up for the second car."

"Just one car at a time?"

"Yep, that's procedure. And take your time coming back up. The walkways on the lift hill always have a film of grease on them. And now they're wet."

I listened carefully to Travis, although just as I couldn't believe what I was seeing, I honestly couldn't believe what I was hearing. And what he was asking. That someone with a significant fear of heights, which I wasn't going to throw into the equation at this point, needed to ascend a narrow greasy rain-soaked maintenance walkway five stories into the air while holding onto a warping waist-high two-by-four railing that overlooked the unyielding asphalt of Playland's southern midway.

This *was not* what I signed up for.

Or even the kind of thing I'd ever had rolling around in my imagination about ride running. I mean, what kind of sick person dreams about all the things that can go wrong with a ride? On the positive side, both walkways had a series of parallel wooden strips that had been laid about a foot apart all the way around the track. And they were significant enough in size to make it look like there was a dual set of steps lining the lift hill. So there were footholds for traction that would hopefully counter the grease and the rain, which had once again started falling lightly out of the sky.

This was all just a bit much, with things piling up so fast that I found it hard to pinpoint which concern was my biggest. But I had a job to do. I had to help get the riders down off the hill. That was what I grabbed onto. For the moment.

"We're coming up to get everybody off," Travis yelled up the hill to the coaster train, where the riders maneuvered in their seats to turn around and listen. "Please stay seated and follow our instructions. We'll be up in just a minute."

"Do you guys need a hand?" said a familiar voice from off to our right. It was Rick over on the Rotor, who had a birds-eye view of the situation because his control post was equal in height to where the coaster had stopped its climb.

"I think we're fine Rick, thanks. If you see any relief people let them know we need Moon and Melvin," answered Travis.

"Ah, I think the coaster being stopped halfway up the hill is enough of a 'Bat Signal' for everybody in the park. They'll probably be along at any moment."

"Yeah, you're probably right. But just want to be 'official' about it and make sure it gets reported."

"Wouldn't sweat it, Travis. I really wouldn't."

Travis gave Rick a halfhearted wave and turned his attention back to me as he moved to the base of the hill.

"Are you ready? This doesn't happen every day you know."

"Yeah, thank God. I'm as ready as I'll ever be," I answered, still unsure if that was ready enough. My fear of heights was a funny thing, as I had no problem pole vaulting, riding tall rides, or even standing where Rick was over on the Rotor. But when it hit, it was like one of those lightning bolts off on the horizon – swift and sudden, with an immediate and devastating impact. That's what had happened during a trip to Niagara Falls when I couldn't bring myself to get within ten feet of the cliffside railing on the Luna Island overlook. The fear that filled every cell of my body was so intense and so involuntary, coming from somewhere deep inside, that my feet froze to the ground as my heart and mind raced frantically, unable to shake irrational yet overpowering thoughts of falling over the side. Even watching my parents stand next to the railing...I was paralyzed by my escalating internal hysteria. This inability to control what was going on in my head set off a wave of panic that I could only make subside by moving onto solid ground, with "solid ground" being something I could neither define nor verbalize, but something that my body instinctively knew when my feet found it.

So, was I going to end up frozen on the lift hill, too panicked and petrified to help our stranded riders? Yeah, that was a possibility. Travis might yet be asking Rick for a hand.

But this was my job – I had to do this. I mean, I didn't really have to. Travis didn't know it, but I was on short time, with Saturday being my last day working the park. So would it really matter if I couldn't do this? Yeah, it would, it would matter to me. Like paddling out on a big day, this was a challenge I had to overcome. And to do that I set about channeling the mindset of a big day, specifically the pre-surf moments when I stood on the beach and assessed what needed to do done to make it out through the roaring walls of whitewater. There was always doubt, in addition to the intimate knowledge of the "caught inside" thrashing I'd likely take somewhere during the session. But despite my unease and second thoughts, I'd never failed to put my board in the water on a big day. Paddling out was just something that had to be done...as was going up to get the riders off the coaster.

The lift hill sloped upward like an intermediate ski run and was modestly lit by several pairs of floodlights, plus spillover from the Rotor. In taking my first step onto the hill, looking up into the starless night sky, everything melted away except for the patter of rain and the irregular flapping of the coaster flags, their worn and ragged edges blending into the darkness as they pointed away from Travis and me in the easterly wind. Underfoot things felt pretty solid. The wooden strips weren't all that slippery and spaced so closely together that I could take three at a time with a normal stride as my right hand clung to the ride's outside railing, which didn't feel as flimsy as it looked and provided track-level luminescence for the climb, being lined with hundreds of flashing light bulbs that hung from an electrical line draped along its outer edge. I didn't dare look over the railing onto the ever-receding asphalt, content to fix my gaze on the chain or even over at Travis, as for some reason looking into the center of the ride didn't activate any sense of dread as we continued climbing toward the immobile coaster.

Travis stopped at the back of the first car we reached (actually the third car in the train) while I continued walking up to its front. The back and front seats were occupied, the middle seat not being used tonight because the restraint bar didn't lock.

"Is everyone okay?" asked Travis.

This elicited a disorganized collection of up and down head shakes from the riders combined with a couple of "uh-huhs."

"Does anyone feel uncomfortable, like they need to get off right away?"

This time it was a disorganized collection of back and forth head shakes with some "un-uhs."

"Okay, good, good. There's no danger of rolling backward because the cars are locked on the anti-rollback device. So, what we're going to do is get you out one car at a time. Please, please be careful when you step out onto the walkway. It's a little slippery tonight," Travis finished, then looked over at me. "Ready?"

"Yep," I said, surprised that I actually was. That we had a purpose, a job to do...I wasn't exactly comfortable with my back wedged against a four-inch-wide railing that was the only barrier between me and a 50-foot drop to the ground, but the task had centered and focused me. Not to mention that our stuck riders didn't need to see a nervous ride oper-ator. It was important for them to be confident in what Travis and I were doing – even if we weren't.

"I'm going to unlock the lap bars, and you guys step out, one seat at a time," Travis said, crouching down to seat level, delivering his instruc-tions to the riders as face-to-face as he could manage. He had their attention as he pulled up on the release mechanism at the back of the car.

"Okay, go ahead and step out," he said, waving at the teen girls in the seat beside me. "Be careful when you get on the walkway."

I really couldn't imagine having a complete stranger ask me to step out into the surreal realm of mist and shadows near the top of the lift hill. And only by being up there did I fully grasp how awkward the exits would be. Even though Travis released the bar, it wouldn't stay up on its own because of the tilting angle of the coaster. That left the girls work-ing as a tag team, with the one on the inside holding the bar up while the girl closest to me crawled under and around its hefty red piping before squeezing through the coaster's slanted side opening, which now angled awkwardly backward into an almost horizontal position. Without hesi-tation I offered my hand to help her get upright, experiencing a flushed second of doubt as I extended out my right arm, not from the height, but remembering how an Ocean City lifeguard once told me that touch-ing a swimmer during a rescue was the absolute last resort because you never knew what a frightened person might do. But I had no regrets and was instantly gratified when the girl pulled hard on my arm truly need-ing the extra point of balance while swinging her feet over the coaster's bulky running boards and down onto the tilting walkway.

"Are you okay," I asked as she gingerly got her feet set in this other-worldly setting high above the park.

"Yes, yes, okay," she said, shaking her head for added confirmation as her hands clasped tightly onto the railing.

"Good, okay, go ahead and step down, I'll help your friend out."

It was obvious that getting the next girl out was going to be more of a challenge. So I let go of the railing and braced my body against the coaster, lifting the lap bar entirely out of her way with my right hand while still being able to offer my left hand to help her out of the back-ward leaning seat. She made a smooth and quick exit from the car, and we all moved down to the last seat where a boy of driving age was able to get himself and his girlfriend out onto the walkway with me being just an observer.

"Yeah, go ahead and walk them down," Travis said to me before turning back to the still stranded riders. "I'm staying here while he takes them down. And then he'll come back for the next car."

There was an attempt at idle chatter as we descended, not on my part as I was preoccupied with getting the riders off and making sure my heels got anchored solidly on the wood strips.

"Does this happen often?" asked the young man innocently enough, although I wondered whether he was really curious or just trying to impress his date.

"First time this year as far as I know. It's the weather," I answered just as we just stepped off the hill and onto the loading platform, my body doing an involuntary shudder as my feet detected solid ground.

"Sorry about all this," I said, removing the chain from the Exit opening. "Thank you for making things easy for us. I'm really sorry."

"Will the coaster be running again tonight?" asked the first girl I'd helped out of the seats.

"I hope so. I hope you get to finish your ride. Check back a little later."

I finished taking them down the Exit ramp then made the climb back up to Travis, again focusing my eyes on the lift chain to keep from looking at the receding ground on the other side of the railing.

"I think we can get them all off in one shot," said Travis as I reached the coaster train. This made sense. There were only six people left – four in the second car, and two in the front seat.

"Sure, why not?" I said, walking up to the very front of the coaster, where a young couple had the honors of being the ones who'd made it the farthest up the hill. I waited for Travis to release their lap bar before pulling it up to let them out. The three of us then took a few steps down to the second car, where Travis and I got the remaining riders out of their seats.

"Alright, let's get out of here!" Travis said in a tone that didn't disguise his relief, although we still had some work to do in getting everyone off the ride. Fortunately, the walk down was uneventful, and when we finally hit the flat boards of the loading platform, I looked up from my focus on the young man in front of me to see Moon and Melvin standing over by the brake lever. Travis peeled off wordlessly, stepping across the empty track to consult with our repair duo while I continued escorting our riders to the Exit ramp. As with the last group, I thanked them for making things easy and apologized for the "thrill" of having to negotiate the lift hill on foot to finish their ride.

Back up on the platform, everyone's attention was on the hill as I tried and failed to covertly turn the trio into a quartet, with Moon offering a nod to acknowledge my arrival at Travis' shoulder. For some reason, he looked different tonight, so much so that I couldn't help myself from staring at him until I figured out why – his trademark mirror shades were sticking up out of his work shirt's breast pocket. This was the first chance I'd had this summer to see his eyes, which were brown and bloodshot, and framed by more than a hint of up-all-night puffiness.

But damn...things must be serious.

"What the hell did you guys do to my ride?" said Melvin with a stern look, which he held just long enough to make Travis and me squirm before he and Moon broke into their familiar stereo laughter. I didn't join them but was relieved that he wasn't serious.

"Had you going, didn't I?" chuckled Melvin, who now turned his attention to a pair of boys who'd come up the "Entrance" ramp. "Hey, can't you see the ride is closed?"

Moon didn't speak but helped explain Melvin's point further by gesturing up the lift hill with his arm, making the boys quickly retreat back into the park.

"C'mon, let's see if we can get this thing going," said Melvin, as he and Moon moved towards a wooden gate next to the lift hill. Moon pulled the gate inward, which gave access to a short set of stairs that both men descended, quickly evaporating into the crisscrossing thicket of yellow beams that concealed the lift chain's malfunctioning motor.

"We just wait?" I said, looking at Travis.

"Yep. They'll do whatever they need to do."

Although Moon and Melvin were out of sight under the lift hill, we could hear conversation and the occasional "clank" from whatever it was they were doing down there. And it wasn't all that long before Melvin's head poked out from an opening in the side of the lift hill's framework.

"You got this thing off, right?" he asked.

"Right – everything is all off right now," answered Travis.

"Okay, then turn it all on, and hit the green button."

Travis went over and switched on the power, pressed the green button, and there was a metallic groan and "clunk-clunk-clunk-clunkity-clunkity-thunk" as the coaster chain began slowly moving, finishing its job of delivering the cars to the top of the hill.

Fifteen minutes too late.

Once the chain clattered back to life Moon and Melvin bounded out from under the ride, with Melvin taking up watch at the brake lever, closely following the movement of the coaster train as it made its way around the track. When the cars rumbled around the final turn and started into the loading area – with more speed than Travis would ever allow – Melvin pulled lightly on the brake lever, maybe only getting it to an upright 90°position before letting the speeding cars run almost a third of the way up the lift hill to catch the still-flawlessly moving chain. After the silver coaster train released for a second time into the horseshoe left at the top of the hill, Melvin eyed it like a mid-ocean Captain Ahab, again letting the cars charge right through the loading area and back onto the chain, which didn't hesitate at all despite the extra forces being put upon it. For the third time the coaster successfully came off the chain and rocketed around the track, creating a platform shaking earthquake as it moved into the loading area, Melvin now throwing a maniacal bug-eyed "It's alive!" grin at Travis and me as the chain lashed onto the coaster for a fourth consecutive time. Joining in the action was a smiling Moon, who'd actually lit his Winston and blown a large backlit smoke cloud that curled around Melvin in a spine-chilling mad-scientist moment that could have been immortalized in the Ghost Ship, or better yet, the live actor fright-fest of the pier's Morbid Manor. (And here we have the "Ride Operator from Hell!") Travis and I remained silent but in "what the fuck is going on here?" eye contact while Melvin ran the coaster through two more times before expertly stopping the cars right at our feet. He and Moon exchanged nods before turning back to Travis and me.

"There – I think she's ready," said Melvin contentedly, dialing his smile down to its standard slightly devilish incarnation. Travis' shock wore off before mine, and he was able to make a rational response to what had been an extraordinary few minutes.

"Thanks, Melvin. Promise we'll keep a close eye on it the rest of the night," said Travis.

Melvin didn't say anything, turning away from Travis to look at me.

"He wants to meet you, you know," he said, my jumbled thoughts unable to make immediate sense of what he said.

"Uh...what?" I responded, finally unscrambling Melvin's riddle just as the words left my mouth.

"Leland, your grandfather. He wants to meet you before you leave Playland."

The words exploded on the end of my nose, knocking my head involuntarily backward while turning into stars before my eyes, like I was on a wet stage and had put my lips on an ungrounded microphone. I blinked hard to ease the tingling sensation still lingering on my face, and also to bring some coherence back to my thoughts. My legs, which had momentarily buckled, felt full of sand.

This was definitely not what I signed up for!

Chapter Forty

Downtown

Just how Moon and Melvin discovered I was on short time at the park was a mystery. Well, maybe it wasn't, they knew everything. And it seemed like they knew everybody, including my grandfather, who they were now insistent that I meet. I'd put them off twice yesterday, and again when I arrived at the park tonight. But then they found me on break from the coaster. Melvin was dogged in pushing for the encounter, as I presumed he had a stronger relationship with my grandfather than Moon did.

"Ah, he's just an old man, what could it hurt?" was Melvin's mantra. It was also his "seal the deal" line – I'd agreed to talk to Leland tomorrow afternoon before my final Playland shift started. After saying yes, my anxiety mounted steadily through the remainder of the night, and by the time Travis and I shut the coaster, my focus was so frayed that I barely heard what he was saying, even to the point where Travis asked if I was okay. Although I appreciated his concern, I still blew him off with a quick "I'm fine," unsure of what to do with the unsettled feeling deep inside me, a continuous vibration that felt like an AM radio being rapidly spun up and down the dial. There were so many questions...not ones that I wanted to ask tomorrow, or even wanted to ever discuss with this long-lost blood-related stranger. But ones I still wanted answers to. My dad, aunt, and grandmother were the obvious sources for answers, but I didn't want them to know that any of this was taking place. Hell, I hadn't even told Greg or Robin, who I was picking up at the bus station after work. She'd quit her job early, too, and we were going to spend the final week of the summer "on vacation" at the condo. Greg was supposed to ride along for the pickup, but as my unease mounted through the night, I'd asked him if he could catch a ride with Gary. Initially, I felt bad, yet it turned out I'd done Greg a favor by eliminating this detour from his evening. Katie would gladly give Greg a ride so their after-work date could get an early start.

It felt strange turning out of Playland onto southbound Coastal Highway, driving past Capt. Bob's illuminated bull and the empty front porch of the glowing Sunshine House before getting stuck at the red light at 62nd Street, where I watched a seemingly endless line of inbound cars stream off the Route 90 Bridge. Traffic was thick, as it should be on the next to last Friday in August, with the summer in its final throes and the weekend throngs from Baltimore and Washington heading "down the ocean" for a final fling in the sun before Labor Day. Once the light went green, proof of this hypothesis was immediately off to my right at the bay end of 60th Street, where a backup of brake lights spilled out of Fager's overflowing parking lot.

My grandfather had always been a riddle, one of those unknowable conundrums, like the exact point in space where the universe comes to an end. I wasn't sure I'd ever heard my father utter a single word about him, which I guess wasn't a complete surprise, as from what I could piece together, my grandfather was out of the picture not long after my father was born. My aunt, on the other hand, appeared to have some actual recollection, characterizing him as an "SOB" who'd not been faithful to my grandmother. And my grandmother, on the rare occasions I'd witnessed my grandfather's name come up in her presence, would just look the other way and say "that's all in the past," seeming to stare far off into the distance as if watching a movie that only she could see. In thinking about it, most of what I knew about my grandfather came from my great uncle. He was the only one who ever had anything positive to say, apparently having spent significant time riding shotgun while my grandfather drove his truck. But what kind of truck? Did he have his own truck? I never knew. But according to my great uncle, he was one of hell of a driver.

Which led to another part of the story, which was just as murky and beyond the Milky Way as everything else. Supposedly, as Melvin confirmed, my grandfather drove race cars. And somewhere in all this he'd gotten in an accident and been badly injured. I wasn't sure if it was in a race car or in a truck, with the story going that he had a choice between hitting people and hitting a pole. A consistent part of the story was that he had taken the pole, and in the aftermath, after a lengthy recovery, he "wasn't right." There was never any definitive pathology beyond that. It also wasn't clear if this had taken place before, during, or after the time he and my grandmother were married.

These thoughts flashed through my head like the countless signs lining Coastal Highway, keeping me preoccupied as I rode the clutch through stop-and-go traffic all the way to where the Jolly Roger pirate stood in darkness off to my right, the park now closed except for the westward pointing floodlights of the driving range. Thankfully traffic opened up here, able to spread out to Baltimore Avenue, where the town's densest cluster of oceanfront hotels set the sky ablaze with neon and lit the area with enough wattage that headlights weren't necessary. Still fully illuminated at 21st Street was the two-story block-long façade of Phillips, where I knew the kitchens were just starting to break down – if they were lucky – as the waitresses attempted to gently shoo their final tables out the front door.

Layton's was still open at 16th Street, and then things turned back into night as I moved into the streets with single-digit numbers, an area that was mostly residential other than the small shopping center at 8th Street and the post office at 6th Street. I kept going, passing the darkened softball field on my right at 3rd Street, then the bus station at 2nd Street, my eyes being drawn to the lifelike steer painted on the rectangular Melvin's Steakhouse sign at 1st Street. Robin's bus had probably just arrived. Unfortunately, she was going to have to spend some time on the wooden benches in front of the station. And live with the little white lie that we ran late at Playland tonight.

In the hopes of getting some answers about my grandfather I flicked on my right turn signal and downshifted into second gear just after the merge of the Route 50 Bridge, turning onto Dorchester Street. As expected, both sides of the street were full of cars as I cautiously moved toward the still illuminated "Ocean City Marina" sign that served as a gateway to the boat docks. Deciding to circle the block, I turned right on St. Louis Avenue, then turned right again at Paul's Tackle Shop, uttering an audible "fuck" upon seeing both sides of Talbot Street completely filled with cars. After Talbot dumped me back out onto Philadelphia Avenue, I skipped Dorchester to turn right at the Ice House. From there I began drifting down Somerset Street, past the White Marlin Restaurant and its illuminated rooftop red letters, finding no vacancy among the diagonal spaces in front of the sleek charter boats lined up on my left. I took my usual nosy look into the Harbor Inn's cigarette smoke-filled interior and went right again on St. Louis. Guess I shouldn't have been surprised that there wasn't an empty legal inch of asphalt available down here.

This left me no choice but to turn back onto Dorchester Street, where I pulled into the already full driveway of the Ocracoke Apartments, leaving the back half of my Sunbird hanging across the sidewalk. I figured I was safe for now, even with the police just a block away, knowing that they'd check with the very prominent property owner inside before taking any action. Quickly climbing the three familiar front steps, I knocked gently on the screen door, seeing that the television was still glowing off to my left in the front corner of the porch.

"Yes?" came Mrs. Bunting's distinctly hoarse voice.

"Mrs. Bunting? Mrs. Bunting, it's Earl Shores." I said softly through the screen.

"Earlie?" she asked, calling me by my childhood nickname.

"Yes, it's me. Can I talk with you for a few minutes?"

"Sure child – is everything alright?"

"Yes...oh yes, I'm fine," I said, realizing she thought I might be in trouble or have a serious problem. Well, I did have a problem, but it wasn't a call the police or the ambulance kind of emergency. "Everybody's fine. Do you have a few minutes?"

"Sure, sure child, the door's open, come on in."

Opening the door and entering the familiar layout of the porch, I could have been six-years-old, ten-years-old, or anywhere between then and now. Mrs. Bunting, like always, was looking up at me from her chair. House dress and apron on, as usual, with a pink sweater over her shoulders despite the warmth of the evening. The porch was entirely dark except for a flickering police scanner and the cathode glow of the television, which reflected off Mrs. Bunting's oversized bifocals.

"Come on in, sit – sit down, Earlie," she said, reassuringly. "You sure do look sharp in that uniform. That's some yellow."

"Thanks. They make them bright so we stand out in the park," I said, sitting down in the wooden chair next to the doorway that led into her house. That being the chair in closest proximity to Mrs. Bunting's chair, as I didn't plan on entertaining the entire neighborhood with our conversation.

"You might be fine, but the look on your face says, maybe you're not," she said perceptively. As usual.

"I'm not sure where to start," I said, noticing my hands were trembling. And damned if this wasn't the first time I'd ever felt nervous sitting in this room – but I continued. "Turns out some people at Playland know my grandfather."

"Leland?" asked Mrs. Bunting, putting her hand up to her mouth so the tips of her fingers covered her lips.

"Yes, he wants to meet me. Tomorrow at Playland."

It was strange to have Mrs. Bunting go quiet and look away from me to stare at the Salisbury newsman on the television.

"I know nothing about him. The only person who ever really talked about him was Uncle Earl," I said, filling in the silence.

"Yes...yes, that makes sense. He was like a big brother to your Uncle Earl. Earl was the baby in the family. When Leland courted your grandmother, Earl finally had a male near his age."

"My aunt despises him, and my dad never ever talked about him. About all I know is that he's originally from this area. That's right?"

"It is. Last I heard Leland was in Salisbury. He was born in Mt. Vernon. That's on the west side of Salisbury."

"Did he ever see, or try to see my aunt or my dad when they stayed with you back in the 1940s or 1950s?"

"Nope. He never bothered. That's because he knew he wasn't welcome."

"You do know the story? You have some idea of what happened between him and my grandmother?"

"I don't know all of it. I know what I saw."

"They got together down here, didn't they?"

"Hmm-mmm. They did. Gimme' a second, Earlie," said Mrs. Bunting, getting up out of her chair to disappear through the doorway into the darkness of the house. After a few moments, I heard some rustling, like the opening of multiple boxes. Then the rustling stopped, and Mrs. Bunting returned with a small rectangular photo that she placed into my hand.

It was a sepia image of a young woman seated on a wooden bulkhead, posing in front of a large body of water that faded off into an infinity-like distance that was far beyond the capabilities of the camera. Her ear-length dark hair had long bangs that flowed into an intentional downward curl on the right side of her forehead, and she was wearing a long, flowered short sleeve dress beneath an overcoat that had been draped across her back and shoulders. The purposeful positioning of the coat allowed her bare arms to extend out to her knees, where her glove-covered hands locked together to make sure the dress remained appropriately in place for the photo. A string of pearls hung around her neck, directing your attention to a tight smile and piercing eyes – I would've guessed blue – that jumped off the yellowing paper like stars on a cloudless night. She was stunning, looking like a silent screen movie star.

"That's your grandmother," said Mrs. Bunting.

"Oh my God..."

"She was younger than you when that was taken. I'm thinking 1930 or 1931. She was something, wasn't she?"

"I just..."

"You never think of old people ever being young, do you?" said Mrs. Bunting with a laugh. "But we were."

I continued to stare at the image. The eyes – they were my grandmother's eyes. But the rest, the youth, the beauty – was it okay to think that? – I was at a loss for words.

"Had to beat the boys off with a stick. Did you know she'd won a dance contest up at the Pier Ballroom?"

"No, I never knew that."

"Yep, she surely did. She was the dickens, too. Those were the speakeasy days. She'd sneak out of here, I'd hear her, I knew – then try to sneak back in. This was when I only rented rooms. Believe me, it was a challenge to get in and out of here quietly."

"Sneaking to a speakeasy? My grandmother?!"

"Yeeesss, indeed!" said Mrs. Bunting, with a big smile and her distinctively chortling laugh, which was comforting to hear at this moment. "Things you never ever thought about."

"So, how did they meet?"

"One of the dances on the pier. Let's see, I'm pretty sure she was 16. That a' made –" Mrs. Bunting held up her right hand, moving her thumb over her first three fingers. "Leland was 19, I think."

With my thoughts bubbling like an over aerated aquarium, there weren't a whole lot of words working their way to my mouth, so I left it to Mrs. Bunting to keep the conversation moving.

"Oh, it was love, those two. Of course, your great-grandmother and great-grandfather didn't approve. She was too young. And he was, well, just not what they wanted for Alice. They thought they was better than him."

"I'm not totally surprised. Why didn't they –"

"Approve? Oh, he was from down here, first of all. You know, backwoods, backward, and all that. He was a truck driver."

"That I'd heard."

"And he did some racing, too."

"I'd kind of heard that. From Uncle Earl."

"From what I heard, he was good at the racing. But once they got married, he had to quit."

"How did they end up married if the family didn't approve?"

Mrs. Bunting took a surprising pause to look off to the street before looking me in the eye with her answer.

"Alice was barely 18 when she had your aunt."

Now it was my turn to pause as I ran the math and the possibilities that Mrs. Bunting didn't say directly, but left open to implication.

"Oh. I see – I think."

"And did you know that Alice lost a child? Stillborn. Would have been between Peggy and your father."

"No, I had absolutely no idea."

"Then not long after your father was born, Leland was back down here."

"Wasn't there an accident or something?"

"Yes, he hit a pole with his truck. Spent some time in the hospital."

"Supposedly he wasn't the same after the accident?"

"That's what I heard. They weren't married by the time that happened."

"Oh."

I took a pause to look at the television, which had a slightly snowy image of Johnny Carson working through his opening monologue. It was nice to have gotten some answers, but it seemed like those answers had only served to create more questions – which might never be answered. Glancing down at my watch, oh shit, I needed to get Robin.

"I've got somebody waiting for me at the bus station, so I need to get going. But thank you, Mrs. Bunting, you've been a great help," I said, standing up to move toward her chair and take her hand.

"Sure child, you take care. It was good to see you. Don't be such a stranger. And tell everybody I said 'hello.'"

She didn't mean anything, but my bouncing stomach completely dropped when she said "everybody," because I didn't want my family to know that this conversation took place. Fortunately, it was a reminder that I needed.

"Oh, I will. I certainly will. Just one thing," I said, looking at the still organized wrinkles on Mrs. Bunting's face. "Can we keep this conversation just between you and me, at least for now?"

"Earlie, you have my word. You just be sure to let me know how things turn out."

"Thanks, I will. You have my word."

Chapter Forty-One

A Meeting

A s usual, things worked out differently than I'd hoped. I mean, how was it that out of my reluctance to lie to Moon and Melvin I was now telling lies to the people who were closest to me? But that's what I'd done in figuring out a way to get to Playland at 12:15 pm without revealing the actual reason I needed to be there early. Greg and Robin were fully accepting of my cover story that Mark and I needed to go over some paperwork because it was my last day. And Greg even seemed glad to have an excuse for another ride from Katie, an arrangement that would continue until Playland closed the following weekend. I was unnerved by the "advantage" I had when telling my lie. That advantage being, I wasn't someone who told lies, so neither Greg nor Robin had a second thought that my explanation might be on the fishy side. Which was fine with me. Essentially my grandfather was and would remain a phantom – if all went well. So why should this meeting not be a phantom event?

But I wasn't going to be meeting a phantom. My grandfather wasn't a ghost, or at least he wasn't going to be for a short time this afternoon. He was going to be completely real. Not only was I going to see him, but I was also going to interact with him. On what level, I had no clue.

The day had started off cloudy, but now the sun was out as I made the turn at 65th Street and cruised by the artificial grassy mound of the Slide N' Ride before getting into Playland's parking lot. Just a handful of vehicles were lined along the go-kart fence, and I could see Moon and Melvin standing beside a rust-stained blue-and-white pickup truck, the brand of which wasn't apparent until I pulled up into the adjacent row and saw the "F-O-R-D" across the back of the tailgate. Moon and Melvin continued talking into the truck's passenger window while I sat and gathered my nerve to step out of the car, feeling my ever-increasing heart rate pound in my ears like a marching band bass drum. I was doing the meeting "naked," leaving my sunglasses and hat in the car, feeling like it was the proper thing to do (confirming that my morals were still intact despite telling a lie to be here). Moon and Melvin both offered nods as I walked toward the truck, with Melvin finally introducing me with a smiling "here he is." Purposely I'd not yet looked in the window. My mouth was as dry as my armpits were wet. And it was a decidedly sandy low-tide dry.

I wasn't sure what to expect when I turned my head, but it took a couple of seconds for the scene to wash over me before I caught my breath. Sitting on the passenger side of the truck's bench seat was a frail, hunched old man. The top third of his head was entirely bald and flanked by close-cropped gray hair on the sides, sheared at a post-harvest cornfield length. A meandering sickle-shaped red scar dripped off his left cheek, while above it, his whited over left eye floated independently of his still working right eye, which fixed me with a penetrating gray-green iris. He was smiling, showing off a pair of yellowing, brown-edged front teeth, which were the last lonely holdovers on an otherwise empty upper gum line. Beside him at the steering wheel was a nervous looking woman with straw-like short white hair and a sleeveless pink top that revealed way too much of the elephant-like skin drooping off of her upper arms. I hated being so judgmental, but I'd spent the entire summer "people watching with prejudice." At this point, it was a reflex.

Quickly my eyes moved back to my grandfather, where I tried hard not to stare at the untethered orb occupying his left eye socket, focusing instead on his right eye and the prominent bridge of his nose. There was no way around it, they looked familiar. It wasn't quite a mirror, but...

"I'm sorry for not getting out, I have trouble moving around these days," were his first words, coming out in a wavering tone. "Earl...Earl junior, right? Nice to meet you."

Out of the window opening came his left arm, a mottled and shriveled limb that reminded me of the branches that trees shed during a windstorm. I couldn't help my slow-motion reaction to this gesture. It wasn't that I had an ingrained objection to shaking his hand, it was just that a left-handed handshake, even for a lefty, was an unnatural thing.

"My right arm doesn't work too well. And since we're both lefties, this kind of works out okay," he said, his smile growing to show off several stumpy bicuspids still lingering in his lower jaw. "Call me Leland."

"Hi, Leland," I said awkwardly shifting my feet to get my left hand up to the window frame and clasp his bony fingers, which had an odd lifeless quality, like I'd grabbed a steamed crab by its side legs.

"I've heard a lot about you over the last couple of weeks," Leland said, pointing to Moon and Melvin. "They say you're a hard worker. Polite, too. And good with the go-karts."

That brought a group chuckle from everyone, and smiles, too, which helped knock some tension out of the warm air.

"I'm flattered," I said, looking directly at Moon and Melvin. "I really enjoyed working here."

"It's funny, those two guys – they kind of look after me these days – said there's a kid named Shores working in the park. I was thinking, 'Nah, it can't be,' but here you are. You're in school, aren't you?"

"Yes, at the University of Delaware. Going into my junior year."

"Good! That's really something. And you work here during the summer?"

"Yes. I worked at Phillips last year. The Crab House downtown."

"I'm glad you didn't go back there this summer. You know, my hair, at least when I had hair, used to be blond like yours," Leland said with a laugh. Then his face changed, going more serious, but still carrying a smile. "How's your father?"

"He's a college professor. At a school just outside of Philadelphia," I said being on my guard not give too much away. But at the same time, our number was in the Philadelphia area phone book.

"I'm so happy to...that's wonderful, that really is," said Leland, his good eye looking directly at me. "The smarts came from your grandmother. Did you know she was a spelling bee champion? And how's your aunt doing? She doesn't think all that much of me."

"She's an executive for a local construction company."

"Is she married?"

"No. Not yet at least. She's too busy spoiling me," I said, thinking that maybe I shouldn't have said it. There was a pause as it looked like Leland was working hard to find his words.

"How's Earl? He would be your...Uncle Earl?"

"He's good, too. He has a landscaping business. He was actually in Ocean City a few weeks ago."

"We spent a lot of time together. I taught him how to drive, and how to work on an engine."

"Oh, he's quite the mechanic. He keeps everything running."

"And how's your grandmother?"

"She's doing well. She retired, but still looks after everyone."

"She was something. Very special."

I nodded in agreement. I thought so too.

"I did love her, I really did. But sometimes things don't work out. Actually, a lot of times things don't work out," continued Leland.

While I wasn't completely uncomfortable having a conversation with a stranger who was much more than a stranger, we were now straying into the realm of where I was getting more information than I wanted. Talking was okay, but I wasn't up for a confessional. Already I was having a hard time finding landmarks in the conversation that I wanted to flesh out with more than a single sentence. And what was just said...I wasn't touching it with a ten-foot pole. It was going to shrivel here in the sunshine until the discussion got pointed in a less weighted direction. So I didn't hesitate in trying to do that.

"How do you guys know each other," I asked, waving my left index finger back and forth between the truck and Moon and Melvin.

"I've known Melvin since he was a boy. His family was neighbors of mine in Salisbury, years ago," answered Leland, and from here the conversation moved into territory I was more comfortable with, and actually interested in. It turned out that once the marriage with my grandmother ended, Leland moved back to Salisbury and began racing cars again. He'd had several minor accidents and couldn't serve in WWII because of a damaged leg, even lying about his age when he tried to enlist. He raced sporadically after the war before finally deciding he'd had enough, saying that it was no longer a risk worth taking. The accident, the big one that even I'd heard about, took place on Route 13 near Nassawadox, Virginia in late 1958. A school bus pulled out in front of his truck and he swerved to avoid it, hitting a telephone pole head-on. It took him several years to fully recover from the accident, and after that, he worked mostly as a mechanic. Nobody wanted to hire a one-eyed truck driver.

More Playland people were starting to fill the parking lot, and I was a little worried that I wouldn't get into the park before Greg showed up. But then Moon and Melvin saved me, looking at their watches and saying they needed to get to work. I took this as my cue for a clean break.

"Well, I think I need to get inside, too," I said, watching Moon and Melvin make their way to the access road.

"Looks like you do. Thanks for taking the time..." said Leland.

"Sure, sure," I mumbled, struggling for some final words.

"It was nice to meet you and hear about everybody."

This gave me an uncomfortable feeling, and a question that needed an answer. Were we done communicating for just the moment, or were we done for good? I wasn't taking any messages home, that was for damn sure. And although I wasn't thrilled about the lies I'd told to get to this moment, I wasn't going to hesitate to tell another one if there was talk about having more contact. Maybe it was the uncertainty in my expression, or maybe it was his plan all along, but Leland cleared the air.

"I won't bother you again, you have my word," he said, sticking his left arm out the window a final time.

"You take care, then," I said, focusing on his good eye while shaking his hand, deliberately not saying "nice to meet you" because I wasn't sure that this traditional sentiment reflected how I felt.

"You take care," Leland said with a wave and a smile as I walked toward my car to get my hat and backpack.

"You too," I answered reflexively.

I didn't look back as I walked up the access road into the park. It wasn't my thing to conjure up an instant hate for someone I just met, especially an old man who was pretty much harmless at this stage of his life. But from all that I knew or at least half of what I knew, I should have been carrying a grudge as big as Playland's parking lot. But that's not what I was feeling. Not that I was ready to forgive and absolve him of whatever wrongs he inflicted on my father, aunt, and grandmother before he disappeared from their lives. "Disappeared" was the best I could do because I didn't know if he'd abandoned them or was shown the door. I had a feeling it was the latter, but I hadn't bothered to ask for clarification. Whatever wounds he inflicted, I didn't know what they were. Which was probably just as well as I had nothing to hold over his head as we talked. That made it easier to suspend reality and just have a conversation with an old man sitting in a car.

Albeit, like no other conversation I'd ever had.

Chapter Forty-Two

Vacation

T he morning session had been a bitch.

A meaty overhead swell was rolling into the beaches of Ocean City. It was the type of swell that could only be generated by a tropical system somewhere out in the Atlantic. It was also the type of swell that I'd been waiting for all summer. Yet as luck would have it, the wind was up, blowing onshore with a flag-flapping force that turned the waves disheveled and dumpy despite a brilliant overhead sun that made the ocean look deceptively inviting. I hadn't gotten far out from the Caine house when I realized that my eyes had given my brain some erroneous information.

That I was still emotionally underwater from yesterday didn't help. Unable to turn off my thoughts, sleep was perpetually one sheep away during the night. Surely, I kept Robin awake with my tossing. But having her here was a great comfort. It was a good feeling to know that we'd be together until school started next weekend.

Thanks to my insomnia I'd gotten up late, and had to suffer the weekend surfing beach crowds at 118th Street, which because of the size of the swell, was a self-selected gathering of the surfers who could make it to the lineup. In being late, I'd also slid my session into dead low tide.

This was usually a good thing at 118th Street, but the waves were mostly jumbo-sized closeouts. Beautiful and tantalizingly hollow, but hard to ride. A steep drop with high odds of burying the nose and going ass-over-head into two feet of water. And even when I negotiated the drop, there was only a short wall to dig into before a half-block long wall of water crashed over all at once with a thundering "foompf!"

With a full summer of surfing behind me, I had no qualms about paddling out into a mid-morning weekend surf scene, knowing my wave catching prowess and summer tan would give me cover as a local. Not to mention that I'd been a regular at 118th Street since early June. I might not have been a true local, but by now I was part of the 118th Street "crew." A couple of guys even backed out and gave me waves during the session, a nice compliment for sure, even if the waves did little but blast the board out from under my feet and push sand into openings of my body that I didn't want to think about.

Still, whether it was the events of yesterday, the lack of sleep, or just coming to grips with the summer being over...I was a mess. A half a beat slow to my feet and a half a stroke short on every wave. Summing up the *Twilight Zone* nature of the session was an event that happened right before I came in.

I'd been hanging with a pair of 118th Street regulars who I'd gotten to know through the summer – we knew each other's names, at least – when we heard multiple lifeguard whistles. The whistles blew shrill and long, which meant there was trouble in the water, so the three of us turned reflexively toward the beach, where we watched the 119th Street lifeguard jump down from his stand and sprint along the waterline to the guard at 118th Street. After a brief conversation that included a lot of pointing out to the vicinity of where we were sitting, the 119th Street guard pulled off his sweatshirt and started swimming out into the ocean.

"Wow, somebody must be in trouble," said Kevin, a dark-haired surfer who lived at 126th Street and rode a slick yellow-railed 6'4" G & S pintail.

"Guess that's not too surprising, it's pretty funky out here," I said, looking over to Mark, who I could always recognize because of his navy Rip Curl wetsuit vest and his red-decked Heritage twin fin. (For whatever reason, I'd made a habit of pairing surfer's faces with the type of board they rode.)

"Thought they'd keep a tighter rein on the swimmers today. Some are venturing out pretty far," said Mark, continuing to look back toward the beach.

"It's low tide. The swimmers won't know they're in trouble until they *are* in trouble," I said, getting nods of agreement from Kevin and Mark.

We watched the lifeguard as he swam out, disappearing from sight when the sizeable sets rolled through, then reappearing out of the back of the wave with his orange rescue buoy trailing behind him on a white line. His smooth freestyle stroke ate up yardage quickly, so it wasn't long before he pulled up in front of us, treading water about 10 yards away all the while swiveling his head back and forth to scan the area.

It was a hell of an effort – but what in the hell was he doing out here?

"Somebody needed help. What happened to them?" asked the lifeguard between heavy breaths.

"Who needed help?" said Kevin, in a serious tone, making sure the guard understood that we weren't asshole surfers playing a game of "who's on first?"

"Someone was waving out here, waving for help," insisted the lifeguard.

"We haven't seen or heard anything, and we've been sitting here for a while," offered Mark, looking directly at the guard and being serious with his tone.

"Yeah, we just watched you swim out, but we haven't seen anyone struggling at all," I said, not adding that we certainly would've done something if we saw someone in trouble. In fact, I'd made a habit of asking people who seemed to be out too far for their own good if they were okay.

"Was it a swimmer or a surfer?" asked Mark.

"Couldn't really tell. Thought it was a swimmer," said the guard, now just catching his breath.

"We haven't seen any swimmers. And we haven't heard anything except the waves and your whistles," said Kevin.

"We would have let you know if someone had a problem. We might not care for the tourists, but we're not letting them drown," I said, generating nervous chuckles and nods from Mark and Kevin.

"Okay," said the guard, not looking totally convinced while still scanning the undulating brownish-green water. "Guess I'll head back."

"Yeah, we would let you know. The waves aren't that good today!" said Mark, trying to defuse the moment with some levity. It worked, as Kevin and I couldn't help from laughing.

None of us said a word as we watched the guard begin his long swim back to shore. And in this long moment of quiet, we all moved our eyes and heads for a secondary scan of the area around us. Finally, I broke the silence.

"Man, that was weird," I said.

"It was. I've never seen that before," said Kevin, who was on his third summer of living in Ocean City.

"Yeah, honestly, that kind of creeped me out. You guys didn't see anything, right?" quizzed Mark.

"No, nothing at all," I answered quickly.

"Uh-uh. Not a thing," said Kevin.

This brought us to another very uneasy silence, with all three of us again looking out to the horizon and then back to the beach.

"I might be done," I said, looking for an excuse to get out of the water.

"I think I'm done, with this spot at least," said Kevin.

"It's not much fun, anyway," added Mark.

"You guys take it easy then. See you during the week," I said, turning my board to paddle north toward the surfing beach's imaginary 119th Street border, looking for a wave to get me in. It wasn't long before a sizeable wall showed up, one that I knew I didn't have much chance of making. But I didn't care at this point, paddling as hard as I could, feeling the wave pick up my board and point its nose down the quickly going vertical wall of green.

The drop was heavy, very much an elevator shaft as I opted to go left and deal with the wave on my frontside. This allowed me to get my inside edge set early and make it cleanly down the face, all the while racing a fast closing guillotine edge which loomed over me as I tried for a quick turn off the bottom. A nice thought, however futile, because there was no way to outrun the glimmering chandelier of water now folding over me. Just before the lip detonated on my back, I turned the board hard toward shore, letting the wave's still building energy rocket me out of the impact zone and into the shallows where the pursuing whitewater would dissipate over the sand. I continued this at-the-beach heading for a few more seconds before making a calculated decision to fall off the back of the board into the foamy "cushion" of whitewater trailing behind me. A controlled and deliberate rear dismount being preferable to falling in front of the board and into the path of my unforgiving fiberglass surfboard fin.

After executing my exit plan perfectly, I was able to walk away from this off-kilter morning session completely intact and spend the first full day of my "vacation" with Robin, instead of with the doctors at the 94th Street Medical Center. And because of my freedom from a work schedule, I was able to paddle back out at 118th Street right as the lifeguards went off duty at 5:30 pm, the swell in the water now more organized and welcoming thanks to the slack wind and high tide.

The paddle out wasn't as challenging as I expected, which I could probably chalk up to being in prime shape after a full summer of surfing. I did feel fully "in tune" tonight, shaking off the vibe of the morning while putting yesterday's encounter with my grandfather a little bit further in the rear-view mirror. Floating over the fast-moving, oil-smooth mounds of greenish water...tonight, I was ready. Ready for what I was pretty sure were the biggest waves I'd been in all summer, something that Robin's telephoto lens could confirm once the film was developed. I was so grateful to have her here and so thankful that we made it to this point. The separation had been more challenging than we thought, but at least now I understood how much I wanted her in my life. And how much I loved her. It was the distance more than anything that made things hard, as I never had any inclination of letting my eyes wander. Playland wasn't really set up for that, although I was happy for Greg and Katie. She seemed like a great fit for Greg. I really hoped they could continue on together, but with Greg going back to Delaware and Katie heading off to the University of Richmond, the odds would be against them.

Only a handful of other surfers were out at the moment, which I found surprising because the conditions were significantly better than they had been earlier. But then again, it was a Sunday evening in late August. A lot of schools were back in session this week, so maybe people were packing up and hitting the road early. I'd discovered last year that the final week of the summer was almost a throwaway week. If you were here and still working, you were guaranteed to be getting overtime (well, maybe not at Playland). Every Ocean City business was short-handed now. There were fewer waitresses, cooks, busboys, lifeguards, and ride attendants throughout the resort. Which translated into additional wait times for tables and food, as well as food that spent extra time under the heat lamps as servers courageously attended to their additional tables.

So, there was plenty of space out in the water tonight, not that it mattered all that much to me. I was floating over the waves in my usual state – alone. I guess I'd gotten used to it, or at the least, accepting of my solo status. I still fought off the "empty" sensation out in the lineup, like something within me that knew the situation wasn't right. But it was how things ended up this summer, and how they'd been for quite a while now. Greg hadn't been on a surfboard for a month, or about one-third of our total time in Ocean City. I never asked him about it or asked him to make an official declaration that he was finished. And I never made any suggestions to him, however innocently, about picking up the board again. We both kind of *knew*, figuring the less said, the better. I still thought about Jack, John, and Harry, looking for their faces anytime I paddled out into the water.

I'd actually heard from Jack. He was back home in Seaford last week for a short stay before heading to VMI. He called, and we tried to set up a final surf session, but like so many things this year, it just didn't work out. I was able to tell him that his Playland body count was still on the Spider control box, something that he got a big kick out of. I also thanked him for helping me land the Playland job, as I'd had another memorable summer in large part because of Jack. He'd been right, Playland was a great place to work. And it meant a lot to me that some type of lineage between us continued with me working in the park. If only we could have worked there together.

Playland had been a trip. Almost the tale of two separate summers, with the finale being one of the trippiest events of my life. Meeting my own flesh and blood – I still wasn't sure what to make of it all. I don't know who else in the park knew about the meeting, but I still hadn't told anyone about it. Not Robin, not Greg, nor my family. Leland said he wouldn't bother me, or anyone else, and hopefully, he'd live up to his word. I half wished that I'd made him promise, but something about that felt wrong, even to have that thought while we were talking. He was thrilled to find out that my dad was a college professor. That was probably the biggest smile I saw from him. And he did seem genuinely happy to meet me, his left-handed grandson who had a knack for going fast (in go-karts, at least). There was something in his face when he shook my hand – a finality, a contentment – that I wouldn't deny him despite what I knew of his past.

This summer, like the last one, had been unlike any other summer of my life. But this summer, starting with my grades, to the frustration of the go-karts, to coming face-to-face with my never seen before grandfather...this summer was much heavier than the previous one. Last summer was like a "totally bitchen" surf magazine article where sunburn and busted surfboards were major events. This one, and hell, I even forgot about registering with the Selective Service, contained much darker shadings. And I was sure that this one probably was the more *real* and adult of the two, even to my understanding and appreciating that Greg wasn't happy surfing. For me to ask him or expect him to keep me company, that wasn't fair of me.

Of my decision not to deny an old man a chance to meet his own flesh and blood...I didn't have the heart to do otherwise. It had nothing to do with whether saying "yes" or "no" was the more adult thing to do. I simply made the decision I could live with for the moment. For the adult I am now, it was the best I could do. Only time would tell if I did what was right, just as only time would tell if I could heal my grades and point my life in an entirely new direction. And what a mighty undertaking that was going to be.

Yet at the moment there was something about the golden light of the evening and the undiluted energy in the swells passing below me that had my adrenaline levels positioned to where everything was clear and sharp. Each distinct ripple on the approaching waves, the rainbow shadings of the beach towels on the Carousel balconies, the telescope-like 500mm lens beside the Caine house that Robin had aimed in my direction...everything was in perfect focus. Even my thoughts were crystal clear, as despite the size of the swell and steady roar of the whitewater, I felt at one with the ocean. In a peaceful place, calm and fully aware that my existence in this world began right here in Ocean City. And that through some unseen pull that I couldn't explain I'd ended up living here, working here, surfing here, and even uncovering hidden parts of my past here – an intense head-to-toe shiver ran through me that had nothing to do with being cold.

Then, as if on cue, a significant set of waves rose up in the distance, their well-defined peaks seeming to glow as they rapidly moved toward me. And I was ready, more ready than I'd been for anything in my life. Quickly I ruled out the first wave, knowing it would likely be the smallest one in the set, and that if I missed it, I could end up getting caught inside. Wave number two had potential, but wave number three was bigger, and holding its enticing A-frame shape as it continued to build in size. My name was on this wave. It was just a matter of whether I wanted to go frontside or backside in taking it on.

I'd not ridden anything like it all summer, of that there was no doubt. So I began taking long, smooth strokes, looking back over my right shoulder at a fast-charging mountain of green that had only blue sky behind it. The thing was a monster and I wanted it, digging at the water with a churning determined rhythm that would have made my bedroom wall idol Mark Richards proud. Up the wave lifted me, higher and higher – c'mon arms, c'mon! – until I looked down onto an almost block-long black diamond wall, and kicked my feet to thrust my trusty 6'2" WRV into the wave. Then I felt it, the wave's extraordinary energy pull my board smoothly forward...the moment of no return had arrived. But there was no hesitation tonight. I pushed both hands into the fresh coat of wax on the deck of my board and popped up to my feet, getting a breathtaking overlook of the most magnificent natural roller coaster I'd ever seen. And I knew I was going to make it. It was something I felt deep inside of me.

All the way down to my Ocean City soul.

Acknowledgements

The idea for this book has been rolling around in my head since the day I left Playland. I even thought the story would make a great play, a bit of youthful hubris that overlooked the fact that I knew nothing about the publishing world at the time. That changed through the years as I learned a thing or two and got my work onto the pages of the *Washington Post* and *Sports Illustrated*. But somehow, the story of my amusement park summer remained a flickering star far off on my writing horizon.

It took an invisible gut punch in the fall of 2014 to make me realize that the book *had* to be written. I'd just pulled onto Dorchester Street and was staring at the empty gravel lot where Mrs. Bunting's house had once stood. Not only was there a big hole in the street, it suddenly felt like there was an equal size hole in my heart. It was *by far* the emptiest feeling I'd ever experienced in Ocean City. And while sitting there staring at the vacant space, I realized how many of my Ocean City memories really didn't exist anymore. The physical places where they had happened were gone.

Never to return.

So I want to acknowledge and thank the "history keepers" of Ocean City. It's through their dedicated efforts that our cherished memories stay alive long after we can no longer stand in the spot where they actually happened. I consulted their work often while piecing *Playland* together.

The Ocean City Life-Saving Museum (www.ocmuseum.org) is the epicenter of Ocean City history. What the Hurley family has done in curating the museum over the last four decades is nothing short of miraculous. And it's such a welcoming place. I learn something new on every visit.

Bunk Mann's beautiful *Vanishing Ocean City* book (https://vanishingoc.com) is another invaluable repository of Ocean City history, as is his weekly column in *The Dispatch*. It's always a good day when there's a "Vanishing Ocean City" post in my Facebook feed

And then there's Brandon Seidl's amazing Haunted House website (www.ochh.net) There's so much information on the site, even beyond Trimper's legendary dark ride. I found Brandon's work inspiring because I realized I wasn't the only person with an amusement obsession.

Jim Futrell, the Historian of the National Amusement Park Historical Association, provided me with a detailed background on Playland, and stunning park images that I'd never seen before. He was also able to confirm for me that Playland's final summer of operation was indeed 1980.

The final history keeper I need to thank is fellow Playland alumnus Rick Machado. His encouragement was invaluable, as was his guidance on park details that had become slightly fuzzy through the years. Rick gave the project a shot in the arm every time we talked. His contributions were vital to the completion of the book.

My hope for *Playland* is that it can contribute in some small way to Ocean City's "story." And if it can also bring some smiles and happy memories to readers...there's not a whole lot more a writer can ask for.

Thank you so much for reading *Playland*. I hope you enjoyed your visit to the park!

References

Ocean City: A Pictorial History
Hurley, George and Suzanne. Virginia Beach, Donning, 1979. Print

Trimper's Rides
Thrash, Monica and Brandon Seidl. Charleston: Arcadia, 2014. Print

Ocean City Volume II
DeVincent-Hayes, Nan, and John E. Jacob. Charleston: Arcadia, 1999 Print

Shores, Earl. "Ocean City Surfmen." *Historical Traveler*, Summer 1996, pp16-19.

Keesey, Lori. "Recollections of a Seaside Village." *Maryland*, Summer 1986, pp 34-39.

"Behind The Scenes Management." *Oceana Magazine*: July 21, 1978, p 3.

The Visitor: June 29, 1964; August 9, 1965; September 1, 1965; June, 1966.

Resorter: July 15-31, 1964; August 1-15, 1964; Summer 1969.

Beachcomber: June 4 1966; June 18, 1966; July 9, 1966; July 16, 1966; July 23, 1966; August 13, 1966; August 20, 1966; August 27, 1966.

Ocean News: July 8, 1966; August 26, 1966.

Ocean City History

Ocean City Life Saving Museum – www.ocmuseum.org

Brandon Seidl's Trimper's Haunted House Online – www.ochh.net

Vanishing Ocean City With Bunk Mann –
www.mdcoastdipatch.com/author/bunk-mann
www.vanishingoc.com

Amusement Park History

National Amusement Park Historical Association
www.napha.org

About the Author

Ocean City 1966

Earl Shores was just six weeks old when he became the fourth generation of his family to visit Ocean City, Maryland. After spending time living and working in Ocean City, Shores landed a Contributing Writer gig at *Eastern Surf Magazine,* and went on to write for publications ranging from the *Washington Post* to *Sports Illustrated.*

Playland: Greetings From Ocean City, Maryland is his fifth book.

Books by Earl Shores

Surf Lessons: Stories Of An Eastern Surfer
The Electric Football Wishbook
Full Color Electric Football
The Unforgettable Buzz: The History of Electric Football

www.earlshores.com